The Use
and Training
of the Human Voice

ARTHUR LESSAC

THE USE AND TRAINING *of* THE HUMAN VOICE

A PRACTICAL APPROACH TO SPEECH AND VOICE DYNAMICS

Preface by Irene Dailey
Illustrated by John Wilson

MAYFIELD PUBLISHING COMPANY
MOUNTAIN VIEW, CALIFORNIA

To Birdie, Fredi, Michael, and David

First Edition © Copyright 1960 by Arthur Lessac
Second Edition © Copyright 1967 by Arthur Lessac

Library of Congress Card Number 67-28352

ISBN 0-87484-845-8

Printed in the United States of America

Acknowledgments

This second and so far most definitive edition of *The Use and Training of the Human Voice* would not be possible had it not been for the encouragement, guidance, and invaluable assistance over the years from my many friends and students. I want to single out for very special thanks and appreciation, Dr. John Reich, Mr. H. Donald Wilson, Mr. David Simon, Miss Beatrice Straight, Mr. Peter Cookson, Mrs. Cissie Blumberg, Dr. Ruth Metzger, Mr. Vincent Park.

Nor could this edition have materialized to its present stage without the significant contributions made by the small but dedicated group of professional teachers who have worked with the Lessac system during the past six years. Their interest, helpfulness, and enthusiasm has been a constant source of both inspiration and challenge. Foremost among them are Professor Sue Ann Park of Chicago; Miss Irene Dailey, Dr. James Scott Kennedy, Mr. Dick Pyatt, Miss Bobby Troka, Mrs. Anita Lande, all of New York; Dr. Robert Hobbs of Boston; Mr. Jack Jones of Oklahoma City.

To David Morgan, who edited and supervised the production of this edition, I am forever indebted. His was a labor of love that can never be repaid except with everlasting gratitude.

And finally, I want to express deep satisfaction with the fact that my son, Michael, has found much in my work to inspire his theatre research and to sustain him in his professional activities as director, teacher, and singer of songs. Of even greater pleasure is the prospect of future collaboration, foreshadowed by our first joint effort with the two chapters on vocal life in this book. He is also the author of most of the poems in Chapter X.

How wonderful is the human voice! It is indeed the organ of the soul. The intellect of man sits enthroned visibly, on his forehead and in his eye, and the heart of man is written on his countenance, but the soul reveals itself in the voice only.

—HENRY WADSWORTH LONGFELLOW

Special Preface to the 1973 Edition

When State University of New York at Binghamton several years ago decided to seek a more productive approach to the problems of speech, communication and theatre education we did a serious survey of the existing state of the art. Our conclusions were that Professor Arthur Lessac's work and methods offered the greatest opportunity for significant advances in this area to take place. It was on this basis that we invited him to join our faculty. In 1970, after 25 years of individual work and study, he became a Professor of Theatre here and we instituted an intensive program of training utilizing his methods.

I am gratified to tell you that there is now a nation-wide and to some degree, international, group using this method and text in many schools and universities. Here, at SUNY-Binghamton, teacher training workshops are held each summer—three will be conducted in 1973.

I have increasingly realized that "the Lessac System" is an approach not just to speech, communication and acting but to physical effectiveness in its fullest sense. Here at the University, over half of Professor Lessac's time in the last year has been directly with the Physical Education Department. There he has utilized his knowledge of breathing, posture and relaxation (see Chapters 4 and 5) to explore the application of his methods to physical training. He has had unusual results and is developing additional knowledge in many aspects of human performance.

Additionally, he has begun to explore the psychological implications of learning through sensation and feeling and its relationship to current research in such areas as bio-feedback and the psychology of suggestion.

Thus, in teaching through sensation and feeling, we have involved ourselves in a new learning process that appears to be applicable in many areas of human behavior—from posture, walking, running, to speaking, singing, acting and on into emotional life itself. In the specific area of communication, many persons feel that the "musical phonetics" and the voice and speech training methods in this text lend themselves to new approaches to such things as teaching reading-readiness, spelling, foreign languages and other applications.

Thus, this text is and will long be considered of great significance to many areas of American education far beyond our original expectations. What is relevant to the user of this book is that he can learn much about voice and speech and gain insight into a fundamental, overall development at the same time.

ALFRED G. BROOKS, Professor   3/9/73
Chairman, Department of Theatre
State University of New York
    at Binghamton

Preface

ALTHOUGH THIS IS A BOOK FOR EVERYONE, I am particularly excited about its revolutionary contribution to the training of voice and speech for the actor.

All of us want a creative, dynamic, challenging, and experimental experience in theatre, whether as audience or craftsmen. We have new theatre plants, experimental in design; young playwrights with awareness of today's complexities; directors with unique approaches to space and time. Only the actors and the teachers of actors are chained by some sort of misguided loyalty to the tried and tired and no longer true.

It is time to introduce a twentieth-century approach to the fundamentals of acting. For Arthur Lessac, it is acting-speech, and he has developed a method that organically integrates the two. For him, acting and speech are not compartmentalized into separate skills, functioning together but still independent of one another. This is mere *organizational integration*. The Lessac system promotes a true *organic integration*, where acting is speech and speech is acting.

Creative acting, as well as creative communication of any sort, is the result of every part of the human instrument functioning to its full potential: the physical instrument; the vocal instrument; the sensory-imaginative instrument, opened, developed, shaped, and inspired. Lessac has developed a method that involves the body, the senses, the imagination in words and sound; that involves melody, tempo, and rhythm; a teachable, learnable method for the modern actor in that long-neglected area of voice and speech.

As both student and teacher of the Lessac approach, I am excited by the possibilities inherent in his methods of correlating voice and speech with all facets of the actor's instrument and the concurrent development of the whole. It affords us an opportunity to develop our craft in a new dimension long desired and sorely needed. And most important, it is a method that deals with a whole life style . . . a life style as relevant to the layman, the professional man, the teacher, as it is to the professional actor.

—IRENE DAILEY

Contents

An Introduction

to the Lessac System

*T*HE SUBJECT OF THIS BOOK IS VOCAL LIFE.
I address it to anyone who is interested in vocal communication: To those who want beautiful voices, to those who want clear, articulate speech—but primarily to those who want to reach their fellow man.

This book does teach the fundamentals of voice production and speech training, but vocal life is more than that. Vocal life is the philosophical and psychological extension of the pure mechanics of voice and speech. To become vocal life, voice and speech must become intrinsically enmeshed with all the life energies—with the emotional and physical energies of the individual. Vocal life is not an isolated function: It is the synergism of all energies involved in vital vocal communication and the expression of the personal culture of each individual; it is the use of the trained voice to express and to communicate every nuance of feeling and purpose, whether it be from the stage or podium, around the conference table, in the classroom, on a ballfield, in a factory, or in the most intimate of personal communications; it is the integration of voice and speech with facial posture and dynamics and expressive and communicative body gestures.

Verbal communication is useful, but it should not be merely utilitarian: Whether on a personal or professional level, it should be creative. The sensitive actor will recognize that vocal life is not only the extension of inner energies but also a creative and controlling influence upon the dynamics of these energies. In the same way, the non-actor should realize that vocal life is not merely an instrument for expressing emotions but a creator and controller of emotions, not only in others but in oneself as well. It is an instrument with which emotions can more effectively be perceived and evoked. Vocal life can educate and inspire: Through its development and creative use, everyone—and especially the underprivileged and under-developed—can seek and find an identity and an image based on the true possibilities within, rather than the accident of outer circumstances. The use, as well as the training, of the human voice must be the constant development and exploration of vocal life.

The approach to voice and speech training pre-sented here was developed out of a concern with the entire communicating personality; as a result, it is equally applicable to the professional creative artist *and* to the layman interested in influencing or affecting others through his verbal and vocal communication.

My own philosophy concerning vocal and verbal functioning has always been that: (1) *all* the vocal arts and *all* the speech skills should be considered a single discipline—a gestalt—and taught with one fundamental training method; (2) such training must reflect the natural functioning of the human organism, must be based on the development of permanent physical habit patterns, and will, therefore, be training that lasts; (3) such training must be designed to produce speech and voice patterns that are neither affectation nor imitation and that will, therefore, be almost immediately applicable in all speech situations; (4) American speech, and indeed all speech, must be founded upon a euphonic standard that will reflect its natural vigor and will not emulate any particular regional standard or any particular theatrical style.

This is an esthetic approach. To some people, an esthetic speech must *retain* all of the regional and individual peculiarities, patterns, and habits of any area or group; to others, an esthetic speech must *remove* most regional characteristics and imitate one specific regional style, such as British or New England or Midwestern. In this book, we will consider voice and speech to be esthetic when an honest, vital, and salutary use of the body and vocal instrument reflects personal individuality in the most euphonic manner.

But an esthetic approach does not imply a totally subjective approach. To avoid the pitfalls of subjectivity, I have devised a method based on physical actions that can be recognized and reproduced exactly and at will by anyone who has learned to experience them correctly. The foundation of this method, then, is the *physical* aspect of voice and speech—the natural way in which the body produces vocal sounds. Voice training should consist of eliminating bad physical habits and strengthening the natural tendencies that emerge as a result. This method is thus both esthetic *and* scientific.

The experienced teacher will immediately see that this book represents an unorthodox approach to the training of voice and speech. The method is essentially different in many ways from other methods currently taught, but the merit of its innovations lies not in their originality but in their efficiency. I believe it to be revolutionary in scope because it is an objective approach applicable to any voice and, indeed, to any language, and one that can be taught by any teacher.

Since the basis of the Lessac system is the experience of certain physical sensations and development of the ability to recall these sensations and actively control the actions causing them, physical feeling must be the reference point—the measuring rod that tells whether or not the voice is being used correctly. The traditional idea of relying on the ear for control of voice and speech is discarded because your ear is not a reliable judge of your own vocal production; it is of primary importance only when sound reaches you from outside. The sounds that originate in your own vocal apparatus are perceived differently, and you cannot effectively compare these sounds with those produced by others. The auditory and sensory areas of the brain—both of which are active when you speak yourself—adapt themselves to bone and air conducted sound in such a way that proper discrimination between the two is impossible. Thus, a dependence on the hearing apparatus will often reinforce bad habits and interfere with the learning of new habits (see Chapter II).

I have found, on the other hand, that the physical sensation of producing sound well can be recognized and understood immediately, and I teach the use of these non-auditory sensation patterns to guide and control the production of sound. The student must first be made aware of the feeling of the physical sensation of using the voice correctly; then he learns to use these feelings as cues by which he controls his voice production. Essentially we are going to create new habits—habits of vocal control and perception that belong to the same areas of awareness that control emotional and physical life.

Physical sensation has always been an essential reference point in my work, both in voice and speech research and in the development of training methods. I began this work from the physical end of voice and speech, from the way that human beings produce and control vocal sounds. Considering the human body as a musical instrument, I worked on the premise that careful observation of how the body *wants* to function— how it *would* function in the absence of adverse conditioning—is the best guide to the production of beautiful sounds. I studied the different parts of the body involved in voice and speech production and used simple common sense criteria as to what constituted rightness or naturalness in any action or position. I considered the absence of tension, for instance, a sign that the muscles were being used most efficiently and were in their most natural positions. It was quickly evident that "natural" was not necessarily the description of actions performed or positions held habitually by most individuals. These were often quite "unnatural"—full of tension, stress, and strain, and certainly not conducive to good and relaxed voice production.

I observed that whenever beautiful tones were produced, the voice was nonthroaty, nonnasal, nonpharyngeal; it was produced and resonated effortlessly; it had stentorian resonant qualities and projection, pitch-range, variety of color, and nuance and body of tone. This is not surprising if we accept the premise that our bodies are naturally good musical instruments: A fine instrument properly used—used as it *wants* to be used— produces a beautiful tone.

As these sounds were produced, I observed that certain facial muscles were particularly active and that the face took on a characteristic posture not previously recognized. I studied this particular facial position, saw that it met all the criteria of naturalness, and called it the "inverted-megaphone" shape (see Chapter V). I also noted that when sounds were created by natural actions, with the face in the natural, inverted-megaphone position, the experience was effortless and balanced. The sound seemed to travel, to become amplified, and to resonate with a kind of self-generated energy that coursed through the porous bones of the face and head without conscious exertion of any force or use of any breath that the speaker could feel.

My next step was to determine how this optimum configuration of actions and positions could best be attained. Some of the actions that produce vocal sounds are clearly not controlled by the performer: He cannot consciously feel or control the passage of the breath stream from the larynx; he cannot move the vocal cords; he cannot determine what parts of the cords are to vibrate (see Chapter IV). I found, however, that he could control any actions and positions that he could learn to sense— those of almost all the parts of the head above the larynx—and those areas were actually the most crucial in the control of vocal activity.

When I embarked on research into methods by which this perceptual learning could be achieved, I found a two-pronged approach: *Both the positions and actions of the relevant parts of the body and the accompanying sensations can be described.* The student tries to attain both a given action and the corresponding sensation: He approaches the goal by two paths at once—but once he has achieved a given action-sensation and the sound it produces, he finds the physical sensation a surer guide to repetition of the sound than the description of the action. *The sensation is built into the action—when the sensation is the control, the control thus becomes built into the action.*

On these general principles, I have developed new standards and techniques that apply to all voice and speech training—all of the vocal arts and all of the speech skills forming a single discipline. To compartmentalize this discipline into polarized fields, as the traditionalists have, is to train the left and right hands of a pianist separately.

By voice we usually refer to the phonation of the vocal cords, which produces vocal sound waves that become amplified and resonated in other parts of the body. Voice is related primarily to the vowels of our language. When these are sustained to any given extent, we say we hear singing; below this threshold of sustention, we say we hear speech. In its narrowest sense, speech refers to articulate sounds—articulation being based principally on consonants, both voiced, such as N, M, and B, and unvoiced, such as S, SH, P, and T. In a broader sense, speech is usually considered to include the above and all other aspects of vocal expression, such as intonation, inflection, accent, emphasis, and nuance—everything used to convey intellectual content as well as emotional impact. Singing, in the broader sense, should be the same thing, except that the vowel sounds are sustained.

Obviously then, voice, when narrowed to non-sustaining or staccato-like vowels, is also part of speech. And speech, broadened into poetic recitation with sustained vowels, approaches chanting or singing. Certainly such aspects of speech as accent, intonation, inflection, and emphasis apply to the entire range of voice, whether in terms of pitch, volume, tempo, or color. The vocal effort of calling out to bridge distance or noise, the expression of enthusiasm, the lyric description, the solemn entreaty, the cry of pain, the adamant emphasis, the forceful but controlled anger, the earnest statement—these are all, in effect, matters of voice. To the extent that these *are* matters of voice, they fall under the general principles of natural action . . . and we can therefore apply them to the speaking *or* the singing voice.

In studying how consonants were produced, I also applied the physical criteria of natural function—the absence of tension in the muscles, a balanced action and position of the muscles, and the most efficient use of muscles. I found it useful to define the qualities of the consonants by likening them to the different instruments of the orchestra: The V may be thought of as the vibrant singing of the cello, the NG as the throb of the oboe, the T as the tap of a drumbeat, the SH as the voiceless murmur of the wind machine—all of the consonants, when produced as action-sensations, have instrumental qualities that can be defined by their orchestral equivalents (see Chapter X). The vowels, always voiced—except in a whisper—and produced with one technique, can be considered fundamentally a single instrument or solo voice in an orchestra. Each consonant, on the other hand, is different from the others in method of production and in effect, and together they make up an entire orchestra.

I found that when consonants were felt as vibratory and tactile combinations of action and sensation associated with orchestral instruments, muscle and vibration memory were developed, and the ear was deemphasized as a controlling guide—the student learned to feel the sounds instead of listening for them. I also found that with this concept as an aid, students were able to produce a desired sound much more quickly, more easily, and more surely than when they were told in detailed description how and where the tongue, lips, teeth, soft palate, and back of the throat must be used—and were exhorted to listen carefully for the sound. Finally, the concept of feeling consonant sound opens up to the student a whole new range of distinctive tonal and rhythmic effects that can color his speech; it provides him, in a practical and efficient manner, with precision, tempo, melodic values, emphasis, accent, and other voice qualities that the vowels cannot provide.

Loss of intelligibility in speech is largely due to the loss of final consonants and those that precede other consonants; yet if they are conceived as orchestral instruments played and felt effortlessly, they come easily. Consonants experienced in this manner not only preserve intelligibility but reveal the inexhaustible variety inherent in the structure of English words—in their contrasting rhythmic patterns, sustained tonal colors, and melodic qualities. For example: When the word *characteristic* is spoken with the C's felt as light, tapping drumbeats and the S as a sustained sound effect, it takes on new rhythm and a new quality of expression. The same principle applies to words like *environment, incestuous, demand, questioned, contract,* and *scientists.*

With this concept of the consonants as musical instruments, students can be taught to produce them by the same methods used in teaching vowels: description and perception of the physical sensations produced by the proper body positions and actions. Having achieved the desired sound and having felt it, the student is able to control and repeat it by the application of sense-memory.

When the essential elements of both voice and speech are subjected to the same training and judged by the same criteria—natural functioning of the body, proper feeling of the action-sensations, audibility, clarity, and intelligibility—we have the basis for a new standard of speech in both its broadest and its narrowest definitions. This standard is not derived from individual personality, talent, effectiveness, custom, character, environment, or example. All of these, together with regional standards, may quite properly contribute to individual speech, but I am concerned here with more objective standards of enunciation, articulation, and voice usage—standards based primarily on euphony and natural function.

A standard need not force a choice among the customary ways of speaking of different social or regional groups: When someone says "reyan" instead of *ran,* the essential fault is not that the pronunciation is wrong or the intonation peculiar, but that the sound is too nasal.

A choice of pronunciation for the R in words like *hard, fir, mother, board, fierce,* and *firm* does not require a choice among various regional preferences but a recognition that the R, when it follows a vowel and precedes a consonant, or when it is the final sound in a word before a pause, is a backward, restrictive, throaty influence that tends to produce poor tone, a tight jaw, and loss of clarity. But if the facial stretch is forward enough to increase the mouth cavity and relax the tongue and jaw, and the tonal sensation is strong enough to direct the vibration forward into the bony area, one can use as much or as little R as one pleases and offend no one.

With proper facial posture, the Westerner will speak most comfortably with vowels that sound remarkably like those of the Easterner or Southerner using the same technique. And learning to feel the consonants as musical instruments with skill and finesse is as easy for the Southerner as it is for the New Englander. The recognition that nasality, throatiness, lippiness, or a tight jaw is a detriment to good speech need not stop at state or regional boundary lines.

Since criticism is aimed, not at the pronunciation of a word, but at the way in which the vocal mechanism is used to produce the word, voice and speech training need never be considered to militate against regional accents. The student is not asked to imitate any speech pattern not native to him. Through the muscular sensation of the facial posture, the tonal sensation of the vocal action, and the orchestral accompaniment of the consonants, objectionable regional influences are eliminated while the flavor of regional individuality is retained to give variety to an excellent common culture of voice and speech.

As the student learns the three physical action-sensations, referred to in later chapters as structural action, tonal action, and consonant action, voice and speech become an inner experience. Since every vowel, and therefore every syllable, is transmitted through bone, not forced out through the lips, speech remains an inner activity. When the student becomes competent at using these inner action-sensations, he can always be confident of being heard and understood, whatever the position of his body or the need for projection. To "throw" the voice to an audience or to force the articulation of consonants is to treat voice and speech as an extrinsic, nonorganic function.

Of even greater significance, when voice and speech become an inner physical experience, is their intrinsic combination with all other inner experience, including emotion. This synthesis of energies leads to an organic functioning in the most exciting sense of the term and provides tools and methods as valuable in clinic, classroom, business, and industry, as in the performing arts.

When characterization in the theatre calls for artificial and unnatural use of the voice, even these effects can be practiced with impunity when the basic controls are established, for then the performer can allow himself the latitude to experiment and explore the many abnormal and ordinarily harmful uses of his voice without fear of damage to the vocal mechanism—and with greater effect. In any of the arts a skill must be learned correctly before it can be distorted effectively, and expertise in handling weak forms of speech and voice comes from putting the strong form through the experiential paces of tempo, facility, flexibility, carelessness, informality—a sort of fifty-year phylogenetic process in a fifteen minute period.

The idea that any particular group of people requires a different kind of good voice or speech from any other group must be rejected. I start with the premise and the promise that everyone can have a good voice—singing and speaking—and I believe that every good speaker should and can be a good singer and that every good singer should and can be a good speaker.

Each of the action-sensations — structural, tonal, and consonant—contributes to the effectiveness of the other two, and working together as a trinity of actions, they make the speaker look good, feel good, and function more effectively. *He will look good* because natural use of his vocal equipment eliminates facial distortion. *He will feel good* because each action-sensation relieves physical tension at the same time that it uses energy wisely and produces controlled but vitalized speech. *He will function more effectively* because he has a conscious and intelligent control over his voice and can be heard and understood in any speaking situation—a conversation with a single person or an appearance before thousands.

I believe that this approach will lead to a superior American speech standard, elegant and beautiful and effective enough for the highest artistic use—and at the same time practical and natural enough for the most utilitarian application.

The Use
and Training
of the Human Voice

Memo to the Reader

Read this book—*then do it*.

The words can only tell you—point a way. Only by doing will you know. A guidebook can set you dreaming of far-away places, but only going can show you the way and only arrival can make them real . . . So this book will describe a goal and a way to reach it—but only by your own effort will you fully understand what complete mastery of your voice and speech can do for you.

To help you reach this goal, this book needs your cooperation as much as you need this book. There will be many questions and problems that arise as you read each chapter; in the studio, they could be answered or solved easily through demonstration and on-the-spot guidance—here you must find your own answers through faithful application of the exercises. You will find that the principles and exercises are parts of a total gestalt . . . a gestalt whose intra- and interrelationships are always shifting but always in balance—the dynamic balance of parts always in motion, always alive, to maintain that balance.

The Lessac system is not a rigid step-by-step progression. The order of this book is an order that has worked well in the studio, although it is actually observed much less strictly there: Let every student feel free to adapt . . . to wander through the system, with concentration and awareness, but at will. Let every teacher adapt for every student, for every particular problem, according to his own predilections. Learn the principles of verbal and vocal life—learn them well—but experiment along the way. If you gain nothing else from this book, I hope you will find yourself exploring the idea that nothing stands alone, isolated or encapsulated. Everything is a part of something, and nothing functions well until it functions in balanced relationship with every other part.

Part One: Building the Foundations of a Good Voice

*B*EFORE YOU CAN BUILD A STRUCTURE, you must understand both esthetic and engineering principles; you must draw up a plan based on those principles; and you must prepare the site. Before you can develop your voice, you must understand the anatomical principles and the physical and physiological actions by which it is produced; you must determine what you want to accomplish and how you are going to accomplish it; and you must prepare your body to carry out the actions that will be demanded of it. In the five chapters of Part One, we will consider all of these things: the physical aspects of voice and speech; the basic principles of the Lessac system; and techniques of breathing, posture, and relaxation that enhance, rather than inhibit, natural functioning of the voice. One can speak without knowledge of these fundamentals, but one cannot repair or perfect anything without knowing how it works.

CHAPTER I

Don't Envy a Good
Voice . . . Have One!

Y OUR VOICE is a very active agent in your personal public relations, working for you or against you every day, whether in social, occupational, or very personal situations. You communicate in many ways, but the response is fullest—for good or ill—when voice, face, and gesture work together to convey a personality in the physical presence of another or others.

Everyone knows the importance of an attractive appearance: We try to remember the smile, the fresh pocket handkerchief, the clean white gloves, but we often forget the decisive role that voice plays in the total impact of our presence. The smile, the handkerchief, the gloves—even great personal beauty—may fade from sight at the sound of a nasal, rasping, inaudible, or otherwise inadequate voice, where a pleasant voice would have heightened the effect.

From even a few words, your listeners will read a quick personal history. Whether you will or not, they will decide your state of mind, your state of health, your social and educational background —all from the quality and use of your speaking voice. When you speak without awareness of your voice, you may fall into a trap you never see. What you consider a normal speaking voice, others may hear as angry or annoyed or withdrawn. They may be hearing echoes of feelings you harbor deeply, or you may simply be using your voice poorly. In either case, proper voice training can give you control of the impression you create; at the same time, learning to feel the control of your voice will increase your awareness of, and your control over, your emotional responses. Through control of the voice, you control yourself: forcefulness can be expressed without force, anger without aggression, anxiety without withdrawal. With this healthier approach, you need not fear the emotional responses that creep into your voice; you can use them constructively. If, at times, you still want to hide such responses, then a more objective use of one or all of the three action-sensations described in the Introduction and more fully in later chapters—a concentration on the natural use of these physical skills—can act as a perfect protective mechanism.

But more—and more important—than merely providing control of emotional responses, an organic kind of voice training can help to liberate, through speech experience, abilities that lie immobilized in most of us. As this training reveals and leads to a valuable reappraisal of these abilities, the voice may set you on the path to new goals.

If you have decided that you want these gifts that come with learning to make better use of your voice, don't be deterred by the adverse opinions of others. Too often close relatives or good friends will discourage voice and speech improvement because they cannot look ahead from the transition period, while new behavior is being explored and experimented with, to the skilled application of the training in normal acceptable behavior. They may say that you are stepping out of character; that people like you for what you are; that if you change, you will be resented; that you don't sound like yourself. But keep on; you will sound like yourself, probably more like your real self than you ever have before.

Conditioning for a Poor Voice

Not everyone needs, or wants, to become a professional public speaker, but everyone *must* communicate in order to deal with other people, and anyone *can* have a good voice. We probably have more control over our voices than we do over our appearance. Anatomically, our vocal mechanisms are all alike, even though they vary in dimensions, and they respond to training as other parts of the body do.

And like the rest of the body, in whole or in part, these mechanisms are *designed* to function efficiently and well. How they *actually* function is the result of a great many habits developed from infancy through childhood and adolescence. Too often these habits are bad, and the bad habits are built up until they undermine the natural, and naturally good, function built into the body. Each generation of poorly conditioned adults passes on a heritage of miserably poor speech and tone quality, as well as poor postural and breathing habits, to each generation of school children.

Infants and very young children breathe naturally and produce free, musical, well-focused, projected voices, but by the time they finish high school they have usually lost these qualities by emulating their elders—and where would the young learn articulation, pronunciation, and enunciation if not from their elders? Some would assert strongly that children learn much from each other—and they do. There is no denying the influence of peer groups, but the peers can only pass on to one another the speech and voice habits they have all learned from watching and listening to the grown-ups around them.

The specific culprits, then, must be parents and teachers. If both would consider the way they speak and do something about it, there would be tremendous changes in the space of one or two generations. Children are much cleverer at imitation than adults, but they can only imitate what they hear and see. If they heard rich, pleasant voices producing articulated, imaginative speech—if they saw well-formed facial posture functioning without muscle strain—there would be no need for speech improvement classes at all. We could devote ourselves to the vocal arts and speech appreciation rather than to vocal repairs and speech correction. Such a renascence would exert a profound influence on our manners, our culture, our social intercourse.

Teachers must bear the brunt of this criticism. They appear suddenly to the child at 5 or 6 as new authorities with tremendous power and influence. Throughout the most important years in his development, the child listens to them as he learns—and how shrill and distracting are many of the tones he hears; how dull, monotonous, slovenly, and flatulent a good deal of the speech. If teachers had to depend on a passing grade in voice and speech to hold their jobs, I doubt whether ten per cent would be employed.

Many schools do assign a teacher or two to act as guardians of good speech and voice, but even these often have inadequate training and unsound, outmoded ideas that unfit them for the task. One has only to interview prospective voice and speech teachers for any length of time to realize what poor speech they often have: Some sound like poor imitations of second-rate British actors; others not much better than the children themselves. Those who are qualified are given impossible tasks. Their few hours with the children cannot begin to reduce the problem—a problem compounded by a disheartening lack of interest on the part of other teachers.

Another failing in our schools is too little singing for pleasure. Singing is fun; it is healthful; it motivates; it educates; and it can serve as an outlet for excess energy. Singing for pleasure is a great aid in developing and maintaining rich, strong, beautiful speaking voices. When a music teacher handles the problem of the child who sings poorly —off-pitch or stridently or harshly—in the most economic and impersonal manner by dubbing the child a "listener" and proscribing him from further singing, he removes a personal inconvenience at great expense to the child. In the anomalous position of listener, the student ceases to be a participant and becomes an outsider. He loses interest in singing, in his voice and his speech, and in music generally; his opportunities have been narrowed rather than widened by what passes for an educational process. Instead of fewer, children should be given more opportunities for singing in school—especially those children who sing poorly. They could do with less listening in music class and more singing in other classes—in gym, in social studies, in language studies, on special projects.

And what of the responsibility of parents for high standards of voice and speech? They recognize these even less than do the teachers, but parents, after all, have mostly learned their speech in the same school systems and the same environments that are producing poor speech in today's children. I have several times suggested to a mother concerned with her child's voice and speech that, for best results with the child, it might be wise if she, rather than the child, were to study. The observation usually came as a shock and, when the mother recovered, was interpreted as an insult.

The adults in a child's world are too busy providing the sustenance of life, the comforts of home, and the content material of a course. Parents and teachers alike forget about the communicating personality. Where voice and speech are concerned, the minimum becomes the maximum, and pride in this aspect of personal culture is an outmoded luxury.

On Building New Habits

Once you have turned away from childhood's natural use of the voice through imitation of bad examples, poor speech becomes one of your more deeply ingrained habits. We speak more often than we read, write, listen—perhaps even think. We use speech to defend ourselves and our personalities, to challenge the positions and beliefs of others, to justify our motives and actions, and to motivate the actions of others. Our voice and our speech are our first line of defense and our chief weapons of offense. One does not easily surrender habits, least of all habits that are so much a part of one's very self, habits whose loss is an attack on the integrity of the self. Without strong motivation, the angry voice will remain angry, the timid, the insincere, and the pompous voices will remain what they are—and their owners will usually call that good enough. A change that involves a renunciation or destruction of something in oneself is always a threat, even when that something is only a pattern of faulty conditioning that inhibits the best that one can be. This is the reason that students, systems, and teachers in voice and speech education spend so much time looking for an easy and painless way—a way to improvement without change.

But whenever real growth takes place, change must be a part of that growth, and the willingness to change must precede it. The process is difficult but not impossible. We cannot set out simply to *break* an established habit; through physical reeducation, we must *create* new habits to supplant the old ones. Once we pass the preadolescent stage, most of our learning takes place this way. At first the old habit is strongly entrenched; the transition period, where learning through new experience begins to take root, is full of discomfort, apprehension, struggle, and self-consciousness. This is the period when motives are in conflict, when one has strong feelings of aspiration and avoidance toward the same goal. But with attention and intention, the new pattern of voice and speech will become familiar, its use increasingly successful, and the new habit will grow and mature while the old weakens correspondingly, until finally the new has joined the other habit patterns as part of natural behavior, and the old is effectively buried.

During the training process you must be aware of change. You may have become dissatisfied with the voice you produce, but the way in which you produce it—like the performance of any habit-formed pattern of behavior—represents for you a natural use of the vocal mechanism. If the training process, then, does not arouse uneasy feelings of strangeness, discomfort, or artificiality, you are learning nothing; if you continue to feel natural and comfortable in the use of your voice, there is no change and therefore no progress. If, on the other hand, you sense and resist the feeling of a changed facial posture or a changed tonal quality, you are resisting progress. A sound that seems peculiar and artificial to you may prove surprisingly good on the recorded playback; a facial posture that feels ridiculous may be quite acceptable when you catch a glimpse of yourself in the mirror. Once you have passed these barriers and realized that the unfamiliarity and discomfort are subjective personal feelings and that the objective results are good, they will begin to seem less strange; the sense of loss will fade away, and a sense of gain will replace it.

You can learn to use your voice so that you sound right, look right, and feel right. What you will do will appear effortless, not because of natural ability, but because of the diligent work with which you have learned a complete set of positive habit patterns arising from new actions, new sensations, and new physical perceptions. A good voice is not an elusive and undependable gift; with correct training you can have a voice that will always function well in any situation.

But training techniques in voice and speech that depend solely on imitation, repetition by rote, descriptive imagery, or the inspiration of a magnetic personality are not scientifically precise, nor can they provide conscious control of the voice. Such methods may seem, temporarily, to be of some benefit, but they do not lay a sound foundation for understanding the processes involved in producing a good voice at all times.

As I pointed out in the introduction, speech and voice are indivisible. Nevertheless, following the general trend toward specialization, speech techniques have unfortunately become isolated from voice techniques until the two are usually taught as separate subjects that have little or no connection with one another. The single technique described in this book will help anyone to develop both a fine voice and effective speech. Although the degree of quality and skill that the student develops will naturally be determined largely by the amount of effort and concentration he brings to the work, this book will demonstrate that excellent and effective speech is the direct result of fundamental *vocal* skills and *vocal* techniques. When you have mastered the feeling of these fundamentals, you need never envy a good speaking or singing voice—you will have one!

CHAPTER II

The Physical Aspects
of Voice and Speech

*W*HERE THE UPPER PART of the trachea, or windpipe, opens into the larynx, are two little freeloose edges or membranes, somewhat inaccurately called the vocal cords. From an anatomical point of view, these membranes were originally intended to serve as a gateway for the breath stream as it comes in and goes out, spreading apart to permit the passage of air and closing during the act of swallowing to prevent passage of foreign matter, such as food and liquid, from the adjacent esophagus into the trachea. Voice teachers call this space between the open membranes the glottis.

How Vocal Sound Is Created

As man evolved, long before history, the visual sense sharpened, less reliance was placed on the sense of smell, and vocal sounds began to develop. Comparative anatomists have pointed out that early man, given the structure of his body, had a choice of developing any of three or four different ways of fashioning the vocal sound from which he created speech. The vocal membranes eventually took over this function, but even today, when the larynx is removed because of throat malignancy, most patients are able to develop a fairly strong speaking voice by substituting the esophagus, which has no equivalent of the vocal membranes. Medical case histories even record claims that some of these laryngectomized patients have developed fairly strong singing voices as well—without mechanical or electronic devices.

But sound created by the vocal membranes is primarily what we deal with in voice and speech. The process begins as a mental one: We decide to speak and the brain sends a message, or nerve impulse, to the membranes to close, just as it does when we swallow. The breath, coming from the lungs through the bronchial tubes and trachea into the larynx, builds up a tiny back pressure behind the closed membranes; when the pressure is strong enough, the breath puffs through, setting the membranes into vibration at a fantastically rapid speed, while the breath-puff, its function over and its pressure dissipated, lazily joins the circulating air in the oral and nasal cavities. The vibrating membranes send out the sound waves that constitute the human voice, and this action is what we mean by the term "phonation of the vocal cords." At this stage, of course, the sound waves, down around the vocal membranes in the larynx, produce inadequate and inaudible tones, but for all practical purposes, *the breath stream has terminated its function and the sound stream is on its own.* It might be said that breath ends where sound begins.

For the breath stream and the vocal sound stream are two separate currents or forces. Breath emerges from the body as a gaseous substance, traveling at approximately 12 feet per second; its characteristic action is to disperse. Vocal sound is a molecular wave action, a kinetic energy traveling at the rate of approximately 1200 feet per second, or one hundred times as fast as the breath stream. When this current comes in contact with any hard, rigid substance, it sets that substance into vibration, causing additional sound waves. The already weakened breath stream passes around such a substance and sets up no vibrations.

Resonance and Wave Reflections

These secondary vibrations produced in any hard substance by the sound waves from another vibrating body create what we call resonance. There are two types of resonance:

1. Direct or enforced resonance occurs when a vibrating body is placed in direct physical contact with another substance—a tuning fork on a desk or piano or piece of metal.

2. Indirect or sympathetic resonance occurs when the sound waves from a vibrating body set up vibrations in a substance some distance away. If, for example, you depress an E and a G key on the piano without hitting the strings and hold those strings open while striking a short, sharp C, the C vibrations will stop as soon as you release that key, but sound will continue from the open E and G strings, which have been set into sympathetic vibration by the sound waves sent out from the C string.

Both types of resonance occur in the human vocal process. The primary resonating structures are the teeth, the hard palate, the bone of the nose and maxillary sinuses (located near the cheekbone), and the forehead and frontal sinuses (above the eyes toward the center of the forehead). Sympathetic resonance occurs when the vocal sound waves, traveling through the air from the vibrating membranes, make contact with the hard palate and then the bone of the nose. Direct resonance is passed from the nasal bone to the forehead, sinuses, and cranium.

In addition to setting up new vibrations in some structures, sound waves are also reflected from these and other structures. They travel in all directions and, in an enclosure or cavity, reflect continuously from top to bottom and from wall to wall. This action creates tone color and body, which vary with the size and shape of the cavity. A well-formed large cavity darkens the tone and gives it fuller body, while a smaller cavity produces a lighter and thinner tone. If you cup your hands to your face while speaking or singing, you add cavity or wall space, but since the palms are covered with flesh and porous skin, which absorb sound, you do not add new resonating material; yet the voice takes on a deeper, fuller, darker quality.

Anatomical Aspects of Voice Production

The voice box, or human sound box, is the cavity or enclosure where the tone is strengthened, amplified, and beautified by resonance and wave reflection. Most musical instruments have a sound box of definite shape and size; a few, such as the accordion and bagpipe, have flexible cavities; and man has both. The larynx has been mistakenly identified as the human sound box, but once the vocal membranes have begun to vibrate, nothing else of importance takes place in the larynx. The true voice box is made up of two parts: a major adjustable area in the oral cavity and a major nonadjustable area in the nose and sinus cavities.

We can exert tonal control and tonal direction in both the flexible and rigid cavities. Proper formation of the oral cavity, where wave reflection takes place, produces a full-bodied, mature, authoritative, warm, expressive tone; coordinating this action with proper use of the resonating areas adds brilliant, ringing, penetrating, stentorian qualities. Wave reflection and resonance must feed each other; deny one and the other loses its lustre. Vocal resonance, without proper form of the oral cavity, becomes tinny, shrill, and strident; while even the best-formed cavity cannot make the voice more than a dull and lifeless instrument without good resonance.

Even the rib cage in the chest cavity, also often mistaken as the principal sound box, will resonate more efficiently and effectively when the oral and nasal cavities are fully used. Then the sound waves, instead of moving incorrectly through the throat into the chest, will travel through the three major resonating structures—hard palate, nasal bone, and forehead—and will continue on through the head, the spinal vertebrae, and the ribs, directly into the chest cavity.

The diaphragm, along with the breathing process it initiates, plays a vital role in posture, structure, athletic feats, physical labor, and maintaining general body condition for all its functions. In voice production, its only specific function is to send the breath through the trachea into the larynx to set the vocal membranes vibrating; there the role of the breath in particular and the diaphragm in general ceases. It does not control the action of the sound waves as they reflect through the oral cavity and set the resonating areas in vibration, any more than the bow or hammers control the sound waves within the cavity of the violin or piano.

Controllable and Noncontrollable Factors

The entire process of originating vocal sounds in the larynx is performed without voluntary control. We do not sense the breath that begins the vibration of the vocal membranes. This unfelt, unmeasured puff of air is supplied *before* we register the sensation of sound,

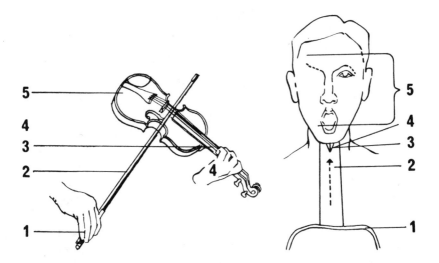

Figure 1. A comparison of violin and voice actions: 1. Initial pressure: violin—right hand, direct control; voice—diaphragm, indirect control. 2. Vibrating agent: violin—bow, direct control; voice—breath stream, no direct control. 3. Vibrators: violin—strings, direct control; voice—laryngeal membranes, no direct control. 4. Pitch: violin—left hand, direct control; voice—vocal cord action and organ of corti, indirect control. 5. Resonance: violin—wooden sound box, no direct control; voice—mouth cavity, hard palate, teeth, nasal bone, forehead, and other facial bones, direct control.

and any breath action, any aspirate sensation or pressure, we feel during vocalization is breath *after* the act, therefore unnecessary breath and a symptom of tension, push, strain, or force. Any good instrumentalist knows that the slightest overuse of pressure or blowing or squeezing destroys the beauty of his tone quality. So it is with the voice; the slightest sensation of breath is enough to spoil the finest vocal effort.

In Figure 1, the components and actions of the violin and the human vocal mechanism are compared. Some of these factors are within the player's control and some are not. Those that can be controlled on the violin are precisely those that cannot be controlled in the voice, and those that cannot be controlled by the violinist can be controlled by the speaker or singer. In playing the violin, the production of tone and pitch are manually manipulated by the right hand with the bow and the left hand on the strings; the vocal counterparts—diaphragm, breath stream, and vocal membranes—cannot be manipulated because they produce no controllable physical sensation in the trachea and larnyx. Only controllable actions are responsive to training.

The factors in vocal production beyond conscious control—the involuntary actions—include the act of respiration and the movement of the breath from the lungs through the bronchial tubes and trachea until it puffs through the vocal membranes in the larnyx; the neural impulse that closes the membranes; and the vibration, and extent of vibration, of the membranes and other muscular actions within the larnyx.

Subject to partial or indirect control are the semivoluntary actions, including supplementary breathing and the memory experience and brain signals that help in approximating pitch.

We have complete conscious or voluntary control over postural actions that aid respiration, including loosening of the knee joints, rotation of the pelvis, firming of the abdominal wall, expansion and extension of the back during inhalation and exhalation, and maximum chest expansion without chest or shoulder elevation; the actions of the cheek muscles, lips, jaw, and tongue that form and control the spatial relationships within the oral cavity affecting tonal quality and vowel formation; the sensation of the vocal sound waves vibrating in the hard palate and bone of the nose, forehead, and sinuses; and the habit pattern of overriding the auditory mechanism.

Bone and Air Conduction

Since sound is a molecular action, it requires a substance to carry or conduct it. Air is one conducting medium. Tiny air molecules, stimulated by an initial vibration, become extended or rarified and then contract again. In the extended state, each molecule in turn stimulates the same process in the molecules surrounding it, until a molecule reaches the eardrum and sets it into vibration, beginning the auditory process in the ear. This movement of sound waves to the ear through air is called air conduction.

But sound may be conducted through other media, such as wood, metal, water, bone, and glass. In the human body, bone conduction takes place in the teeth, the hard palate, the nasal bone, the sinuses, the cranium, and sometimes other bones.

A simple experiment can demonstrate the difference between air and bone conduction: Take a tuning fork, pluck it, and

hold the vibrating end near your ear; the sound you *hear* is transmitted by air conduction. Now pluck the fork again, but this time rest the base against the outside surface of your upper teeth; the sound you *feel* coursing through the teeth, nose, and head is transmitted by bone conduction (fig. 2).

A variation in the experiment demonstrates that the ear plays no part in bone conduction: Place the tuning fork on someone else's teeth and you hear

Figure 2. Tuning-fork experiment.

absolutely nothing, however close you are, while he feels and hears a big, brilliant, ringing sound. This means, of course, that he does not hear this sound through *his* ears since you hear nothing through *yours*. When you place the tuning fork to your ear, you hear what you listen to through the air, but when you place it on your teeth, you hear what you feel through the bone. Both the sensory and the auditory cortices of the brain have been stimulated by the bone-conducted sound waves—and the sound has registered in both, *without* the aid of the ear.

Overriding the Ear

Strictly speaking, the ear can listen, but it cannot hear—if we think of listening as the simple act of receiving the sound waves, while hearing is the physical act of registering sound, which takes place in the brain. We hear when the eighth cranial—or auditory—nerve is stimulated and sends an auditory impulse to the brain. The stimulation can come from vibrations initiated within the body and transmitted by bone conduction or from outside vibrations transmitted by air conduction through the outer ear. We can still hear the inner vibrations even if both ears are stopped up and outside sounds are inaudible, as long as the inner ear and one of the auditory nerve branches remains intact. Block your ears off completely when you speak, and you will hear the inner vibrations even more dynamically than when you listen with your ears, but the sound will be quite different from the sound that others hear when you speak.

When we listen to others, the ear is an active participant and transmits the sound it receives by air conduction with complete objectivity. But since we hear our own voices by means of bone conduction, the ear must be considered a nonessential agent in the process— and a nonobjective one if we try to judge the sound by it.

Conditioned by previous experience, the ear acts as a protector of the existing state of vocal production and speech patterns by standing in the way of attempts to establish new voice and speech habit patterns. An interesting example of this occurred a number of years ago in my studios. A student with a particular accent problem said, in one of his exercises, "I want to go *beck* home." I told him not to say "beck" but to say "back," and he replied, "I didn't say beck . . . I said beck." Even when he heard himself on a tape recorder he insisted, becoming more puzzled and anxious all the while: "But I didn't say beck. . . . I said *beck.*" From this, it should be obvious that the ear does not provide effective guidance to our own vocalizations because it does not effectively discriminate between bone-conducted and air-conducted sounds.

When you have acquired bad habits of speech, your ear reinforces them and so adapts itself that it cannot distinguish between your error (which you perceive primarily through bone conduction) and someone else's correct sound (which you hear solely through air conduction). Only when proper training has inculcated the ability to *feel* the sound does the ear finally become conditioned to the correct sound, as it was previously conditioned to the incorrect sound. At all times, the ear is an ineffectual instrument for changing deeply inbred vocal and verbal patterns.

To say all of this is not to deny the natural role of the ear or the value of ear training, which does develop sharper and better hearing for sounds that come from outside through air conduction. When you listen to your voice on a recording, your ear is entirely reliable and aids in an objective judgment, but when you listen to your voice as you produce it, your ear is undependable and a deceptive guide.

To train the voice, you must learn to ignore the auditory mechanism and rely instead on a new sensitivity to—and a new concentration on—other perceptions: the vibratory, kinesthetic, and tactile sensations that travel principally by the facial and trigeminal sensory and motor cranial nerves. The auditory cortex of the brain does take part in this action, but it is your awareness of the stimulation of the sensory cortex that will be the most vital and fundamental training experience.

When you speak or practice voice exercises, *do not think* the sound first! Such mental control is fickle at best and may very well compound existing vocal deficiencies. Nor will purely mental control provide the active "doing" process you will need to free yourself from undesirable vocal and speech habits.

Do not listen to the sound first! The new sounds and changes that the ear will automatically reject as unrealistic or awkward are precisely those that represent progress in training.

Learn to *feel* the sound first! These new perceptions result from sensations that *do* lead to the doing process, and by doing you will lose the old and find the new.

CHAPTER III

The Three Energies

*E*VERYTHING THAT LIVES MOVES, and all motion is action or energy. In the last chapter, I pointed out that speech and voice begin with involuntary actions—actions we cannot sense or direct—and go on to voluntary actions that we can control at will. My method of training deals only with the latter actions and energies—those that can be controlled consciously and intelligently.

The most important of the many actions that make up the complex process of vocalization and speech can be sorted out into three major categories: (1) structural action, (2) tonal action, and (3) consonant action. When these actions are correctly performed, speaking and singing are physically effortless but never lifeless. When the three are properly integrated, they help to relieve physical tensions, and the very act of speaking brings with it a sense of well-being and vitality. This chapter is only an introduction to the concepts; each action will be explained more fully in later chapters, and exercises will be given for mastering each.

Structural Action (see Chapter VI)

The first concept involves muscular sensations and kinesthetic memory—the tendency of muscles to assume accustomed positions—and leads to physical awareness of the contours and movements of the face and the oral cavity that help produce the most satisfactory vocal tones. Through the structural stretch exercise, certain cheek muscles are extended and the face takes on a specific form or facial posture. The feeling, or action-sensation, of this posture is very much that of a megaphone turned around inside the oral cavity—the wide end expanding the middle-posterior area of the cavity at the cheekbones, beneath the eyes, and the narrow end rounding and protruding the lips (fig. 3).

When the stretch exercise is faithfully practiced and the inverted-megaphone form achieved, not only will vocal qualities

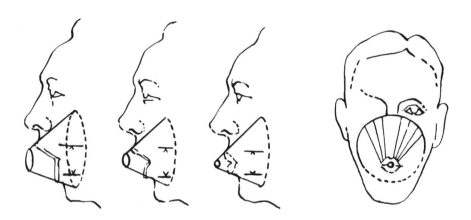

Figure 3. In the inverted-megaphone shape, the space between the side teeth, as indicated by the parallel lines and arrow heads, remains the same whatever the lip opening.

improve, but important by-products will appear—supportive habit patterns effortlessly producing a facial posture both functional and attractive, maximum expansion of the oral cavity or voice box, a soft rounding of the lips, greater flexibility of the tongue, a new approach to phonetics, and a newly discovered reflex action that relaxes the jaw, lowers the larynx, relaxes the vocal membranes, and even contributes to dental health.

Structural perception is not static; if it were, the speaker using proper facial posture would sound as if he were speaking inside a barrel. It must be dynamic and flexible—a constant awareness of muscle and membrane moving as they accommodate themselves to the inverted-megaphone shape in action. Nothing should be tight or taut; there should be only the dual feeling of relaxed energy and energetic relaxation.

This new facial posture may seem strange at first, but you will, in fact, look perfectly natural and probably better than before. A speaker whose lips curve back, pulling the mouth into a permanent wide smile, is under a great handicap. This backward facial posture tends to promote not only faulty jaw position and defective voice production, but weak and undesirable facial expressions; it inhibits projection of a positive personality.

Tonal Action (see Chapters VII and IX)

With the second concept, you will learn to experience the sensation of vocal vibrations. When the voice is properly used, the tones are consciously transmitted through the hard palate, the nasal bone,

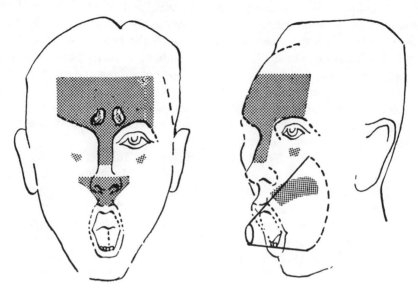

Figure 4. The major areas of tonal action—indicated by shading—are the hard palate, the bone of the nose and nasal sinuses, and the forehead and frontal sinuses.

the sinuses, and the forehead. Some of the sound waves continue on through the frontal sinuses, cranial bone, spine, and ribs, to produce chest resonance, but the conscious action takes place in these four areas of the head (fig. 4), and the more tonal action felt in these structures, the greater the chest resonance. When sound is transmitted in this way, we feel the vibratory-tonal actions.

All vowel sounds should be produced and felt as vibrations, because all vowels are voiced tones. The belief that pure vocal tones or vowels are expelled through the lips is a common misconception; only in whispering or the transmission of voiceless consonants do we feel the projection of sound through the lip opening.

The characteristic sensation of tonal action may be a buzz, a tickle, resonance, or a fairly strong vibration. You will learn to feel it first on the gum ridge of the hard palate and then through the rest of the bony areas. The intensity of the sensation and the concentrated density of the vocal sound waves will vary with circumstances—whether you are outdoors, in a large auditorium, in a classroom, or across a dinner table—but the essential feeling of the tones will be the same.

Control and command of tonal action rests on learning to *feel* this buzz or call instead of *listening* for a vocal tone. When this tonal sensation is combined with the proper use of the structural form, you will enjoy a sense of energy, of relaxation, and of exhilaration. Occasionally, even without training, one unconsciously adopts the right facial posture and focuses the voice properly through the bone conduction areas. When this happens, whether in a choral anthem, a performance on stage, or a shout to a taxi, the single vowel and tone come booming out with great vibration to everyone's pleasure—not least, one's own. With this sense of pleasure, the body announces that the voice is functioning properly, that it is properly controlled, that the vowels are correctly resonated and trans-mitted through the bony sounding board.

Tonal action develops the full pitch, range, power, and projection of the voice and improves quality by eliminating nasality, muffled tones, throatiness, and breathiness. With good tonal action, no breath and only the mildest warmth is ever felt on the lips at any level of voice production—the most conversational or the most projected. Tonal action feels good; it stimulates and relaxes the speaker because it functions properly only when all parts of the vocal process are in proper balance. Thus physical tension is relieved while beautifully rich and dynamic tones are produced.

Consonant Action (see Chapter X)

Consonants are the framework, the components of the skeletal structure, of the word, and they make three important contributions to speech: (1) They convey and crystalize the intelligibility of the word; (2) they give rhythm, tonal color, and melody to speech; (3) they furnish contrasts and variations through percussive, melodic, and sound effect qualities. Like both structural action and tonal action, the consonants can be felt.

Since the vowel is sustained in singing, the vowels are often compared with a solo musical instrument, and the singing voice *is* an instrument, not quite like any other. The musical qualities of the consonants, however, are rarely discussed; they are seen as utilitarian tools for the control and clarification of speech and little attention is paid to their esthetic functions; yet every time you feel a consonant, you feel a particular character of sound that *can* be related to a particular instrument, and a variety of consonants will simulate a variety of instruments. In speech, then, unlike singing, the consonants come to the fore; they are primarily responsible for rhythm, tempo, tonal variety, and sound effects, while the vowel sound dominates only in moments of special vocal emphasis. The vowels are a single instrument; the consonants make up an orchestra. It is interesting to note that in Greek, the consonant is called *symphona*, which means "consonance, or a harmony of sounds," while the vowel is called *phonienta*, which means sound.

Consonant action explores the instrumental identity of the consonants in detail (fig. 5); each has its own individual identity and physical sensation. The V, for example, if the sound is made as vibrant as possible, simulates the tone of the cello; the N, which has the greatest range and resonance, is a violin; the Z, the bass viol; the B, D, T, and K are percussive instruments. Some of these sensations are sustained or legato,

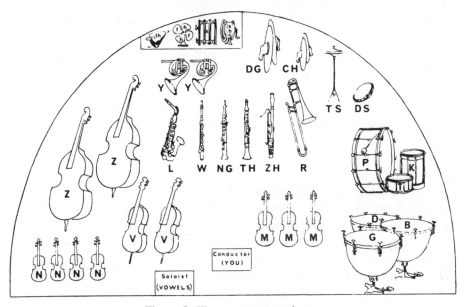

Figure 5. The consonant orchestra.

others short or staccato; some have special timbre, color, and tonal quality; others are voiceless sound effects. The correct sound for each of the consonant instruments can be repeated precisely if the proper physical sensation is memorized—not mentally or by listening, but through a physical sense memory. This method also eliminates the need for complicated, hard-to-coordinate, and impractical tongue, lip, and jaw drills. Some practice, of course, is necessary, but if you work with a little imagination, the pleasure, satisfaction, and skill to be derived will follow almost immediately.

Consonant action is important, not only because it supports and contains tonal and structural action, but because it is entirely responsible for intelligibility in speech. The margin for error is extremely wide in the pronunciation of vowels, but extremely narrow in the use of consonants without loss of meaning. Even singers must learn that beautifully clear diction in singing comes, not from careful formation of vowels as they are used in speech—which often destroys a good tone—but rather from skill at feeling the consonants, qualitatively and artistically, as musical values or instruments.

Each consonant must be a complete action-sensation. Too often, a singer or speaker *prepares* carefully for the execution of a consonant—tongue, teeth, and lips in position—and then, instead of following through with the proper percussion, legato, or sound effect, he assimilates this preparation into the vowel that follows, leaving behind an aborted consonant; yet because of the preparation, he feels that he has followed through. The esthetic satisfaction to be found in feeling skillful consonant action will guard against this unwitting neglect.

The Three Energies Combined

The three actions must not be thought of as separate, isolated entities, but rather as three basic components of a single whole—a trinity of actions that produces dynamic voice and speech. The three are always at work as an integrated unit, a coordinated team shifting the position of leadership to fit the speech need. One of the physical sensations will usually dominate the other two; which one will depend upon the strength of the speaker's involvement in his material, his distance from his listeners, the balance of all the elements in his total situation. Out of doors or in a large auditorium, tonal action will carry the speaker's voice to his farthest listener; in a conference room or a class room, structural action will give him quiet authority; in conversation or in sotto voce communication, consonant action will add precision and clarity to intimacy.

As you learn, you will take one step, one action, at a time, but the goal is a total result—a unified and coordinated set of speech and voice patterns deeply ingrained and gratifying. Not only will proper practice and execution of this trio of actions improve voice quality, articulation, and diction, but thorough mastery of them will counteract any tendency toward monotony, carelessness, lethargy, ineffective tempos, or poor projection. The process will, in fact, develop a built-in physical gauge for proper tempos, quality, and clarity, while adding vitality, vibrancy, and excitement to both voice and speech.

The Connecting Links (see Chapter VIII)

Structural, tonal, and consonant action are the framework on which I have built the method of voice and speech training presented here, and the consonants and major vowels—the principal elements of speech—fit comfortably into this framework, but there are two groups of vowels that stand somewhat apart: (1) the R-derivative, a consonant-like vowel, usually followed by the letter R, as in *learn, word, turn;* and (2) the neutral vowels, which are weakened forms of strong parent vowels that have become, over the years, specific vowels in their own right; there are four simple vowels, as in *took, tick, tech,* and *tuck,* and four diphthongs, as in *poor, peer, pare,* and *pour.* They occur frequently in conversation and only a little less often in formal communications.

In a sense, the importance of both of these groups is negative: The R-derivative and the neutral diphthong are always colored by the R, but this coloring must not be allowed to draw the voice or the word back into the throat. The neutral vowel is a fragile bridge between two consonants, and it must be crossed deftly so that it appears to become a contiguous part of consonant action rather than vowel pronunciation. Whether a neutral is stressed or unstressed, it should be thought of as the shortest distance between two consonants.

The unique virtue of this combination of the neutral link-vowels and consonant action is that a much more sophisticated skill at articulatory liaison has evolved out of it that makes possible a much more dynamic, and yet a more natural, linking technique than that which exists in either French or Italian, or even in the best British speech.

The End Result

Most of us admire the consonant precision of British speech at its best, the rounded vowels and tonal timbre of the French, the melodiousness of the Italians, the vitality of the Russians; to each of these languages, these qualities add not only excitement and beauty, but subtleties of meaning and expression. If you use the three energies with full vibratory, kinesthetic, and orchestral feeling, you will find that you have at your command the ability to add to your own speech any one or all of the admirable qualities inherent in these other languages and cultures; yet you will not, to the slightest degree, sound like an imitator of British, French, Italian, or Russian speech. You will sound like an American whose speech is thoroughly indigneous while at the same time a product, a reflection, and an intrinsic part of your individual culture and personal pride.

With this chapter, the basic exposition of the theory, philosophy, and logic behind the Lessac system of voice and speech is complete. There will be further discussion and amplification of these topics, but at this point you are now ready to begin the work of building a good voice and effective speech.

CHAPTER IV

Breathing and Posture

OICE AND SPEECH not only reflect your personality, as I pointed out in the first chapter, but the physical condition of your body. An excellently conditioned body is necessary for excellent use and control of any body action, and voice production and speech skills are the results of body actions. Illness, pain, fatigue, depression, or poor posture will quickly affect the quality, volume, rhythm, and pitch of your voice.

Nothing is more important to good body condition than correct breathing and correct posture. The two are interrelated: How you stand affects the way you breathe, and your breathing habits determine your posture. Breathing habits affect body balance, body alignment, distribution of body weight, and the relaxation and appearance of the body. When you stand and breathe properly, you will be free from unnecessary muscular tensions, aches, and strains. No physical act, whether it be walking, dancing, lifting a weight, skipping a rope, throwing a ball, climbing the stairs, playing the piano, talking, or singing, can be carried out efficiently and pleasurably unless it is supported by well-conditioned habit patterns of breathing.

The Mechanics of Breathing

To understand the complementary action of posture and breathing, you must understand the breathing process. The primary purpose of breathing is to provide the body with oxygen and to carry away its waste products, especially carbon dioxide. All this is accomplished by the passage of air in and out of the lungs.

Inhalation begins when the brain signals the diaphragm, a muscular membranous partition separating the chest and abdominal cavities, to contract, an action that lowers and flattens the muscle. As a result the chest cavity increases in size and the density of the air in the cavity *outside* the lungs, the pleural spaces, is reduced. The air *inside* the lungs, now proportionately denser, expands and pushes the elastic walls of the lungs outward to equalize the pressure in the chest cavity. Since pressure within is now less than the air pressure outside the body, new air rushes into the lungs through the trachea and bronchial tubes to restore *that* balance. (fig. 6). The process is reversed, and exhalation occurs, when the diaphragm relaxes and returns to its original position. As the chest cavity is reduced, the increasing density of the pleural air compresses the lungs and forces the

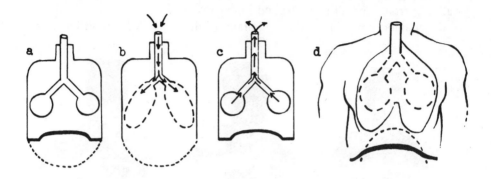

Figure 6. An experimental demonstration of the breathing mechanism: A. The bottle cavity represents the chest cavity; the rubber stretched across the bottom, the diaphragm; the balloons, the lungs; and the glass tubes leading into the balloons, the trachea and bronchial tubes. B. As the rubber is pulled down, the bottle cavity increases, the balloons expand, and air rushes into them through the tubes. C. When the rubber returns to position, the cavity is decreased and the air is pushed out of the balloons. D. The human lungs.

breath out through the bronchial tubes, trachea, larynx, throat, and finally the mouth or nose.

Just as air can be exhaled through either the nose or mouth, so can it be inhaled in either way, and in breathing exercises, the two methods should alternate. There are three ways to inhale through the nose: (1) with lips closed in the position used for saying M; (2) with lips open and the back of the tongue touching the soft palate in the position used for saying NG; or (3) with lips open and the top surface of the tongue against the hard palate, approximating the position used for saying N. The last is the easiest, quickest, and quietest way; therefore an excellent choice when using a microphone. For ordinary purposes, breathing through the nose is more hygienic than breathing through the mouth because the nasal passages warm and cleanse the air before it reaches the larynx, but since mouth breathing is both inevitable and efficient in speech or singing, it should be included in your practice. Of course mouth breathing is hardly advisable outdoors whenever the weather is cold or windy or the air polluted.

The Posture for Breathing

The chest should never be unnaturally puffed out during inhalation; it should, in fact, be at nearly full expansion at all times. What we call chest expansion means inflating the chest cavity, not changing its position or girth; it does not mean lifting the front of the chest while contracting the back. Every internal cavity must have a back and sides as well as a front, and all must expand in expansion. In the exercises at the end of the chapter, you will learn to maintain a fully expanded, broad back area,

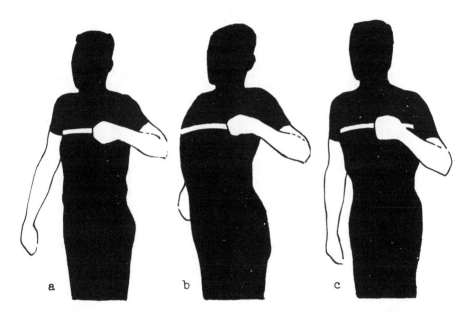

Figure 7. The effects of breathing and posture on chest measurements: A. Normal chest measurement with incorrect posture—33¼ inches; B. Measurement with incorrect chest expansion—36 inches. C. With correct breathing and posture, the normal and expanded measurements are about the same—39 to 40 inches. These measurements were all taken on the author.

which will bring about the fullest chest expansion without puffing. (fig. 7). Correct breathing and posture will restore almost a half inch to your height and one-and-a-half to three inches to the chest circumference—neither of which will be additions, but natural attributes now hidden by incorrect function. With a full broad back and shoulder line, free of any protrusion of the shoulder blades, the body will look as it was meant to look—straight and strong, yet relaxed and graceful. With more room inside the chest cavity at all times, such vital organs as the heart, lungs, trachea, and larynx will be less crowded, and the whole body will feel lighter and more comfortable.

Some bad posture is carelessness drilled into habit, but too many of us, young and old alike, have been conditioned into poor posture by poor but potent influences. We have deliberately taken, or been given, as models the stiff look of the soldier at parade attention; the puffy, heavily hunched look of the improperly trained wrestler or weight lifter; or the majestic, thrust-bellied stance of the old-fashioned opera singer (fig. 8).

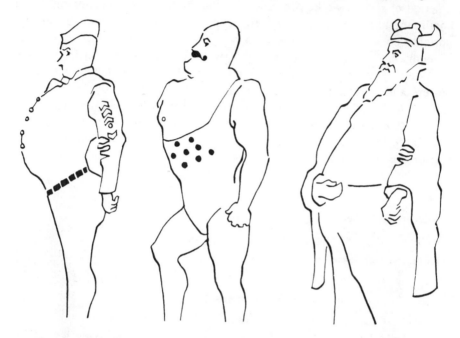

Figure 8. Three incorrect versions of correct posture: the soldier, the wrestler, and the overpadded tenor.

Perhaps few people today would imitate these examples completely, but it is a mistake to think that there is *anything* to be learned from such models. Even partial imitation is harmful and to be avoided.

With good posture, you will never stand with knee joints locked and tense thigh muscles pushed to the rear; pelvis pushed backward, incorrectly bending the lower spine and stiffening it into rigidity; abdominal wall sucked in or pushed out; upper back contracted, thrusting the shoulder blades out; back muscles of the neck so tightly constricted that the head is forced backward, the chin forward and up; shoulders lifted and thrown back; chest lifted and puffed out.

With good posture and breathing you will look taller if your are short, less gangling if you are very tall.

How the Body Wants to Breathe

Again, taking the natural, functional approach to breathing, the first question is how does the body *want* to breathe when it is not subjected to poor conditioning? Fortunately, correct breathing and correct posture are relatively easy to achieve—you can demonstrate this for yourself and you can be your own teacher—but concentrated practice over a period of several weeks is necessary to build the proper functioning into a continuing habit. Although very few people breathe correctly while standing upright, no one can breathe *in*correctly while bending over, squatting, kneeling, crouching, jumping, sitting forward, or lying on his back. In these positions, the muscles fall naturally into the relationships that lead to good posture and counteract faulty conditioning, allowing the body to breathe as it wants to breathe. Observe what happens when you inhale and exhale in any of these positions and remember the sensations; observe particularly the physical feeling of the stomach, the sides, and the back; then, with the sense-memory of what it feels like to breathe correctly, try to reproduce those

Checklist

1. Crown of the head is highest part of the body.

2. Head in easy swiveling position.

3. Chin is level—never raised.

4. Back of neck extended upward.

5. Front of neck always loose—never stretched.

6. Shoulders sloping and somewhat forward.

7. Entire back expanded, with maximum space between shoulder blades.

8. Spine, with slight convex curve, in easy contact with wall from pelvis to upper back.

9. Overall chest cavity expanded.

10. Pelvis rocked forward; abdominal wall curves inward and upward as part of the forward movement.

11. Hands fall a bit in front of the thighs.

12. Thighs forward and loose.

13. Knees always unlocked and loose.

14. Calf muscles loose.

15. Heels against wall; body resting lightly on both heels and soles.

Figure 9. Correct posture.

sensations while standing upright.

At first, you may find it necessary to change your usual upright posture quite radically. As your body responds, to accommodate the unfamiliar expanding movements of natural breathing, it will begin to assume the position shown in figure 9. In the check list that accompanies the illustration you will find the characteristics of the posture that accompanies correct breathing, but let correct breathing be the way to achieve correct posture. Use the list only to check whether you are breathing correctly; if you are, then you will be standing correctly, too.

Like bending and squatting, many common activities break the wrongly conditioned posture patterns that inhibit natural breathing: a batter waiting to swing, a boxer looking for an opening, a violinist playing, a golfer ready to tee off, a woman mopping, a gardener hoeing, a couple engaged in ballroom dancing—all of these people will breathe naturally and correctly, but when the activity ceases and they stand upright again, breathing and posture may fall once more under the control of conventional conditioning. Yet in some of these activities, the participant, temporarily conditioned by his activity, breathes naturally even in an almost upright position, his shoulders, back, and pelvis only slightly more rounded forward than in the correct posture illustrated in figure 9. It should be relatively easy, then—by carrying over the sense-memory from the activity—to retain the comfortable expansion of the shoulders, back, and pelvis while adjusting the head, neck, and legs to the completely upright position.

Expert swimmers and divers, who must combine the maximum chest expansion of natural breathing with maximum body extension, are also assisted in an easier action by the physical support of the water. As a result, perhaps, they often carry over good breathing and postural habits into everyday life. But anyone can do so by learning to recognize and reproduce at will the sense-memory of natural breathing.

Breath and Sound

Before moving on to the exercises, let me emphasize that although natural breathing is a necessary support for good voice and speech action, the breath stream should be understood as a distinctly different and separate current from the vocal sound stream. Remember that vocal sound is amplified and strengthened by resonance and wave reflection; breath, being windlike in character, tends to obscure or disperse the sound waves, creating a breathy, forced tone quality (see Chapter II). If the breath stream were really the same as the sound stream and traveled at the rate of sound, it would, as Dr. Douglas Stanley points out, "have to blow more than ten times as hard as the worst hurricane: to blow the audience out of the hall—to blow the auditorium itself into bits."[1]

For beautiful singing tones or beautifully projected speaking tones, exhalation must be kept to an irreducible minimum. Today, as in the past, the technique of pumping the diaphragm is often advocated for strong speech and voice production. Its advocates still claim that if you breathe well, you will sing and speak well. They have observed an association but turned cause and effect around: The truth is that if you sing and speak well, you will breathe well. If you become aware of the use of breath while singing or speaking, you are already indulging in extraneous and harmful manipulation of the breath. The best tones will be felt when a minimal amount of breath is used, an amount so minimal as to deny conscious use of it. Strenuous pumping or pushing of the diaphragm or the abdominal muscles, then, can have little to do with volume or projection of tone.

Breath is necessary to vibrate the vocal cords, but the amount required, even for a strong tone, is infinitesimal when compared with the amount available. Some French scientists hold that breath is non-essential even here, that vocal cord vibration is stimulated entirely by neural impulses.[2] Should their experiments prove valid, the Lessac system of voice and speech training will be even more significant.

The diaphragm and other respiratory muscles, as well as the whole body, must be maintained always at the peak of condition, but the dispersant stream of breath must never be permitted to interfere with the stream of sound. Remember that breath control does not regulate voice production—rather, voice production regulates breath control.

Natural Breathing Exercises

These exercises will teach you to feel the natural breathing function. While in the exercise positions, breathe easily; don't *try* to breathe correctly or to do anything unusual or difficult. You will find that inhalation and exhalation are different from what you usually feel when you stand; nevertheless, they will feel entirely natural and automatic. As you do the exercises, note carefully the various action-sensations that accompany them; try to remember these sensations; try to associate them with some natural activity you enjoy and practice them as if you were engaged in that. If you concentrate completely on becoming aware of the natural breathing processes, you should find the exercises pleasurable as well as instructive.

[1] Stanley, Dougles: Your Voice: Applied Science of Vocal Art. New York, Pitman Publishing Co., 1950. p. 3.
[2] Freud, E. D.: Voice and breathing: a report on some new concepts, AMA Archives of Otolaryngology 67: 1-7, 1958.

Exercise one—Supine Position (fig. 10)

step 1. *To take position:* Lie on your back on a firm mattress, a pad, or a blanket.

step 2. Make yourself feel as light as possible; with every muscle loose and soft, your whole body should feel as if all weight had been eliminated.

step 3. Gently stretch your body; make it as long as possible, from the bottom of your heels to the crown of your head, with the back of your neck fully extended and as close to touching the supporting surface as possible without tension in the throat.

step 4. Keep the knees loose but not raised, which will allow the pelvis to tilt forward just enough to relax the small of the back against the supporting surface. The rest of the back will be fully expanded while the shoulders, rounded gently and comfortably, will not touch the floor.

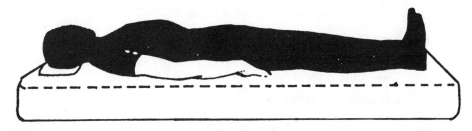

Figure 10.

step 5. Now observe how the body feels. Comfortably relaxed and breathing naturally, you have in this supine position, achieved perfect posture with exactly the body alignment you want to achieve when you are standing: In an upright position it will feel sloping and slightly forward, but it will not make you look stooped or hollow chested.

step 6. Now turn your attention to the natural breathing process in the supine position: when you breathe in, your abdominal muscles, just below your rib cage, swell out; when you breathe out, your abdominal muscles go in. This in-and-out motion accompanies every breath rhythmically and quietly. The sides of your body in the vicinity of your waistline also gently expand. Memorize the action-sensation of the movements in these areas.

step 7. Stand up and try to reproduce these sensations as you breathe quietly. Don't be discouraged if at first you find that the abdominal wall moves inward during inhalation and outward during exhalation, the exact opposite of the actions you observed while lying down. Just lie down again; observe once more the easy, natural breathing pattern; memorize the feeling of the action that produced it; then stand and repeat the feeling and you will repeat the action.

Do this three or four times; then proceed to the next exercise.

Exercise two—Bend-Over Series (fig. 11)

A. Full Bend-Over (fig. 11A)

step 1. To take position: Bend over from the hips with top of head below waistline, arms and hands hanging loosely and comfortably about six to eight
inches from the ground, and knees slightly bent.

*step 2. Inhale easily a*nd naturally without permitting even the slightest lifting of
the body above the waist.

step 3. Memorize the action-sensation of strong expansion of the side muscles all
around to the small of the back occuring simultaneously with abdominal wall expansion, as if you were pushing against the circumference
of a belt, so that you will be able to repeat it when standing upright.
Think of the expansion of the entire waistline as "filling up the bottom
of the bucket."

step 4. Exhale; repeat the exercise several times.

B. Half Bend-Over (fig. 11B)

step 1. To take position: From full bend-over, lift body until forehead, still hanging easily, is about five inches above waist level.

step 2. Inhale easily and naturally.

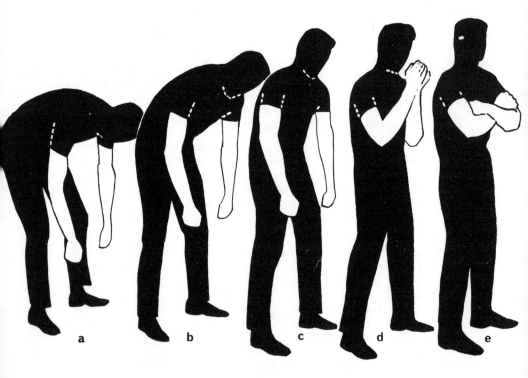

a   b   c   d   e

step 3. Memorize the action-sensation of additional expansion, now moving up into the lower back area just above the sides, so that it, too, can be carried over to the upright position.

step 4. Exhale; repeat several times.

C. Quarter Bend-Over (fig. 11C)

step 1. To take position: From half bend-over, lift body until you assume the golfer's "putting" position, or until your chin is about ten to twelve inches above the waist.

step 2. Inhale easily and naturally.

step 3. Memorize the action-sensation of expansion now moving through the upper back under the armpits and forward into the upper chest. Think of the expansion of the entire upper back as "filling the bucket to the top."

step 4. Exhale; repeat several times.

Comment: If you do not immediately feel this full expansion moving forward, tie a string around your chest just under the armpits across the pectoral muscles and note the pressure against the string during inhalation. If necessary, tie a string around the waist or stomach area as well so that both strings will signal the filling up of the entire breath bucket.

D. Almost Upright Position (fig. 11D)

step 1. To take position: Straighten the knees but leave them flexible enough to jiggle back and forth at least half an inch. Keep the pelvis under to create a slightly convex curve in the lower back; the abdomen will become gently firm and flat, or even somewhat concave. Now lift the upper body as if it were suspended from a string at a point between the shoulder blades, so that the shoulders remain rounded forward and the head and neck slightly bowed, while the rest of the body comes to an upright position.

step 2. Raise your cupped hands to about two inches from your nose with your upper arms touching the pectoral muscles, as if holding a flower and bowing your head a bit to inhale the fragrance.

step 3. Inhale the imagined fragrance realistically.

step 4. Memorize the action-sensation of the expansion starting from the abdominal wall, moving through the side muscles around to the small of the back (the bottom of the bucket), then up the lower and mid-back into the muscles under the armpits, and around into the chest, which completes filling up the rest of the bucket.

Comment: Note that the chest really expands from back to front; since it is not lifted or puffed out unnaturally, there should be no strain or discomfort in neck, shoulders, or back. Note again that your position is almost upright.

E. Upright Position (fig. 11E)

step 1. To take position: Stretch the back of the neck upward, from the flower-smelling position, until the crown of the head is the highest part of the body, the chin level, and the front of the neck soft. Fold the hands easily in front.

step 2. Inhale easily and naturally.

step 3. Repeat the complete expansion of natural breathing as it felt from beginning to end of the bend-over series and you should be breathing correctly with correct upright posture.

Comment: In all of these exercises, the action-sensations emphasize back expansion rather than chest expansion. The back thus expanded feels strong and powerful, seems to move the arms a bit forward as a result of the overall chest expansion, and gives the entire body a feeling of much better overall balance. This action follows the law of forward direction; breathe with your back, and everything moves forward; breathe with your chest and everything moves backward.

Exercise three—Diving or Broad-Jump Position (fig. 12)

Figure 12.

step 1. To take position: Stand upright with arms stretched forward at shoulder height; the entire body, especially the knees, should feel loose and free.

step 2. While inhaling, swing your arms down and back; at the same time, bend your knees into jumping position; keep your buttocks down and your face up and stay on your toes.

step 3. Hold the position, and your breath, long enough to memorize the strong action-sensation you will get from the extraordinarily rapid expansion of your abdominal and side muscles (the bottom of the bucket) during this swing into position while inhaling.

step 4. Practice repeating the experience of full, rapid waistline expansion in an upright position, without lifting the shoulders, head, or neck.

Exercise four—Crouching Series

These positions are like those taken in a football scrimmage.

A. At Rest Position (fig. 13)

step 1. To take position: While on your toes, squat down, placing your left fore-arm just above left knee and knuckles of loosely-clenched right fist on floor between spread knees to maintain balance (fig. 13A).

step 2. Inhale easily and naturally.

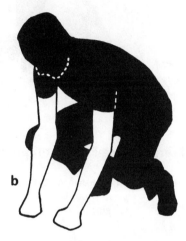

Figure 13.

step 3. Memorize the action-sensation of expansion spreading in the back.

step 4. Exhale and repeat two or three times; then reverse positions of right and left arms and repeat the exercise; then place both hands in loosely clenched fists, on floor between knees (fig. 13B) and repeat the exercise.

step 5. Stand upright and try to reproduce the action-sensation of back expansion as you inhale. You may need to let the shoulders relax and round forward to accommodate this expansion.

B. Charging Position (fig. 14)

step 1. To take position: While on your toes, squat as in previous position, except that the clenched fist is about one foot farther forward; keep your pelvis down (fig. 14A).

step 2. Inhale easily and naturally.

step 3. Memorize the action-sensation of full expansion of the back and sides while abdominal muscles feel comfortably firm.

step 4. Exhale and repeat two of three times; then reverse positions of right and left arms and repeat the exercise; then place both hands on the floor ahead of the knees (fig. 14B) and repeat the exercise.

step 5. Stand and try to reproduce the feeling in the almost upright position.

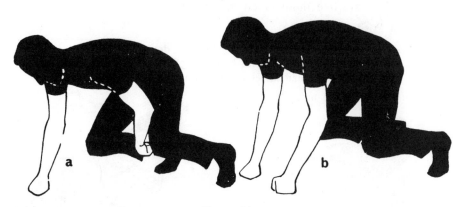

Figure 14.

Exercise five—Floor-Scrubbing Position (fig. 15)

step 1. To take position: Get on your knees and place your hands well ahead of
your shoulders; keep the back nicely rounded in a convex line with no
sagging.

Figure 15.

step 2. Inhale easily and naturally.

step 3. Memorize the action-sensation of added expansion as you breathe, so that
it can be carried over to the upright position; note the firming of the
abdominal muscles.

step 4. Exhale and repeat two or three times.

Exercise six—Push-Up Position (fig. 16)

step 1. To take position: Starting from the floor-scrubbing position, raise your knees about six inches off the ground and balance on hands and toes; keep the knees somewhat bent and flexible and the pelvis low.

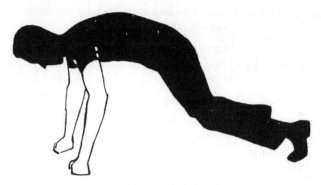

Figure 16.

step 2. Inhale easily and naturally.

step 3. Memorize the action-sensation of expansion in the entire back area and all the way down into the lowest spine and pelvic region and the comfortable firming of the abdominal muscles after inhalation.

step 4. Exhale and repeat two or three times.

step 5. Hold your breath during the last inhalation and stand up, trying to retain the same sensation as in the push-up position.

step 6. Exhale, then inhale while standing and check for the same breathing action as in the push-up position.

Exercise seven—Deep Knee-Bend Position (fig. 17)

step 1. To take position: Squat comfortably on your toes, keeping the pelvis low and rounded comfortably forward and avoiding a rigidly straight back; rest your elbows easily just above your knees with your hands loosely between the knees.

step 2. Inhale easily and naturally.

step 3. Memorize the action-sensation of the complete breathing cycle, beginning with expansion of the

Figure 17.

abdominal muscles and continuing into the sides, back, and chest, ending with the comfortably firm feeling in the abdominal muscles.

step 4. Exhale; repeat two or three times.

step 5. Hold your breath during the last inhalation and stand up, trying to retain the same sensation as in the deep knee-bend position.

step 6. Exhale, then inhale while standing and check for the same breathing action as in the deep knee-bend position.

Comment: This exercise begins as a bellows action in the abdominal muscles and ends with the same muscles acting as a firm control—a kind of body governor.

Exercise eight—Sitting Position (fig. 18)

step 1. To take position: Sit forward with the very edge of the posterior portion of the bony pelvis, or sacrum, resting on the front edge of the chair; rest your elbows just above your knees with your hands hanging loosely between the knees and your feet comfortably flat on the ground.

step 2. Inhale easily and naturally.

step 3. Memorize the action-sensation of the complete breathing cycle, ending with the firm feeling in the abdominal muscles, similar to that of the deep knee-bend exercise.

step 4. Exhale and repeat two or three times.

step 5. Hold your breath during the last inhalation and stand up, trying to retain the same sensation as in the sitting position.

step 6. Exhale, then inhale while standing and check for the same breathing action as in the sitting position.

Figure 18.

Exercise nine—Leaning Position (fig. 19)

step 1. To take position: Stand with feet about fifteen inches away from a table, desk, or chair back, bending forward somewhat, and leaning with your hands on the edge, as if you were examining a letter or a drawing.

step 2. Inhale easily and naturally.

step 3. Memorize once more the action-sensation of back expansion and the firm abdominal muscles at the end of the breathing cycle.

step 4. Step back, letting your hands hang comfortably a bit in front of your thighs, trying to retain the action-sensation of the end of the breath cycle.

step 5. Check your posture and exhale.

step 6. Inhale while standing, trying to retain the same sensation as in the leaning position.

Exercise ten—Combined Leaning Position (fig. 20)

step 1. To take position: Crouch on your toes with your hands and arms resting on the seat of a chair (fig. 20A). Inhale easily and naturally and memorize once more the action-sensation of the entire breathing cycle. Repeat several times.

Figure 19.

step 2. Stand and bend over with hands resting on the seat of the chair (fig. 20B) and repeat exercise in step 1.

Figure 20.

step 3. Lean on the arms of the chair (fig. 20C) and repeat exercise in step 1.

step 4. Lean on back of chair (fig. 20D) and repeat all of exercise nine.

Exercise eleven—Pelvis Rocking (fig. 21)

step 1. To take position: Stand firmly on both feet, hands on hips with thumbs behind, fingers in front.

step 2. Rock the pelvis back, pushing with the fingers, so that the back is contracted into an S curve and the shoulders thrown to the rear into a completely wrong posture (fig. 21A).

step 3. Reverse the hand position—thumbs to the front, fingers behind—and rock the pelvis forward, simultaneously extending the shoulders and expanding the back, moving the entire torso forward into the correct posture (fig. 21B).

step 4. Repeat these movements from extreme back to full forward position of the pelvis and back several times.

step 5. Memorize the action-sensations that accompany forward movement of the pelvis: loosening of the knees, relaxation and forward movement of the thighs, filling of the small of the back, firming of the abdominal muscles to an almost concave feeling, straightening and lengthening of the spine from an S curve to a slightly convex C curve, broadening of the back, and forward movement of the shoulders.

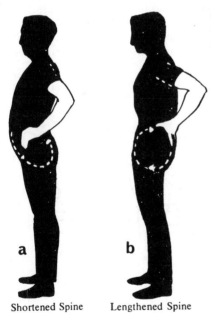

a   b

Shortened Spine   Lengthened Spine

Figure 21.

Comment: The importance of this exercise is its demonstration of the extent to which the pelvis can move backward and forward and the importance of training the pelvis, as well as the torso above the waist, to stay in the proper forward position. Remember that the concave curve in back and the convex in front, with the abdomen hanging out, is wrong; the slight convex C curve in back and the concave abdomen is correct. There must be this slight convex curve to the spine, from the forward rotation of the pelvis to the gentle forward rounding of the shoulders and back, to maintain a straight line through the center of the body. If you attempt to maintain what you think is a straight spine, you will curve it the other way and throw everything off center and off balance. As you practice the pelvis-rocking exercise—and you should repeat it as often as possible—you will feel the tightening of the muscles in the thighs and back in the wrong position and the relaxation and physical relief in that area as the small of the back fills out with the forward movement of the pelvis. The other aspects of good posture, from loose knee joints to broadening and forward movement of the back and shoulders, will follow.

Exercise twelve—Posture Check (see fig. 9)

step 1. To take position: Stand with your heels against a flat wall, balancing your body on both the heels and soles of the feet.

step 2. Inhale and exhale easily and naturally.

step. 3. Feel the correct action-sensations of the breath cycle.

step 4. Observe the characteristics of correct posture: heels against wall; knees loose; spine long and straight and in contact with wall from bottom of pelvis to top of shoulder blades; no open hollow in the back; neck extended, lowering the chin and elevating the crown of the head and moving it away from the wall.

step 5. Move away from the wall and move around freely and easily.

Comment: Keep this posture whether standing or walking. Remember that the proper head position will make the still unfamiliar overall posture feel comfortable.

Exercise thirteen—Abdominal Muscle Strengthening (fig. 22)

step 1. To take position: Bend slightly from the waistline, keep the knees loose, and grasp the thighs firmly.

step 2. Suck the abdominal muscles in until you feel a hollow in the abdominal wall.

step 3. Swallow, to tighten the abdominal muscles further.

step 4. Relax the abdominal muscles; repeat exercise once or twice.

Comment: Do not repeat this exercise more than three times without a few hours rest in between because of the strain on the abdominal muscles.

Exercise fourteen—Exhalation Control

Although exercises fourteen and fifteen are both exercises in breath control, concentrate on your posture as you do them. Do you feel the slight C curve? Are your knees loose? Is the back of your neck straight? Can you swivel your head easily from extreme left to extreme right on a perfect level? Is the crown of your head the highest part of your body?

Figure 22.

step 1. Inhale easily and naturally.

step 2. Exhale slowly while sounding the letter S, with the tongue up toward the gum ridge and the side teeth gently touching.

step 3. Concentrate on making the S very thin, high-pitched, and sharp, but exceedingly soft, at the same time; avoid jerkiness, changing quality, or a heavy, pressured hiss, like air escaping from a tire.

step 4. Try to soften the S when it gets thin and sharp; then *try to sharpen* it when it gets extremely soft.

step 5. Check with the back of the hand or a mirror to make sure there is no noticeable escape of breath. At the same time, note how the abdominal muscles gradually, almost imperceptibly, contract inward like a sponge being squeezed very slowly until all the water is gone.

Comment: This exercise will develop skill in using a minimum of breath in the production of either voiced or unvoiced sound. Do ten consecutive repetitions three times daily. In the beginning, you should be able to sound the S for fifteen to twenty-five seconds; if you hold the sound as long as you possibly can each time, you should finally achieve a duration of forty to fifty seconds. When the S is perfect, do the same with Z, SH, ZH, TH, F, V, M, N, and NG. (See Chapter X on Consonant Action.)

Exercise fifteen—Duration-Capacity Improvement

step 1. Inhale easily and naturally and hold for as long as you can without straining.

step 2. Time the duration of breath holding and divide in half to provide a 50 per cent norm.

step 3. Inhale again and hold breath for norm time.

step 4. Exhale: repeat exercise immediately.

Comment: Do ten consecutive repetitions three times daily. Each week, add from three to five seconds to the previous week's norm. Be precise: If you begin with a norm of twenty seconds, do not hold to twenty-two seconds or stop at eighteen. If you feel constriction in the throat, try swallowing while holding your breath. If swallowing is difficult during the exercise, collect some saliva, which not only helps to relax the throat muscles, but acts as a lubricant. The body handles the first half of the duration quite comfortably and naturally; then note the very gradual and almost imperceptible firming of the abdominal muscles, from about midway through to the end of the exercise.

CHAPTER V

Relaxation: Harmony

and the Art of Resting

*I*n *An Actor Prepares,* Stanislavsky wrote:

> It seems that if you lay an infant or a cat on some sand to rest or to sleep, and then carefully lift him up, you will find the imprint of his whole body on the soft surface. But if you make the very same experiment with a person of our nervous generation, all you would find on the sand are the marks of his shoulder blades and rump—whereas the rest of his body, thanks to chronic muscular tension, will never touch the sand at all.

The secret of the infant and the cat is relaxation.

By relaxation, I mean a dynamic process. The term should not imply the absence of action or motion—without disease there is no such thing as an inactive muscle or an inactive nerve—but the most efficient application of all the muscles of the body to the task at hand, be it action or rest. This implies a constant harmony among the muscles, and action and rest cannot really be separated, for in each action—including rest, which is almost zero action for the voluntary muscles—some muscles contract or shorten, which is action, and others are released or lengthened, which is rest. But each group helps the other: Just as correct breathing aids good posture and good posture leads to correct breathing, so muscle contraction aids release and muscle release permits contraction; whatever the individual function at the moment, all of the body's muscles function together as a whole. In that sense, every muscle has a role to play all the time; there is never a loss of tonus. In this state of harmony, the whole body functions in proper balance, which we experience as genuine relaxation.

In discussing breathing, posture, and relaxation thus far, I have dealt primarily with the voluntary muscles, but when we relax the voluntary muscles, obviously we tend to exert a direct effect upon the semivoluntary and nonvoluntary systems of the body. When we relax those skeletal muscles over which we have control, the visceral organs and internal muscles will tend to relax as well. I believe it physically impossible to be thoroughly relaxed in any one part of the body while tense in any other part. The salutary effect of physical relaxation on the nervous system is well known. All this means that relaxation can be consciously induced, controlled, and felt. Being relaxed should mean simply that you experience the *feeling* of being relaxed. You can learn to recognize the presence or absence of body tensions—and you can learn to ensure their absence.

Energy and Rest

There should be no sense of opposition between energy and rest; rather they should work together like two children balancing a seesaw. The one is essential to the other and both are a part of every action. When one rises, the imbalance between the two sets up a potential rise for the other.

When any voluntary physical act is accomplished with the greatest degree of relaxation, a state of *restful energy* has been achieved: The total effort required to perform the task has been distributed among the largest possible number of muscles; excessive tensions are completely absent; the muscular relationship is balanced, with no overloading anywhere—in effect the body as a whole has performed the task instead of delegating it to any specific muscle group.

When a man relaxes easily into physical inaction, he approaches the state of *energetic rest:* He has taught his muscles to feel so free and weightless—never limp or heavy—that he loses his sense of contact with bed, chair, or ground; every muscle possible is in a state of release—*the sensation of repose and the readiness to spring alertly into action have melted into one feeling.*

To achieve these states, you must learn to observe the functioning of your own body. With continued practice of such concentrated observation, you will slowly begin to identify body actions that may at first have seemed too subtle to be perceptible. You will become more vividly aware of the sensations of both tension and relaxation and of the equilibrium of rest and energy. This experience, and the knowledge you gain from it, are the first step in developing your ability to choose the appropriate balance between rest and energy at any time and in any action. In this manner, you gain mastery of your body and freedom in the use of it. As you gain control over the subtler actions, you will also find new sensitivity in the use of the body.

Control and Consciousness

With practice, you can gain such control over your

body as a whole and over the individual muscle groups, that you can choose the appropriate balance between action and rest in any act effortlessly and at will. The control has become habitual, *but this does not mean that it is exercised routinely.* The body cannot begin to establish an appropriate balance without a conscious command from the brain: That this is a habit means only that the body can execute the command easily and accurately.

This kind of control can be compared to that which you exercise when you drive an automobile. The physical acts of shifting gears, pushing pedals, slowing down, or passing other cars are habitual and may be almost on the level of reflex action. The hand and the foot know, without being told, how far and how fast to move to accomplish the desired action—but because the brain is in constant command, they do not begin to move until they are directed to do so, and the action can be suspended or altered at any given moment; thus, the driver is not driven by the hand or foot but the hand or foot by the driver. He knows *why* each action is performed; though the hand or foot can guide the action without conscious control once the command is given, the driver retains the right to command and to regulate if necessary. For this reason, these actions cannot be called purely automatic or mechanical. This priority of command will also govern the use of the habits you acquire in vocal production and speech skills.

The ability to balance rest and energy is particularly advantageous during periods of stress. At such times, the tendency is toward greater tension and muscle contraction. If you have practiced relaxation as a dynamic process, you will be able to reverse this tendency and will significantly increase your physical and nervous endurance in times of severe pressure.

Natural Ways of Relaxation

Before we begin the specific relaxation exercises, a word about some natural techniques of relaxation. First of all, the breathing and posture exercises in Chapter IV could very easily serve as excellent relaxation exercises, but more basic than those are four relaxing actions we come by naturally—stretching, yawning, shaking of muscles, and swallowing. Man has the power of positive relaxation in these actions, but he does not indulge in them often enough. Observe how spontaneously and how often the cat and dog stretch, shake, and yawn. These are the natural ways of controlling and directing the state of feeling good. And they do not have to be learned—they are there for the asking.

The yawn reflex has two characteristic forms. In the first, and the more involuntary, the facial muscles are stretched backward and respiration stops for a split second; then comes a deep, involuntary

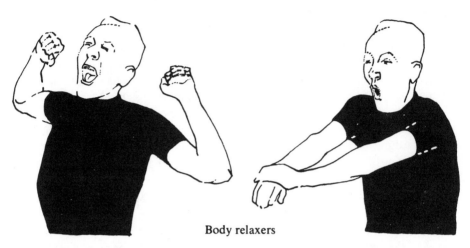

Body relaxers

Figure 23. The two yawns: A. Backward and focused on the soft palate;
B. forward and focused on the hard palate.

intake of breath, sometimes followed by several successive attempts at short
inspiration (fig. 23A). If this yawn is voiced, the soft-palate focus produces
a high-pitched, nasopharyngeal sound of importance in training the upper
third of the male singing voice. The second form is more controllable and
may be induced by forming the face into the full inverted megaphone shape
described in Chapters III and VI (fig. 23B). When this yawn is voiced, the
sound is usually a comfortably produced AW or O vowel sound, cleanly
focused on the bony resonating areas, and of major importance in training
the lower two thirds of the male singing voice and the entire range of the
female voice.

Yawning and stretching often go together. Aside
from increasing the intake of oxygen, the yawn relaxes; it stretches the
muscles of the face, thus helping to eliminate muscle-cell waste matter; it
produces free, healthy vocal sounds; and it releases tension. Whether voluntary or involuntary, this action cannot be called passive for there is vitality
in its seeming laziness—the vitality of dynamic relaxation. It should not be
stifled if at all possible—rather it should be encouraged.

When we stretch and spread out arms and legs
and back, we feel as if we could move the world. There is more pushing or
holding power behind a relaxed stretch than in any similar forceful action.
The absolute truth of this observation may require controlled laboratory
experimentation, but our own pragmatic experience will support the thesis:
Try lifting, pushing, chinning, or separating two resisting forces, such as
people, or heavy, movable posts; try first with a natural stretch feeling,
using the appropriate balance between rest and energy; then try again,

thinking of the action as an exertion of force in the usual, muscle-tight way. Notice which is easier, which is lighter, which is more enjoyable, and which is more effective.

Shaking or slapping the muscles is a wonderful way to relax them (fig. 24). Start with your wrists, then your elbows and

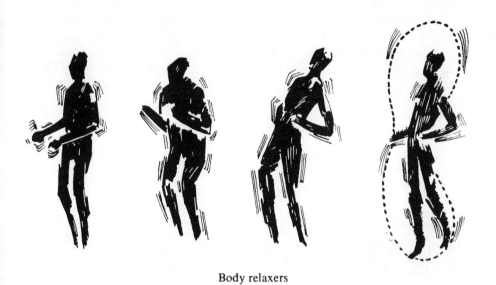

Body relaxers

Figure 24. Muscle-shaking improvisations.

shoulders and neck muscles; then begin with your toes and proceed up through the calves, thighs, and hips. Improvise different rhythms—you will find yourself tap dancing and creating other interesting primitive or modern dance movements. Lightly skipping down four or five flights of stairs is also a wonderful way to shake up the muscles of the body and feel relaxed and exhilarated at the same time.

A more subtle relaxing action is swallowing. For natural and comfortable swallowing, remember to gather saliva in the mouth so you have something to swallow; then the action not only relaxes but lubricates as well. Sucking on a mint is an aid in the swallowing action.

These actions do not have to be learned; we all do them, even if we don't do them often enough. They all evoke the sensation of feeling good; a stretch, a yawn, a shake, a swallow, or a comfortable filling of the breath bucket from the bottom feels good because it induces looseness where previously there was tension. They all represent *natural* relaxation in action.

Relaxation Exercises

To create these exercises, I studied anatomy and some neurology; interviewed dancers and physiotherapists and studied with some of them; observed and studied animals, babies, and adults in various stances and positions; and tried to correlate the results. Along with the breathing exercises, they are specifically designed to eliminate tension and to rid the body of every unnecessary muscular contraction. They will help to produce the relaxation that Stanislavsky observed in infants and cats, and they form a marvelous adjunct to his acting exercises. Practice them with a feeling of uninhibited curiosity, imagination, and anticipated pleasure. Consult your doctor before doing the more strenuous exercises regularly.

Exercise one—Muscle Spreading (fig. 25)

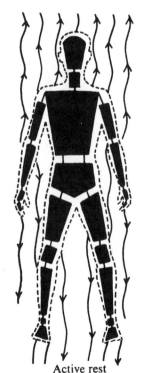

Active rest

Figure 25.

step 1. To take position: Lie flat on your back on a firm surface.

step 2. Think of your body as groups of muscles, made up in turn of myriads of cells, the cells as separate and distinct, one from the other, as little atoms in space. Slowly try to spread these muscle cells farther and farther apart. Wherever you feel tension or body weight, try to spread that weight and rest the area into weightlessness.

step 3. As you feel the weight oozing out of the various parts of the body, start extending them: The neck gets longer; the crown of the head gets higher; the back gets broader; the shoulders, hands, heels get lower; the small of the back is flatter; every joint is now looser and freer. Your overall posture is perfect; you are longer, broader, lighter— you have never felt so relaxed before.

step 4. Imagine the surrounding air to be a body of water or a thick pea soup, and lift first one arm, then the other; one leg, then the other; then the head and neck; then the back— through this water or pea soup. The imagined resistance will create a beautiful sensation of restful energy. When you lift the arms move them all the way beyond your head and back again without stopping to rest, for you should need no rest.

Comment: Since the object is to free the body of obstinate muscle tensions, you must search out the groups of muscles in the body that are heavy and contracted and try to dissolve them—to rid yourself of muscle weight and mass. This conscious untangling and loosening of recalcitrant muscle tension should continue until you have localized those muscle groups that are tensed to support the body or maintain equilibrim. When you have done so, conscious awareness of even those muscles will fade away. As your body becomes lighter and seems emptier and more rested, the sensation of contact between it and the surface on which it rests will disappear. This freedom and feeling of complete relaxation can be achieved best when your efforts to reduce tension are accompanied by correct breathing patterns. The advantage of this tension-release exercise is that breathing tends to function most naturally in a supine position, even for the very poorly conditioned or incorrectly trained individual.

Exercise two—Block Building (fig. 26)

step 1. To take position: Stand upright with correct posture and simulate smelling an imaginary flower in your cupped hands about four inches from your face.

step 2. Inhale and exhale quietly through the nose, with the tongue in the N position, once or twice.

step 3. Drop your hands to your thighs, extend your neck and the crown of your head, and think of all the major segments of the body as blocks.

step 4. Build a straight and well-balanced column of blocks from the ground up: Place the foot blocks gently on the ground; then carefully place the ankle blocks on top of the foot blocks, the calf blocks on the ankle blocks, the knee blocks on the calf blocks, the thigh blocks on the knee blocks, and so on, until you place the neck block on the shoulder block and the head block on the neck block.

step 5. Walk around the room feeling extremely tall and firmly balancing all of the blocks upward, as if you were a weightless moving Greek column.

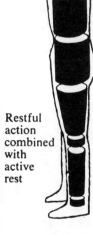

Restful action combined with active rest

Comment: During this step-by-step process, you feel yourself growing taller as the column grows. You feel that as every block-part of you is placed upon the block beneath, it rests down lightly and gently, while at the same time it rests up, preparing to receive the next block, with an inner energy maintaining a sense of perfect balance. As you move, you will begin to develop an unusually keen sense of ease, lightness, alertness,

Figure 26. and grace.

Exercise three—Arm Floating (fig. 27)

step 1. To take position: Stand with arms and hands outstretched.

step 2. Think of your arms resting on the air, as if the air were water in which they could float.

step 3. Feel the weight oozing from the neck, shoulders, and arms and out through the finger tips. Wherever fatigue sets in, loosen the muscles in that area.

Restful action

Figure 27.

Comment: You will feel your arms not only resting on the air below but floating up. You will achieve a serene lightness that makes it possible to keep the arms outstretched for an almost indefinite period of time.

Exercise four—The Long Rise (fig. 28)

Restful action
Figure 28.

step 1. To take position: Crouch on the floor in a deep knee bend, head and arms hanging loosely toward the ground.

step 2. Think of a straight vertical line starting from your feet and going up through the mass formed by your body.

step 3. Beginning with the part of the body nearest the floor, rise slowly . . . slowly . . . Think of resting up along the straight line while at the same time, concentrating deeply on resting downward like the root of a plant in the earth.

Comment: If you feel contraction of the thigh and calf muscles, try to eliminate all feeling of effort by thinking of yourself as being pulled up gently

Restful
action

Figure 29.

by the small hairs on the back of the neck or pushed up by an outside pressure applied to the mastoid bones. Think only of a straight line; like an animal coiled to attack, let no excess energy creep in. If you reach your full height with surprise — did I really move to any appreciable extent?—you can claim a modicum of success.

Exercise five—Upright Bounce (fig. 29)

step 1. To take position: Stand with your arms extended along the sides of your body, hands slightly in front of thighs.

step 2. Think of yourself as a rubber ball or as having strong wire coils attached to your feet.

step 3. Start bouncing lightly.

Comment: Do not attempt to throw your weight upward; rather, concentrate on resting both down and up at the moment your toes touch the ground. As you rest down, you will gain the bounce to go up again effortlessly, each time higher and higher.

Exercise six—Deep Knee-Bend Bounce (fig. 30)

step 1. To take position: Go into a deep knee bend.

step 2. Perform exercise five in this position.

Comment: Remember to feel the coils on your feet, which send you up even as you come down.

Exercise seven—Leg Raising (fig. 31)

step 1. To take position: Stand with arms extended along the sides of your body, hands slightly in front of thighs.

step 2. While resting down on the left leg, rest up from the left hip joint to the very top of the back of the head, creating a sense of looseness and extension in the entire left hip and waist area.

step 3. Let the right leg raise itself effortlessly, beginning at the heel, toe still resting gently on the floor; then flexing at the knee until it has floated up waist-high.

step 4. Repeat the exercise, resting on the right leg while the left leg raises itself.

Restful action
Figure 30.

Comment: While doing this exercise, do not keep a rigid posture, but let the back go into a C curve as though you were about to sit. The more you feel tension dissolving and leaving the localized muscle groups in the supporting leg, the higher. lighter, and easier will you feel the lift in the other leg.

Exercise eight—The Walk (fig. 32)

step 1. To take position: Stand upright, taking a few minutes to get a feeling of lightness and emptiness through the body.

step 2. Think of resting up and resting down with each segment of the body, starting with the feet resting into the ankles, ankles into the calves, calves into the knees, knees into the thighs, thighs into the pelvic area, pelvis into the hips, hips into the waist, waist into the back, back into the shoulders, shoulders into the neck, neck into the head.

Restful action combined with active rest

Figure 31.

step 3. With each segment resting on the segment below and into the segment above, begin resting on the left foot while the right foot floats up as in exercise seven. Feel the sense of enlarged extension throughout the left hip and waist area.

step 4. As the right foot rises and comes down easily—not on the toes but on the outer portion of heel and toe simultaneously —to be rested on in turn, let the left foot rise. Do this two or three times, as though marking time or walking in pantomime, until you begin to move with a heel and toe action.

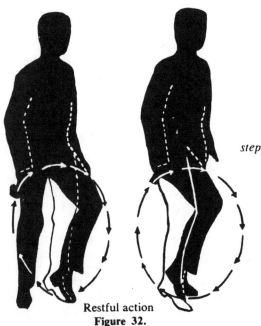

Restful action
Figure 32.

Comment: With this exercise you will learn to walk gracefully by resting on the heel and sole of each foot while the other is released, and this resting and release is done in perfect rhythm, as if your two legs were two wheels, always turning and resting straight down on the ground. You do not feel that your feet are being directed forward; as these leg-wheels move, you feel as if you were floating through the air, moving like a sailboat in a steady, gentle breeze.

Exercise nine—Heart-Beat Movement (fig. 33)

step 1. To take position: Lie flat on your back on a firm surface.

step 2. Rest your body into complete weightlessness with exercise one.

step 3. Concentrate on feeling the pulsations of your heart until you are conscious of that heartbeat as the only energy in your body.

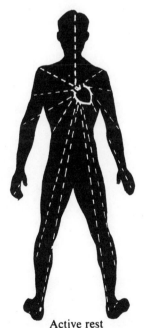

step 4. Feel the pulsations of that heartbeat spreading to every part of your body—your head and neck, your arms right into your fingertips, your legs right into your toes.

step 5. Let the pulsating energy move and lift your fingers and then your entire arm; let it move effortlessly and restfully with the stream of energy-feeling provided by your heartbeat.

step 6. Now do the same with your other arm, then each leg, then both arms, then both legs, then your head and back.

Comment: If you do not succeed at first in feeling the heartbeat, do not be disturbed; your concentration is not yet strong enough; tensions and tight muscles still stand in the way, and you must work longer on the other relaxation exercises. This exercise takes much concentrated, skillful practice, but even partial success is extremely rewarding. To the extent that you do succeed, you experience the very essence of the balance between energetic rest and restful energy.

Active rest
Figure 33.

Part Two: Building a Good Voice

*T*HE HUMAN BODY is a musical apparatus capable of great precision and versatility: It can register, remember, implement, and play itself creatively. But man, so used to using his fingers or his lips or his tongue to play other instruments, seldom thinks of what he uses to "play himself." He gets along with a note or two—and those often as unpleasant as the first efforts of an untrained clarinetist—leaving melodies unheard and rhythms untried. Yet *any* human voice can range from light, high, and bright to deep, rich, and dark. It can express sorrow, anger, melancholy, joy—and so adapt itself to each emotion that it seems the ideal instrument for each expression. Like any instrument, it must be played with skill and artistry if its possibilities are to be realized; yet once you have acquired the skill, you will find it easier to play well than it was to play badly. In the five chapters of Part Two, you will learn to play it skillfully; you will learn to play it for pleasure as well as communication, and the pleasure will improve the communication.

CHAPTER VI

Structural Action

*H*ERE WE BEGIN the actual training of the vocal instrument. The first step is to mold or shape the instrument—to establish the form and function of the oral cavity, and to develop the proper facial posture. The term "structural action" is to be taken literally and dually: It means both the muscular actions that control the adjustable sound box—the oral cavity, cheeks, and lips—and the kinesthetic action of perceiving these muscular actions and controlling them through sensory recall.

The Structural Stretch Exercise

When you open your mouth wide to say AH and then very slowly alter the sound until you get to the vowel OO, you probably feel the teeth gradually closing with the lips, so that by the time you reach the smallest lip opening, the oral cavity is also greatly reduced. If this cavity reduction were really necessary, the entire theory of structural action would topple. But a simple experiment will demonstrate that you can maintain the cavity size unchanged while sounding all of the structural vowels.

To perform the experiment, place a slice of cork about a quarter-inch thick and one and a quarter inches in diameter between the upper and lower molar teeth (fig. 34A). Now, with a large lip opening, sound the vowel AH and gradually reduce the opening until you come to the vowel OO. Try not to bite hard on the cork, and make the action easier by inducing a mild, comfortable yawn sensation in your cheek and lip muscles as you complete the experiment. You will move from the largest to the smallest lip opening, pronouncing an entire series of vowels correctly, without once reducing the space between the teeth—because you can't—and without reducing the over-all space within the cavity.

Now remove the cork and in its place, put the tips of the third and fourth fingers on your cheek between the side teeth, about a quarter of an inch from your lips (fig. 34B). Beginning with the mouth open wide and the tongue gently touching the inside of the lower front teeth, stretch the facial muscles forward so that the lips begin to protrude softly,

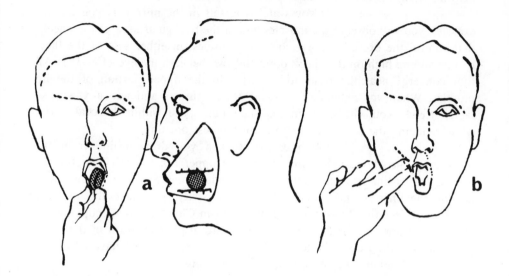

Figure 34. To maintain separation between the teeth in the structural stretch exercise, place slice of cork inside the mouth between the upper and lower molars (A). To check the space without the cork, place third and fourth fingers between the teeth outside the cheek (B).

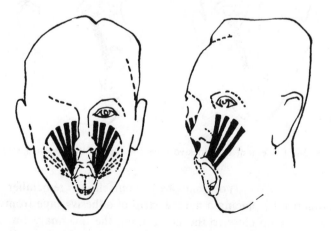

Figure 35. Triangular patches of muscle that help form the inverted megaphone shape.

almost in a pout, and gradually reduce the lip opening while running through the vowel sounds from AH to OO. Again, don't bite down on the fingers, and do induce an incipient yawn sensation in the cheek and lip muscles to help maintain the full two-finger cushion of space.

If you watch yourself in the mirror as you do this exercise, you will observe the muscles within the triangular area of the cheeks that control the exercise. There are four muscles on either side of the face, two beginning high on the cheek bone and two beneath the eye (fig. 35). All four converge near the nose and insert into the upper portion of the lip muscles. When you extend or elongate these muscles and add a yawn-like facial stretch, you will maintain the maximum space within the oral cavity while reducing the rounded lips to their smallest opening.

Observe, too, that if you draw a line from the protruding cheekbone under the eye to the upper lip, a small oval for the lip opening, a line from the lower lip to the jawbone, and a large oval connecting the lines in the middle of the oral cavity, you have the inverted megaphone (see fig. 3)—which we discussed in Chapter III—occupying the vocal sound box. This is the symbol of the natural physical form of the vocal instrument in the Lessac System, and the basic experiment I have described will be our fundamental structural stretch exercise.

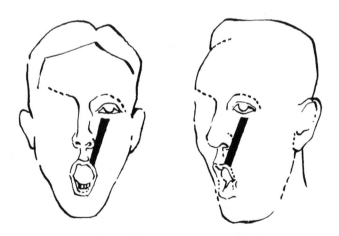

Figure 36. Placement of adhesive tape for feeling the forward stretch.

You can help yourself to remember the basic stretch in practice by placing a narrow strip of adhesive tape from the cheekbone to the upper lip close to the nose, along the imaginary line that forms the upper part of the inverted megaphone (fig. 36). As you practice the stretch, feel the gentle but definite pull of the adhesive tape as it is stretched by the action of the face muscles.

Never begin this exercise by lowering the jaw or pulling any of the facial muscles downward; concentrate exclusively on the forward action of cheeks and upper lip in coordination with a potential yawn sensation in the muscles of the face. Unless this extension is felt as a forward action, not a downward one, various cause and effect relationships with the jaw, lips, face, and larynx will not take place. The feeling of reaching forward is the key to eliminating sensations of fixation, impingement, or undue pressure in the lips, cheeks, throat, and jaw, and the key to some beneficial by-products as well.

Rounded Lips for Rounded Vowels

As you consciously urge the cheek muscles forward in the basic stretch exercise, the lips, too—fully relaxed and cushiony soft in the fleshy part—will gently thrust forward as if consciously attempting to avoid contact with the gums, almost in a pout, and they will take on a symmetrical form without any effort on your part. The basic stretch exercise thus provides a natural rounding of the lips that becomes an intrinsic aid to vowel formation.

Relaxing the Jaw

A rather remarkable result of the stretch exercise—and one I have not heard previously discussed—is the reflex jaw relaxation. As you stretch the cheek and lip muscles fully forward, you slacken the lower face and you automatically induce the maximum separation of the teeth, which floats the jaw downward and slightly inward in an unconditioned reflex action. This reflex is highly significant in view of the recalcitrant problem of fixed and tense jaw that plagues teachers and therapists. Yet the cause of the problem is obvious: Whenever the jaw is consciously *pulled or forced* downward, most of the muscles around the lower jaw and upper neck and throat area become hard and tense, crowding the larynx and impinging on the freedom of the vocal cords. But when the jaw *relaxes* into a lower position as part of a compulsory, natural reflex induced by the upper facial stretch, these same muscles remain relatively soft and loose. The larynx, too, relaxes into a lower position—sometimes as much as half an inch lower—and there the vocal cords occlude and vibrate more freely and more efficiently.

The full forward stretch, and thus jaw relaxation, can be achieved only with correct posture. When the face is lifted, tilting the head back and the chin up, the jaw leads and becomes the dominant element in facial posture and the formation of vowel sounds. The vitally important actions of the cheek and upper lip muscles, on the other hand, are restricted and these muscles are relegated to a relatively passive function. With the chin level and the crown of the head high, however, these muscles of the upper face come into full play, the jaw loses its constricting dominance, and the whole facial posture becomes dynamic and flexible.

Enlivening the Sluggish Tongue

I often hear complaints from students that the tongue is too big, too heavy, or too clumsy. Actually, the tongue, which is made up of many muscles, is potentially extremely agile and this agility is constantly in play when one eats. The tongue can form shapes and dart in any direction.

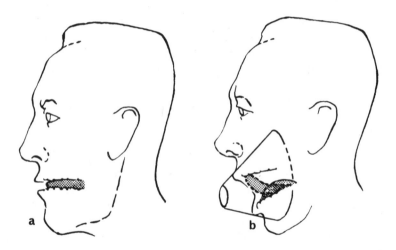

Figure 37. Minimal oral cavity crowds the tongue (A); inverted megaphone shape enlarges cavity and encourages full play of the natural muscular agility of the tongue.

If you speak with a fixed jaw and cramped buccal cavity, the tongue *may feel* large, flabby, and crowded, and it may well interfere with good speech (fig. 37A). But if you concentrate on the tongue while you do the stretch exercise again, you will observe that with the space it now has to maneuver and exercise its muscles, it feels relatively small, flexible, and active (fig. 37B).

Stretch and Relaxation

Yawning, as I pointed out in Chapter V, is one of

the body's natural methods of relaxation, and the stretch exercise simulates a comfortable but stimulating yawn sensation in the cheek and lip muscles; it is, in fact, essentially the voluntary and controllable type of yawn described in Chapter V. Try stretching your back, shoulders, and arms pleasurably and easily as you do the stretch exercise (fig. 38). Note that every part of

the body stretches forward. At the same time, sound out a comfortable, sustained, low-pitched tone on the vowel O, and the effect will be very much like a good early morning yawn and stretch with a surprisingly rich resonance felt up front in the bony areas of the face.

This yawn sensation on the vowel O or AW induces a well-focused and head-clearing vocal sound that resonates in both the hard palate and the nasal bone. At the same time it relaxes the facial, throat, and jaw muscles. This simple adaption of the structural stretch exercise quickly relieves tension and leads to a wonderfully salutary feeling.

Figure 38. The forward yawn stretch.

Phonetics by Feeling

The structural stretch exercise is also the first technique in a new phonetic approach that does not depend upon the listening ear. If you voice the exercise clearly as your lips move from the largest to the smallest opening, you will find that you form a number of specific vowels. These vowels—which will be described in detail later—include AH as in *father*, O as in *beyond*, AW as in *law*, O as in *phone*, OO as in *school*, and, if you move quickly from the widest to the smallest opening, OW as in *found*. You will come to know each specific stretch position as a physical sense memory, and whenever you recall and reproduce a position, you will produce a particular vowel, automatically and perfectly, guided by the way it feels rather than the way it sounds. With this technique, even deaf children can be taught to form the structural vowels perfectly by feeling the sound they cannot hear.

Stretch and Dental Hygiene

The stretch exercise tends to prevent habitual contact between the upper and lower teeth and grinding away of the surfaces of the teeth—which can mean less work for your dentist. The hinge-like spring action of the jaw, which tends to clamp down, as in chewing, or snap shut, is reversed by the proper stretch action. The concept of the inverted megaphone promotes a tendency for the jaw to spring open, which maintains a consistent space cushion between the teeth, even during silence. Dental hygiene alone is enough to call into question theories of chewing action in speech.

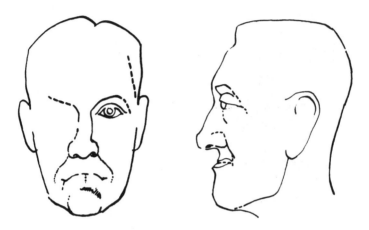

Figure 39. Functional malocclusion.

The habit of speaking with a closed jaw can also lead to a condition known as functional malocclusion (fig. 39). When the jaw appears to be the only moving part, the tendency is to thrust it forward in attempts to speak more precisely, more intensely, or with more volume. In time, the jaw becomes unhinged and the upper and lower joints become permanently dislocated, which upsets the natural alignment of the teeth. At the same time, it alters both the form and the expression of the face.

The Speed of Speech

The structural and other habit patterns you will acquire will contribute to the development of a highly efficient control system, regulating the speed and pitch of your speech. If you maintain the structural form and feel it in every vowel, your speech can be as fast as you like, and it will never be too fast; or as slow, and you will never sound sluggish. A physical mechanism functioning properly and registering all signals cannot operate too rapidly, and the proper interplay of its moving parts will prevent monotony at any speed.

Facial Posture

        Finally, the structural stretch exercise and the inverted megaphone position have a decisive effect on the way the face looks and feels. The concept of good facial posture is a new but a logical one: Just as the body must be held properly to function properly, so must the face, and for the face as well as the body, the functional posture is the most attractive posture.

        Your face will never look its best if, when you speak or sing, the facial muscles pull back, the upper lip and cheek muscles remain inert, the jaw is tightly fixed, the upper and lower teeth clamp together, or one side of the face and mouth is favored over the other. All these actions will encourage premature age lines and grooves, particularly the aging groove that runs from above the nostrils to the corner of the mouth (fig. 40A).

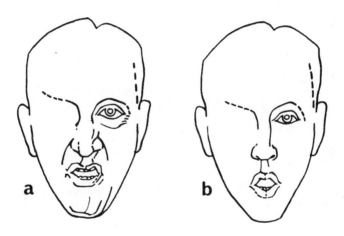

Figure 40. Effect of facial posture: A. Poor posture leads to unattractive and aging lines; B. the forward stretch restores youthful, expressive contours.

        Professional photographers always ask their models to suck their cheeks in a bit to highlight the cheekbones, bring the lips forward, and firm the cheek and jaw tissues. The oval, high-cheekboned face is always the most photogenic, and the facial posture conditioned by the stretch exercise will always tend to produce this contour, regardless of individual structural differences (fig. 40B). It thrusts the cheeks and lips forward, produces a consistent space between the upper and lower teeth, highlights the cheekbones, and smoothes the premature grooves. Nor should you feel, if you are young, that this doesn't yet apply to you. Premature

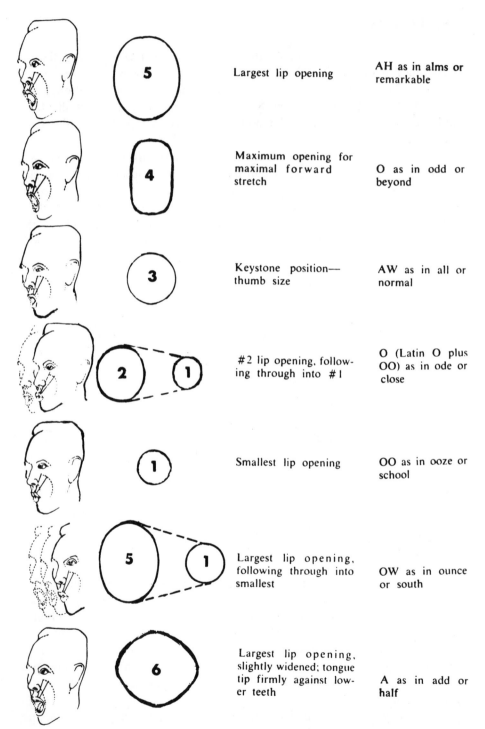

5	Largest lip opening	AH as in alms or remarkable
4	Maximum opening for maximal forward stretch	O as in odd or beyond
3	Keystone position— thumb size	AW as in all or normal
2 1	#2 lip opening, following through into #1	O (Latin O plus OO) as in ode or close
1	Smallest lip opening	OO as in ooze or school
5 1	Largest lip opening, following through into smallest	OW as in ounce or south
6	Largest lip opening, slightly widened; tongue tip firmly against lower teeth	A as in add or half

Figure 41. Structural vowel chart.

aging begins in youth, and if you speak or sing with a facial posture like that in figure 40A, you may end by sounding just like you look.

Good facial posture also promotes tissue health. The muscles stretching action helps to eliminate excess fatty tissue from the face and assists the muscles in getting rid of waste products by permitting the metabolites, or residual and possibly toxic substances, to flow more freely. The kind of exercise provided by the yawn stretch is necessary for the physical well-being of the muscles.

The Structural Vowels

Despite the many secondary benefits to be gained from the structural stretch exercise, its primary purpose in voice and speech is the proper production of the vowels inherent in the voiced exercise (fig. 41). Throughout the book, these vowels will be designated by numbers that correspond with lip openings. A diphthong, or vowel made up of two sounds, will be designated by a combination of symbols—numerical, alphabetical, or mathematical. As you repeat these vowels, make certain that you have the full forward stretch in the cheeks and lips and the full two-finger space between the teeth; keep the fleshy part of the lips soft and flippable. Do not anticipate these vowels—discover them in the structural action.

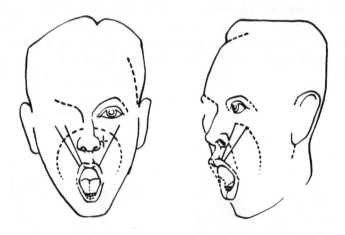

Figure 42. Structural vowel #5.

#5—AH (fig. 42). The largest stretch opening, which you have practiced as the beginning of the basic structural stretch exercise, is called #5. It automatically produces the vowel sound AH, as in *father*. From now on, to produce this vowel, think only of feeling the

largest lip opening and the most forward stretch compatible with this opening.
      #1—OO (fig. 43). The full stretch with the smallest lip opening is called #1. It produces the vowel sound OO, as in

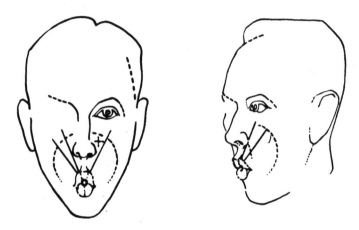

Figure 43. Structural vowel #1.

ooze. From now on, to sound the vowel, think only of feeling the smallest opening while executing the fullest stretch. In this position, be careful not to purse or harden your lips. Unlike the pure Latin or Italian vowel sound OO, the #1 vowel is diphthongal in effect. Though you may not be aware of it, you reduce your lips for the #1 and then, as you sound the vowel, reduce them still further as if to pronounce the consonant W. To my knowledge, this diphthongal character of the English OO has not been previously mentioned.

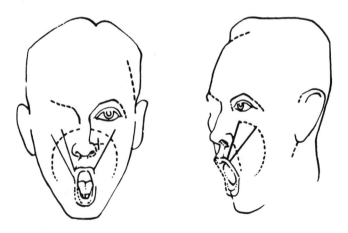

Figure 44. Structural vowel #4.

#4—O (fig. 44). To achieve the #4 position and vowel, begin with the #5 position and stretch your cheek and lip muscles as far forward as you can, still thinking of the #5 vowel. This will change the opening slightly from an oval shape to one a bit more rectangular and produce the vowel sound O, as in *odd* and *yonder*. From now on, to sound this O, think only of maximal forward stretch and the largest possible opening in this position.

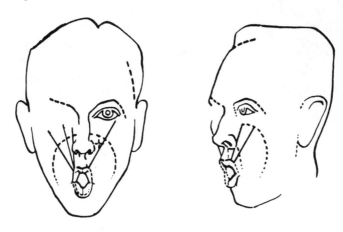

Figure 45. Structural vowel #3.

#3—AW (fig. 45). The midway lip opening with the full inverted megaphone stretch is the #3 position. It produces the vowel sound AW, as in *all*. From now on, when you sound this vowel, make sure that the space between the teeth is full, the cheek muscle stretch complete, and the lip opening just large enough to permit easy passage of the thumb.

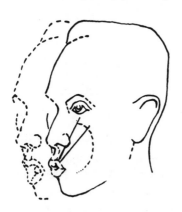

#21—O (fig. 46). Ordinarily, the lip opening slightly larger than #1 and slightly smaller than #3 should be called #2, but it produces a vowel sound not used in American speech—the Latin or Italian O, as in *amor*. In English, this vowel becomes a diphthong, beginning with this #2 position but continuing into the smallest lip opening, #1, and is called #21. It produces the vowel sound O, as in *ode*. From now on, to produce this vowel, think only of feeling the full stretch with a lip opening slightly smaller than #3, and the reduction

Figure 46. Structural vowel #21. of this opening as you sound the vowel.

#51—OW (fig. 47). The combination of the largest lip opening, #5, with the smallest, #1, forms another diphthong, called #51. It produces the vowel sound OW, as in *ounce* or *loud*. From now on, to sound this vowel, think only of feeling the full cheek and lip stretch into the largest forward lip opening and its rapid reduction to the smallest.

#6—A (fig. 48). To achieve the #6 position, which you have not practiced in the basic stretch exercise, begin with #5 and widen the lips elliptically just a bit, while urging the tip of the tongue firmly

Figure 47. Structural vowel #51.

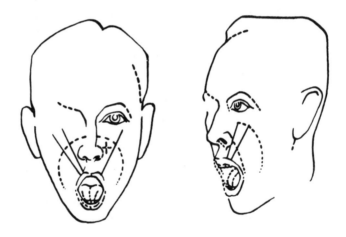

Figure 48. Structural vowel #6.

against the inside of the lower teeth as the tongue widens a bit. This position will produce the vowel sound A, as in *add* or *demand*. From now on, to sound this vowel, think only of feeling a slight elliptical #5, tongue-tip pressing against the lower teeth, and the full stretch position.

These seven sounds are the basic structural or stretch vowels. There are two additional diphthongs that include the Ybuzz, which will be discussed in the next chapter, as the second sound, but both rely entirely on the structural form for the dominant feeling. The Ybuzz vowel EE, as in *eel,* is weak and unstressed in both of these forms.

3y—OI. The combination of the #3 structural vowel with the weak Ybuzz is called 3y. It produces the vowel sound OI, as in *oil*. From now on, to sound this vowel, think only of feeling the midway lip opening and a slight resonance on the hard palate and nose as the sound ends.

6y—I. By combining the #6 stretch vowel with the weak Ybuzz, we get diphthong 6y. It produces the vowel sound I, as in *isle* or *aisle*. These pronunciations may seem strange and difficult at first because the diphthong is commonly formed with a #5 stretch vowel, rather than a #6, but as you master the sound, you will find that the #6 is the more accurate. From now on, to sound this vowel, think only of feeling the slightly elliptical full mouth opening, proper tongue-tip placement, and a slight buzzing on the hard palate and nose as the sound ends.

In forming any of these vowels, remember that it is not the ear that determines the sound, but a specific, physically memorized stretch position.

A Simpler Phonetics

Phoneticians may criticize my phonetic approach as too general: It does not, I admit, accommodate the different phonetic designations they give to the vowel sounds in *băck* and *demånd*. These fine distinctions amount to a didactic position. To avoid nasal quality and poor diction in words like *ran, demand, pass,* and *fantastic,* and also to avoid unnecessary Briticisms, I prefer to use a single category, the #6 stretch vowel. Curiously enough, this serves to improve both sounds. Phoneticians also create separate categories for such vowel sounds as O in *obey,* O in *soft,* and U in *cūbe, ûnite,* and *menü.* I consider these various O's and U's to be weakened, or altered, forms of #21, #3, and #1, rather than distinct entities in themselves. These forms are weakest in conversations; in more formal or more vigorous speech, where the speaker must project, they become proportionately stronger and begin to approximate the formal stretch positions. To superimpose vague, in-between symbols, such as sŏft in contradistinction to sôft or sŏft, is frustrating and burdensome; pronunciation becomes didactic or pedantic at best; at worst, in rebellion against this artificiality, it capitulates to the neglect and vulgarization of lazy, sloppy, and misinformed usage. Actually, specific vowel pronunciation is not essential to communication of meaning. As evidence, one can point to an often overlooked phenomenon that occurs in both singing and speaking: *Vowels are subject to radical modification and change in direct proportion to changes of pitch, volume, emotional intensity, and emphasis.* Curiously enough, neither the speaker nor the listener recognizes these changes even if the word *fool* sounds like *fowl,* or *mean* like *mine,* or *bed* like *bad.* Regardless of these so-called distortions, the diction in both singing and speech, sounds absolutely perfect if the consonants are properly experienced (see Chapter X).

The inverted megaphone stretch applies the perfect form for the so-called "pear-shaped" vowels to *all* vowels, and it accomplishes this automatically, even while it adds vitality and a deeper color to the voice. Obviously, then, no matter what vowel you are using, you should apply as much stretch as possible without distorting the pronunciation of the word. Try it with these words: *nerve, scintillate, easy, stimulate, weekend, western, slovenly, destruction, highway, likelihood, obey.* Most of the vowel sounds in these words are not structural but Ybuzz, R-derivative, or neutral vowels, which will be discussed in later chapters. Nevertheless, the forward stretch of the cheek and lip muscles can be applied to these words. The only difference will be that the space between the teeth which remains full for the stretch vowels, will vary for the other vowels. In other words, the forward stretch of the cheek muscles is constant for all vowels, but the space cushion is variable. To make the vowels and words sound natural to you while you apply the new facial posture, you may use your ear to prevent obvious distortions. Since you will be listening for familiar and accustomed pronunciations, the ear will not seriously mislead you, but the stretch will provide a new phonetic quality that the ear will never notice.

Exercises and Word Lists

In practicing these exercises, check with your third and fourth fingers between the teeth, outside the cheek, to assure maintenance of the maximum space. Do not attempt to impose the stretch on consonants; it serves the vowels only. In both word lists and sentences, test each word with the maximum stretch position without disturbing the seemingly normal pronunciation. You will find that the wrong position will invariably distort the word, while the right position may produce a formal pronunciation if the stretch is grossly applied. but never any distortion.

Exercise one—Woo . . . Woe . . . War . . . Wow Exercise

This is an exercise to develop flexible lip movement while maintaining the full inverted megaphone stretch. Think of the movements of the mouth of a fresh water fish.

step 1. Prepare for the exercise by forming the full stretch with the lips in the #1 position.

step 2. Make certain that you have a two-finger space between the side teeth. If necessary use the cork.

step 3. Repeat each of the words—woo, woe, war, and wow—at least ten times in unbroken rhythm; then again as spontaneously as possible.

Comment: In repeating woo, woe, or wow, make certain that each final #1 lip position becomes the beginning of the very next W. Practice this basic stretch until you feel uncomfortable and strange without it.

Exercise two—Word List for Structural Perception

Consider these words as body movement training in facial flexibility, not as diction or pronunciation exercises. Do not anticipate the vowels—discover them. (In polysyllabic words the representative structural vowel is underlined.)

step 1. Using the full inverted megaphone stretch, practice each column of words from the top down.

step 2. Now practice the words across the page, going from #1 to #6 in each line. Note the gradual enlargement of the lip opening while the rest of the megaphone shape remains the same.

#1	#21	#3	#4	#5	#51	#6
ooze	ode	all	odd	alms	ounce	add
boon	bone	born	bond	barn	bound	banned
booed	abode	bawdy	body	bard	bowed	bad
boot	boat	bought	bottom	Bart	bout	bat
cool	coal	call	column	Carl	cowl	canned
doom	dome	dorm	dominate	darn	down	Dan
fool	foal	fall	follow	far	foul	fallow
grew	grow	McGraw	grog	garage	ground	grand
who'll	hole	haul	hollow	harlequin	howl	hallow
June	Joan	jaunt	John	jar	jowl	Jack
lieu	low	law	lock	lark	allow	lack
mule	mole	maul	Moll	Mars	mouse	mass
moon	moan	mourn	monster	Marne	mount	man
pooch	poach	porch	pomp	parch	pouch	patch
root	wrote	wrought	rot	hurrah	rout	rat
sue	sew	saw	sod	sarge	sow	sad
tune	tone	torn	tonsil	tarnish	town	tan
toot	tote	taught	tot	tart	tout	tatter
wound	won't	warned	wand	bourgeoise	wound	wagon
uke	yoke	yawn	yonder	yard	yowl	yak
zoo	zone	zorgite	zombie	Czar	zounds	zig-zag
crew	crow	craw	crock	carp	crowd	crack
through	throw	thrall	throb	Arthur	thousand	thrash
shoe	show	shore	shock	shark	shout	shack
choose	chose	chores	chop	char	chow	chap
schooled	scold	scald	scholar	scarred	scowled	scabbed
news	nose	gnaws	nostril	gnarl	now	nasty

Comment: Remember to maintain the full structural stretch throughout the
sounding of the vowel, even when the voice inflects up or down, and even
at the moment you terminate the vowel. This is particularly important while
practicing #1, #21, and #51. In pronouncing the #51 do not fall into the
common trap of sounding a #61. The #6 is not as far forward as the
#5 and in the diphthong is usually nasal and therefore wrong. In polysyllabic
words the structural vowel is underlined, but be certain that you maintain
the *constant* forward stretch throughout all syllables. In fact, keep the
inverted megaphone shape even during the silent pause as you move from
word to word.

Exercise three—Structural Perception Drill

These sentences involve primarily stretch-group words. In the first three
sentences the structural vowels are given their numerical symbols. For
additional practice assign the correct number to each vowel in the rest of
the sentences. To do this properly, do not refer to the word lists or figure
it out from memory; prove each one physically. Do not anticipate—discover
the vowels through the stretch.

step 1. Practice each sentence with a complete, and grossly applied, inverted
megaphone stretch.

step 2. Once you have gained facility in reading the sentences with the formal
stretch, read them again a bit more rapidly, but retaining the stretch.

step 3. For normally effective speech, practice reading the sentences more rapidly
with a slight easing up of the gross stretch.

1. Joe Robert's powerful chauffeur scolded the shrewd Paul Jones.

2. Lord Cashmore sought out all the old, romantic New York musical shows.

3. On Tuesday morning's call-board, the students saw the following notice:
   "No More Roles or Parts for Tomorrow Afternoon."

4. The two tallest soldiers marched proudly and smartly down
   through the vastly crowded north and south halls.

5. Howard, who fancied himself a coward, was astonished at
   being chosen to try his doubtful prowess in the round-by-round
   bout against his powerful and monster-like opponent.

6. The old and forlorn traveler foolishly followed the four noisy small children across the last two strongly guarded, war-torn borders.

7. Joe Scott and Paul Pasternak always moved forward far too slowly and cautiously.

8. The large round ball bounced over the huge stone barrier into Jackson's cool, beautiful garden.

9. Martha and Margrit walked arm in arm to the charming park not far from their father's house.

10. The lawyer's awfully awkward daughter ought to be taught to draw.

11. The erratic band manager was shocked, frantic, and angered at the masterfully planned pamphlet which automatically attacked the amateur standing of the fascinating and talented young actress, barring her from acting the important part in the show.

12. When in the course of history, moral issues become blurred and crass attitudes are forced to the fore, it behooves all who are honest and strong to look around, take stock, evaluate anew, and have fortitude to stand up and be counted.

Exercise four—Word List for 3y and 6y

Remember that in these vowels, the initial sound is the dominant one. Emphasize the full inverted megaphone stretch with the #3 or #6 opening and just the barest suggestion of EE as the second sound. Whenever a consonant follows, it should be made almost simultaneously with the mild EE to avoid a second syllable: *oil* as *oi-yul*, *foist* as *faw-eest*, *style* as *sta-yul*, *child* as *cha-yuld*, *mind* as *ma-yund*. There are a few exceptions, such as royal and loyal, which *are* two-syllable words. Note that the words in the second and fourth columns contain the #3 and #6 vowel sounds that dominate the 3y and 6y vowels. Use these companion words as a check to be certain that you do start the 6y with a #6 as in column four; and the 3y with a #3 as in column two.

3y	**#3**	**6y**	**#6**
oil	(all)	aisle	(alley)
boys	(born)	buys	(bad)
coined	(cawed)	kind	(canned)
Doyle	door)	dial	(dally)
foil	(fall)	file	(falcon)
foist	(force)	fight	(fat)
exploit	(explore)	plight	(platitude)
groin	(McGraw)	grind	(grand)
hoist	(horse)	height	(hat)
joy	(jaw)	jive	(jack)
loin	lawn)	lined	(land)
moist	(moss)	mind	(manned)
noise	(gnaws)	nice	(nasty)
poise	(pause)	pies	(pass)
employed	(implored)	plied	(plaid)
quoit	(quart)	quite	(quack)
roister	(raw)	rile	(rally)
soy	(saw)	sigh	(sad)
toys	(toss)	ties	(tacit)
voiced	(vortex)	vice	(vascular)
void	(vault)	vied	(value)
choice	(chalk)	why	(whack)
boisterous	(Boston)	thy	(that)
broil	(brawl)	China	(chat)
adroit	(drawn)	shine	(shallow)
Des Moines	(demoralize)	scribe	(scab)

Exercise five—Sentences for 3y

1. Dr. Doyle from Des Moines carefully voided the Freudian opinion as he adroitly employed the oily ointment for the boy's thyroid goiter.

2. The unemployed oyster-pickers, devoid of choice during the embroiled negotiations, noiselessly and fearlessly deployed their boys, while the so-called envoy loitered about, voicing his annoyance at what he considered their boisterous exploits.

3. Roy filled his small warehouse with all sorts of peculiar items—

there were alloy metals, toy quoits, hoisting tackle, pictures of asteroids and a wartime royal convoy, wire coils, old coins, embroidered doilies, stacks of unused invoices, cans of soy sauce, and what not!

Exercise six—Sentences for 6y

1. The exciting arrival at the height of the mighty mountain made our final night hike a delightfully enterprising assignment.

2. The tired dog, wide-eyed and frightened, cried quietly while frantically trying to find his blind master.

3. The high altitude final trial flight was made in a light Atlas nose cone which skyrocketed the test pilot and five highly nervous scientists nine miles high into the ionosphere.

Exercise seven—Reading Selections

In practicing these selections, remember to use the full stretch, not only on stretch vowels, which are enumerated or underlined, but on all other vowels, to a point just short of distorting them, and remember that the inverted megaphone stretch may vary in size or degree from word to word but *never* in kind or basic shape. Even in pauses, practice the sense of the stretch—the law of forward direction.

1. I found the raucous and persistent honking of the automobile horn frustratingly annoying and wandered down the road to investigate the disturbing noise and, if necessary, to communicate my feelings to the motorist—I was positively in a mood to be rude.

2. The Autumn leaves in bold golds and deep, dark reds were falling profusely all around me. Each leaf floated slowly flake-like, toward the earth after which it nestled down as though, with a self-satisfied sigh, it had happily fulfilled its assigned task and was now, without resentment, waiting for its new cycle of absorption and rebirth. Standing right in the middle of this glorious, joyful process, I felt myself in intimate communion with the holiest of all forces—lifegiving nature at work.

3. Tis not thy words which fall from thy mouth, but how thou speakest them that show us the beauty and the hope and the joy of the world all 'round us.

4. A good sound body, which does not disturb the equilibrium in man, is a divine gift. . . . But it is not impossible to conquer a bad constitution by training. Oh, God, Thou hast formed the body of man with infinite wisdom and goodness. Thou hast united in him innumerable forces incessantly at work like so many instruments, so as to preserve in its entirety this beautiful house containing his immortal soul, and these forces act with all the order, concord and harmony, imaginable. If weakness or violent passion disturb this harmony, these forces act against one another . . . then Thou sendest Thy messengers, the diseases, which announce the approach of danger, and bid man prepare to overcome them.

—MAIMONIDES

5. The flowering moments of the mind drop half of their petals in our speech. Talking is one of the truly fine arts . . . And its fluent harmonies may be spoiled by the intrusion of a single harsh note.

—OLIVER WENDELL HOLMES

6. Fourscore and seven years ago our fathers brought forth on this continent, a new nation, conceived in Liberty, and dedicated to the proposition that all men are created equal.

Now we are engaged in a great civil war, testing whether that nation, or any nation so conceived and so dedicated, can long endure. We are met on a great battlefield of that war. We have come to dedicate a portion of that field, as a final resting-place for those who here gave their lives that that nation might live. It is altogether fitting and proper that we should do this.

But, in a larger sense, we cannot dedicate—we cannot consecrate—we cannot hallow—this ground. The brave men, living and dead, who struggled here, have consecrated it, far above our poor power to add or detract. The world will little note, nor long remember what we say here, but it can never forget what they did here. It is for us, the living, rather, to be dedicated here to the unfinished work which they who fought here have thus far so nobly advanced. It is rather for us to be here dedicated to the great task remaining before us—that from these honored dead we take increased devotion to that cause for which they gave the last full measure of devotion—that we here highly resolve that these dead shall not have died in vain—that this nation, under God, shall have a new birth of freedom—and that government of the people, by the people, for the people, shall not perish from the earth.

—ABRAHAM LINCOLN

7. The sky was cool and stormy black and the newly sprouted saplings rocked from their not-yet-strengthened roots. The young men in the village were in a pantomime of frenzied action preparing for the tumultuous grand festival of the year. The farmers, imbued with the spirit of tradition, set aside their farming implements. All was in readiness; a sentinel-like atmosphere endured throughout. The participants eagerly scanned the huge tracts of verdant sod, mist-shrouded and heavily pregnant. Trees in the distant forest placated the heavens, rising with inexorable strength to protect the virgin fragility of this season's magic—Then the music came.

Exercise eight—A Personal Project

You should practice structural action at all times—when you are in rehearsal or doing improvisations or in casual conversation. You should, in fact, be in permanent training. As an aid to such constant practice, work on the following exercise:

step 1. Select an editorial or a controversial news story from any good newspaper.

step 2. Prepare it by enumerating the stretch vowels as in the first selection above; in later assignments, merely underline them.

step 3. Now practice reading your selection, very slowly at first, with the fullest structural form, always keeping in mind the content of the material you are reading.

step 4. As you improve, read the selection more rapidly, with normal, smooth utterance, while still holding on to the form; then incorporate your intention and objective in the reading into the action.

step 5. After several readings, speak extemporaneously on the subject of the editorial or story. Assume the character of a serious protagonist of the views expressed; then take as many other views as will prove the assignment an exciting one, always remembering to combine your involvement in the subject with structural action.

Comment: The objective in this exercise is: (1) to maintain and carry over the structural posture to spontaneously rapid, or intense and involved, speech; (2) to improvise, characterize, and create, while you occupy yourself with your basic training; and (3) to practice the natural application of structural action in all sorts of speech situations.

Exercise nine—Improvisation in Communication through Structural Action

The object of this exercise is to communicate with another person through pure sound, in this case the sounds of the structural vowels.

step 1. Select a partner and sit facing him.

step 2. Conduct a discussion, using no verbal content or actual words, but attempting to communicate various objectives, emotions, and feelings through the structural vowels. Attempt to influence your partner: persuade, cajole, attack, plead, using all the possible melodies and inflections of structural action. Try to communicate a purpose, an idea, or a state of being. Try to tell a lyric story with the melodies of the structural vowels.

Comment: Do not let yourself get into a rut; use all the vowels, the full gamut of structural action. You may use any pitch, any intensity, any characterization as long as the inverted megaphone shape is not sacrificed; the shape can be varied in degree from the full forward stretch to the most reduced facial posture, but it should still be outwardly recognizable and inwardly felt as the inverted megaphone.

CHAPTER VII

Tonal Action I—

The Ybuzz

*T*HE TERM "TONAL ACTION" is to be taken literally and dually. It means the action of the tones—the vibrations of the vocal sound waves transmitted through bone conduction—and it means our action of feeling those tonal vibrations and controlling them through sensory recall. These actions are of primary concern in the development of both the speaking and the singing voice.

People still contend that since you cannot see or touch the voice, conscious control of something so intangible as the vocal sound waves is impossible. Yet vocal sound waves are no less real than sound waves coming from a violin, a trumpet, or a tuning fork. Vocal sound waves *are* tangible, physical forces, and they *can* be seen through mechanical devices, measured electronically, and felt through the nerve ends. Feeling the tone is an accurate description of the sensation.

It is true that we do not have conscious control of all of the actions of the sound waves, but sensitivity increases in direct proportion to receptivity—you cannot control what you are not aware of. As I pointed out in Chapter II, when you place the base of a vibrating tuning fork against the outside surface of your upper front teeth, you will *feel* brilliant tones surging through the entire bony section of the face and head, and you will also *hear* these tones because they are transmitted by this feeling to the auditory as well as the sensory cortex of the brain. Since vocal sound waves are as much a physical force as the sound waves coming from a tuning fork, you can also learn to feel the vocal vibrations within the body. Just as the tuning fork transmits vibrations from outside the body through the facial bones to the brain, so can the body transmit its own internally produced sound waves, and the sensation is essentially the same.

In the last chapter, I referred to the ability of the deaf student to learn to form perfect vowels through structural action. He can also be taught to feel the sensations of tonal action and can learn to control these sensations, and therefore control the vocal sound waves, without hearing. Thus, tone-deaf students can also be taught to sing perfect chromatic scales by feeling the tones and ignoring what they hear. If these students, who *must* bypass the auditory mechanism, can learn to control their voices solely by feeling the tones, then obviously the technique is practical and can be adopted by those with normal hearing, who will gain more sensitive power of concentration in the process.

The sensations of tonal action are an internal event —you must feel them, from beginning to end, *within* the body. Resonated sound is transmitted to the outside through bone conduction—the vibrating bony section of the sound box, not the breath, sets up sympathetic vibrations that amplify the vocal sounds—and you must never try to project to an audience, whether of one or of thousands, by throwing the voice through the mouth or nose. When your voice functions solely as an inner vibrating current, never pushed and never impeded, you will experience it as a vibratory feeling that uses energy without using it up—a feeling, therefore, that stimulates, energizes, and relaxes.

The Resonating Area

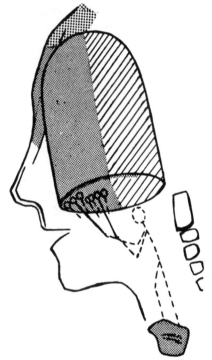

Figure 49. The bony resonating areas must function like the kettle drum, which vibrates in every part whenever any part is tapped.

Tonal action begins when the vocal sound waves contact the bony structure of the face and head and set it vibrating. Every action in voice production that takes place earlier—vibration of the vocal membranes and passage of sound waves by air conduction through the throat and mouth—is nonvoluntary and must be performed without conscious sensation. The three primary resonating areas are the hard palate, including the teeth; the nasal bone, including the nasal sinuses; and the forehead, including the frontal sinuses. These three areas, however, must be considered a single solid mass of resonating materials; like a brass gong or kettle drum (fig. 49), the entire mass vibrates whenever sound waves strike the hard palate, no matter where you feel the specific action of the vocal tones. The beginner may be aware primarily of the action-sensation in the hard palate, while the more experienced singer or speaker, already accustomed to this feeling, may concentrate on controlling the vibrations in the nasal bone and lower forehead, but in either case the tonal radiation will be distributed instantaneously throughout the entire prime bone area. Both the beginner and the professional must be aware of this action if they are to use the tonal vibrations most effectively.

The Vibrating Y

Your training in tonal action will begin with the Ybuzz. This concept replaces one of the conventional approaches to voice building, the use of M, N, or NG. These consonants are totally nasal and can be voiced only with the nostrils open. If you close the nostrils firmly while sustaining an M, N, or NG, the sound will cease. There is nothing wrong with nasals as consonants—they bring to our speech the color of certain musical instruments—but they are not the proper models for tone and vowel production. The entire voice should not be patterned after an intrinsically nasal sound that makes the vowels strident and unpleasant.

Instead, we need a nonnasal model that will create the proper action-sensation, will be a healthy influence on the voice, and will produce a desirable esthetic tone. The choice of the Ybuzz is not an arbitrary one; the Y—a vowel-like consonant or, like the W, both vowel and consonant—is highly adaptable and peculiarly suited to our preliminary tonal objective: the vibratory sensation on the front of the hard palate, including the gum ridge, and in the nasal bone; you cannot sustain a clear consonant Y without feeling these inner vibrations.

Feeling the Action of the Ybuzz

To feel the Ybuzz, say "yes" and linger on the Y as if in hesitation: Y-y-y-yes. Say it naturally and easily, in a speaking not a singing voice, and on a *comfortably low pitch*. Do not try to practice the Ybuzz on the higher pitches; it operates only in the lower third of the vocal range, over no more than approximately five to six whole tones. If you have placed the tone right, you should feel a buzz or vibration on the forward section of the hard palate and in the bone of the nose.

If you do not feel the buzz immediately, try saying the word "easy"; say it easily and languidly, lingering over both the first and second syllables: Ea-ea-ea-ea-ea-sy-y-y-y-y. Now go back to "yes" and sustain the Y while thinking EA, or continue with "easy" and sustain EA while thinking Y.

A third approach is to sound an EE firmly while concentrating on bringing the cheek and lip muscles forward as in the inverted megaphone stretch. But since this vowel sound cannot be made with the maximum space between the side teeth, the space for the Ybuzz will vary from about a thirty-second of an inch on the low pitch to about an eighth of an inch on the medium pitch; at no time will it be more than a quarter of an inch, even for a high Ybuzz pitch, which is, of course, still in the lower third of your range. What does *not* vary is the forward direction of the lip and cheek muscles, particularly around the nostrils and the upper lip. In this Ybuzz position you should feel the cheek area above the lip, and the lip itself, moving out and away from the gums. The tongue should be forward, the tip gently but firmly hugging the inside of the lower teeth, while the sides fit into the space between the side teeth, arching a little toward the upper molars (fig. 50).

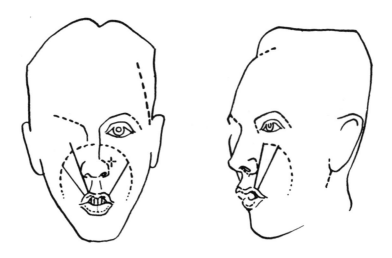

Figure 50. The facial posture for the Ybuzz.

Remember that the *maximum* use of the inverted-megaphone facial posture for the Ybuzz is the *minimum* form for everyday speech; even in quiet conversation, this minimum facial stretch will expand spontaneously to accommodate whatever special emphasis or accent grows out of an increased involvement in the communication. Primarily, you must realize that in effective informal speech the facial posture or form is never less than for the Ybuzz.

As you practice the Ybuzz, you will find that because of the improved facial posture, you are really sustaining the vowel

EE with a far better vocal placement and a more interesting tonal color. This sound and facial position will serve you better than the orthodox injunction to smile and show your teeth when saying EE, which usually produces a flat, nasal, or pinched vowel tone. To remind you of this, the letter Y, or the Ybuzz, will be our tonal-sensory phonetic symbol for the vowel sound EE.

Developing the Ybuzz

When you have succeeded in feeling some vibration or buzz on the gum-ridge portion of the hard palate and in the nose bone, cultivate this feeling and work to improve the Ybuzz until you can feel it coursing throughout all the bony areas, including the forehead. Remember that the Ybuzz is possible only in the lowest third of the vocal range and that you must experience it exclusively as a bone-conducted sensation, not as a sound rumbling about in the mouth or throat and not as a tone propelled through the lips. Even the relatively pleasant throat or soft-palate resonance is not a desirable part of the Ybuzz; the vibrations must be kept flowing forward. In a well-executed Ybuzz, you feel no pressure, no squeezing, no pushing with the back of the tongue; there will be no abrasive or consonant-like noises—just a clear, clean, free-flowing tonal current of the EE vowel felt on the gum-ridge area of the hard palate and in the nasal bone and eventually in the forehead.

Since the Ybuzz is naturally rich and comfortable only on the lower pitches of the vocal range, practice it only on *approximately the lower eight to ten half pitches,* which represents most of your conversational speaking range. No two voices are precisely the same in range, classification, or structural dimensions, so try not to imitate the pitch of another, but choose the one most comfortable for yourself. The buzz must not feel heavy or forced but extremely light in weight and volume, though at the same time dark and vibrant in color and energetic in motion. It is an unusual experience in tonal equilibrium during which you will sense a vibrato or tiny quiver in the bone of the nose as the Ybuzz current continues to move onward and upward.

At no time during the Ybuzz should you be aware of the use of breath. Rather you should feel a *holding back or suspension of the breath* current while the tonal current moves actively through the bones—your attention so completely focused on this action that the gentle inspiration of sound upward through the bony substance seems to have taken the place of breath current and control: You should almost breathe sound instead of air. The breath will already be firmly under control when the tonal action is fully felt and controlled. Feel as if you were trying constantly to sharpen the tone without actually moving into a higher pitch; feel the action of the sound as an internal event rather than a breath-propelled expulsion through the lips.

While you sustain the EE as long as you comfortably can, be sure that the vowel does not tend to become OO but remains an authentic EE as in *keep* or *feed*. If this seems difficult, concentrate on bringing the tongue a little more forward. In urging the cheek muscles around the nostrils forward into the upper lip, remember to keep the lip itself well forward and flippable. The lips in the forward position, whether for the Ybuzz or any other vowel, should never feel wrinkled, pursed, hard, or pointed; they should feel as if they were deliberately pouting forward, away from any contact with the gums. The only time a tense or tight lip position is justified is when it is part of a specific dramatic characterization.

The correct, relaxed posture is important in this, as in all of our sensory techniques. Never lift your face so that you seem to be leading with your chin. Keep the crown of your head as high as possible and the back of the neck extended, and let the shoulder muscles slope forward and downward so that the arms and hands also tend to fall forward. The front of the neck should not be visible and should feel free and relaxed. You should be able to swivel your entire head easily and completely from side to side while you sustain a rich Ybuzz.

In practicing any of the sensory techniques, make a point of not being too careful. This may seem a strange admonition, but to concentrate on being careful is a confining experience; to do anything too carefully encourages apprehension and inevitably destroys spontaneity. But neither can you afford to be careless, for that comes dangerously close to working without purpose or understanding. The objective is to be carefree or free of the oppression of care; it should mean working intentionally and intelligently, but easily, uninhibitedly, and always with imagery.

It is better to work on improving and correcting the tone *during* prolonged sustentions of the buzz than to stop and start over. You will learn more quickly and more surely from correcting a continuing process than from making many fresh starts. Check periodically for nasality by closing the nostrils. If the tone is right and the feeling of the buzz is radiating properly through the gum ridge of the hard palate and the bone of the nose, resonance and tone quality will not change, but if the Ybuzz is not right, the tone will change noticeably. In the word and sentence exercises do not use this test with words that include N, M, or NG, since these consonants are purely nasal and cannot be sounded with closed nostrils.

It is quite evident, I think, that the NG has a strong influence on vowels that precede it. For this reason I consider some vowels to be Ybuzz sounds though phoneticians give them other designations.

These include the I in *-ing* and *-ink* and the final unstressed Y. I cannot agree that the description of these as a short I, as in *sin,* is phonetically accurate. Instead, I consider the I in *singing* or *zinc* or the Y in *lovely* to be an extremely short Ybuzz. Similarly, the A in *hang* is not the A in *hat,* but a very mild version of the 6y.

The Ybuzz sensation is a protective device against strain and throatiness. The inverted megaphone shape, though reduced, still relaxes the jaw as it does in structural action. When produced without extraneous breath or force, the Ybuzz relieves tension and provides a built-in vibratory beam to give directional guidance to your speech; it attacks and helps cure such vocal bad habits as throatiness, nasality, de-nasality, and breathiness, all of which stem directly from wrong placement and pressure.

This effectiveness of the Ybuzz — and of tonal action as a whole—as a defending force is directly due to its influence as a progressive force. The vibrations of the Ybuzz focus induce so relaxing and refreshing a sensation that you will begin to anticipate, search for, and welcome it whenever you speak. The test in proving your mastery over tonal action is to be able to hold on to this tonal guide in moments of stress, anger, strain, overexuberance, and other situations that produce pressures. To the extent that you are able to maintain tonal control in your speech, you will be able to maintain your own equilibrium and reduce disturbing behavior. In this way, the control of the tonal focus in your speech and voice helps you to a better control of yourself. Naturally, it is a disciplined and conditioned control—but it is an extremely discriminating and an exhilarating one as well.

Ybuzz Exercises and Word Lists

Exercise one—Ybuzz Drill

step 1. Practice the Ybuzz on the words *weepy, heed, peace, squeezy, deep,* and *evening,* using a progressively lower pitch for each word over as wide a range as you comfortably can.

step 2. Practice sliding the Ybuzz like a siren sound, first down and up, then up and down, starting neither too high nor too low.

Comment: As the pitch is lowered in both steps, an overall small reduction occurs: The buzz creeps somewhat closer to the upper teeth and seems to fill a smaller pocket on the gum ridge; the lip opening gets a bit smaller; the side teeth come a bit closer together. Maintaining a rich fresh buzz requires a progressively gentler treatment as the tonal action vibrates more delicately in the smaller area. As the pitch is raised, the process is reversed and the buzz expands to a slightly larger pocket on the gum ridge; the lip opening and space cushion between the side teeth enlarge slightly. Neither change, however, should perceptibly change the outward appearance of the facial posture.

Exercise two—Muscle Shaking (fig. 51)

step 1. Practice the Ybuzz while shaking one hand and arm.

step 2. Observe the way this action vibrates the entire body and seems to bounce or pulsate the Ybuzz into the bones of the face; remember this feeling as a sense memory.

step 3. Continue the Ybuzz and try to reproduce this sense memory without shaking the arms.

Comment: Shaking the muscles is a relaxing technique that helps you achieve an uninhibited tonal action and permits you to concentrate on such aspects as form and the direction of the buzz. Begin with one hand in something like a gesture used in expressive speech; then use both hands, pretending to shake the

Figure 51. Body shaking during tonal action.

maracas. The shaking should be energetic though gentle—the muscles free enough to permit the entire body to vibrate in a pleasurable and stimulating muscle-loosening exercise that relaxes and vitalizes the vocal pulsations at the same time.

Exercise three—Ybuzz Word List

Do not practice these words for precise diction, but rather to develop your tonal perception of the Ybuzz as a voice training exercise. Hold each Ybuzz for at least three seconds.

be	bead	beatific	beacon	being
fee	freeze	feast	deemphasize	feelingly
he	heed	instinct	heated	Hebrew
key	keel	Keith	keeper	kingly
lee	relieve	reinvest	lethal	lovely
me	demeaned	meek	meekness	meekly
knee	canteen	niece	nieces	linking
pea	appeal	peace	Peter	peony
she	unsheathed	sheaf	shingle	leashing
see	obscene	seat	seepage	precinct
tea	fatigue	teetered	tincture	beastly
thee	theme	thesis	think	theory
we	wield	weekly	wink	weary

Comment: In normal conversation, the Ybuzz vowels fall into two categories according to length: (1) long (columns 1 and 2), where the Ybuzz vowel is either the final sound or is followed by a voiced consonant; (2) short (columns 3-5), where the vowel is followed by an unvoiced consonant or an NG sound or is a final unstressed Y. The N alone sometimes represents the sound of NGK as in *instinct*.

Exercise four—Ybuzz Sentences

step 1. Read the sentences, sustaining every underlined vowel for two or three seconds.

step 2. When you are satisfied with the consistency and richness of the Ybuzz resonance, shorten the sustention until you can read at a normal pace while continuing to feel the buzz.

1. He sees me ski every single week.

2. We are pleased with these three seats.

3. Leroy breeds really keen steeds.

4. We need steam heat immediately.

5. He keeps bees in his three leafy trees.

6. She freezes beef each spring.

7. Deep green seas bring me feelings of relief.

8. Keep these three greedy people here.

9. The evening breeze seems to seep between the leaves of these trees and flee easily beneath the ceiling of stars.

10. Peter's niece seems to think she needs three free meals each week to increase her meager diet and create a reasonably meaningful weight increase.

11. We mean to keep these leading people free of routine responsibilities.

Exercise five—Ybuzz Improvisation

step 1. Practice these words with emphasis on the Ybuzz vowels.

step 2. Improvise simple phrases or short sentences using one or more of these words; maintain the proper facial form throughout.

thieves	demeaned	decree	complete	reasonably
wheel	creeds	deemphasize	Ethan	instincts
seize	pristine	sheaf	king	precinct
keyed	conceived	wreath	street	seemingly
obscene	meager	lethal	cheating	shrinkage
breathe	Hebrew	weeping	ink	merrily
congeal	seizure	priest	jinx	easy
squeezed	plebeian	ether	tincture	think

The Plus Ybuzz

A variation of the Ybuzz is its application to the vowel sound A, as in *fade,* a diphthong combination of E plus EE. Ordinarily a diphthong should be accented on its first sound; in the diphthong A, however, to ensure the proper tonal placement and forward facial posture, the concentration should be on the second sound, *which is the Ybuzz.* The first sound, while very short, is felt as a tonal emphasis on the bone of the nose, accompanied by full lip protrusion and the smallest opening between the side teeth. It is nothing more than an infinitesimal tonal impulse feeding into the Ybuzz; this first sound will be designated by a + sign and the diphthong will be called the plus Y, the Lessac symbol for the vowel sound A.

To practice the +Ybuzz, begin with a sustained Ybuzz; then add a pulsating rhythm with the consonant Y: eee-Yeee-Yeee-Yeee-Yeee; this is already the beginning of the +Y. Now repeat the exercise and while saying Yeee, think Yey. It is as though, while sustaining the Ybuzz, you let the sound of the E drop in at the nasal bone for a split second, like a very slight quiver; Y-Y-Y-eY-Y-Y-eY-Y-Y-Y-eY-Y-Y-Y-eY-Y-Y-eY-Y-Y. The +Y does not break or destroy the Ybuzz—it simply gives it an added impulse.

As with the Ybuzz, don't be too careful in practicing the +Ybuzz and don't stop and start over if the tone is not right; improve it during sustention. Maintain both facial and body posture, and keep checking for nasality.

Plus Ybuzz and Carry-Over Exercises

Exercise one—Muscle Shaking (see fig. 51)

step 1. Practice a series of +Ybuzz tones while shaking one hand and arm.

step 2. Observe the way this action vibrates the entire body and seems to bounce or pulsate the Ybuzz into the bones of the face; remember this feeling as a sense memory.

step 3. Continue the +Ybuzz and try to reproduce this sense memory without shaking the arms.

Comment: Remember that when you sustain the +Ybuzz, you will sustain only the Ybuzz portion.

Exercise two— +Ybuzz Word List (In polysyllabic words the +Y is underlined)

As with the Ybuzz list, do not practice these words for precise diction, but hold each +Ybuzz—the EE, not the ĕ —for at least three seconds.

obey	bale	bait	baker
day	dames	date	tasty
fey	fade	face	fateful
gay	engaged	gait	gaping
decay	caged	dedicate	case-load
lay	lame	lace	lengthy
may	maimed	make	Macy's
neigh	inane	innate	nation
pay	escapade	pace	pathos
portray	arranged	rake	racetrack
say	saved	safe	insatiable
stray	strain	strength	strengthen
convey	vain	vapor	vacate

Comment: In normal conversation, the +Ybuzz vowels fall into two categories according to length: (1) long (columns 1 and 2), where the vowel either is the final sound or is followed by a voiced consonant; (2) short (columns 3 and 4), where the vowel is followed by an unvoiced consonant

or by an NG sound. The NG turns the preceding E into a +Ybuzz: The E
in *strength* is not the same as the E in *tent* but an extremely short +Ybuzz.

Exercise three—+Ybuzz Sentences

step 1. Read the sentences, sustaining every underlined vowel for two or three
seconds.

step 2. When you are satisfied with the consistency and richness of the +Ybuzz
resonance, shorten the sustention until you can read at a normal pace
while continuing to feel the buzz.

1. They came late.

2. They also stayed late.

3. Babies play whenever they may.

4. She creates extremely tame plays.

5. We may be late but please wait for us.

6. It may rain today.

7. In Spain it rained yesterday.

8. On the plains of Spain it rains and rains.

9. James gave the baby his daily wafer.

10. We aim to please everyday in every way.

11. Mr. Nathan's eighty-eight acres may be made to yield a great
    deal more grain than previously obtained, but it may take
    eighteen days before the changes may be made.

12. The pale waiter was upbraided and chased from the table by
    the lady who ate the cake—she complained that the ale came
    too late for the steak.

13. They may take trains late today or sail away the eighth of May.

Exercise four—+Ybuzz Improvisation

step 1. Practice these words with emphasis on the +Ybuzz vowels.

step 2. Improvise simple phrases or short sentences using one or more of these
words; maintain the proper facial form throughout.

play	strayed	stage	naming	safely
danger	strength	phase	saleable	inmate
prey	traded	escapade	ungainly	created
famous	maimed	proclaim	safe	berate
gazing	range	remaining	nation	satiate
aid	wail	occasion	debatable	shapely
vaguely	framed	belabored	elated	occupation
crave	cable	failure	cape	embrace
shave	derailed	vaguely	grace	lengthened

Exercise five—Carry-Over Drill

Up to this point we have considered the Ybuzz as a formal, concentrated tonal action. The following exercises are designed to encourage the carry-over of the concentrated Ybuzz sensation to a dilute but still resonant tonal action in all vowels, especially the structural vowels. Everyday speech calls for continuous tonal action in a generally nonconcentrated focus, a dilute current, spreading itself throughout the palate and nasal bone and resonating pleasantly, if diffusely, in the oral cavity.

step 1. Begin with a rich, vibrant Ybuzz

step 2. Stretch as smoothly as possible into each of the structural vowels below, carrying over as much of the tonal color and tonal action as possible without permitting the sound to become throaty.

step 3. Now practice the phrases, carrying over the focus of the Ybuzz words to the other vowels.

1. Y-Y-Y-Y-Y-Y-Y-Y ⟶ OO (#1) Keep cool, Mimi.

2. Y-Y-Y-Y-Y-Y-Y-Y ⟶ O (#21) We'll go see.

3. Y-Y-Y-Y-Y-Y-Y-Y ⟶ AW (#3) He called me.

4. Y-Y-Y-Y-Y-Y-Y-Y ⟶ OY (#3y) These toys break.

5. Y-Y-Y-Y-Y-Y-Y-Y ⟶ O (#4) We're odd people.

6. Y-Y-Y-Y-Y-Y-Y-Y ⟶ AH (#5) He'll calm thee.

7. Y-Y-Y-Y-Y-Y-Y-Y ⟶ OW (#51) Read aloud, please.

8. Y-Y-Y-Y-Y-Y-Y-Y ⟶ A (#6) She asked me.

9. Y-Y-Y-Y-Y-Y-Y-Y ⟶ I (#6y) Green eyes I see.

Comment: The sensation is like moving from hot sun to a semi-shade; or better still, like gliding swiftly in the center of a current and then drifting more slowly into the outer edges—but you must stay *within* the current;

never leave it. You must become so aware of the tonal action that whenever you do find yourself outside the free-flowing tonal current, this loss of the action-sensation of the Ybuzz will seem a positive act of omission and a signal for you to move back into the current. If the dilute resonance seems to feel a bit nasal at first, check for nasality by closing the nostrils; if there is no tonal change, what you feel is nasal resonance, not nasality.

Exercise six—The Alphabet

Daily practice with the alphabet is a good exercise for incorporating tonal action into your everyday speech.

step 1. Recite the alphabet, sustaining every Ybuzz and +Ybuzz letter, which are all underlined; the slashed letters represent #1 or #21 stretch vowels, which also provide a pleasant buzzing tonal vibration when done on a slightly higher pitch with full structural stretch. The remaining letters should be executed with good facial posture and a well-directed dilute tonal focus.

step 2. Go through the alphabet again, pretending that each letter is a word used conversationally, with a reasonable degree of emphasis, accent, and inflection, in an attempt to communicate meaning. Tell a story with the alphabet.

A b, c d,   Ø r, s t,

E, f, g...   Ø and v . . .

H i, j k   Dou-ble Ø and

L m n ø p...   X, y, z!

Exercise seven—Ybuzz Communication

step 1. Begin with a rich, vibrant Ybuzz warm-up.

step 2. On the same Ybuzz track, communicate the whole message of each line as if you were seriously trying to convince someone.

Y-Y-Y-Y_____→This is the way to feel the focus.

Y-Y-Y-Y_____→Feel the focus and keep it this way.

Y-Y-Y-Y_____→If we feel the focus and really keep it this way . . .

Y-Y-Y-Y_____→Then we will always be able to feel an easy control over our voice and speech!

Exercise eight—Reading Selections

In these selections concentrate on feeling the Ybuzz with the most reduced facial posture. Read with a maximum feeling of involvement but do not let your involvement disturb, destroy, or pollute the Ybuzz sensation. On the contrary, concentrate on making the Ybuzz current a stimulating expression of involvement that adds a new quality to your interpretation of the reading.

Displacing the seeds of reason,
The traitor screams with peals of hate;
But for the patriot, there is relief of pain
In freedom's sweet embrace.

Pitiless waves,
  Scraping 'cross the heaving seas,
    Unsheathe the razor peaks
      of scaly reefs
        That wait beneath
          To reap the sails
            Of fools who dare
              To venture deep.

Weeping moonbeam tears,
The sea breathes deep
As waves waste away the years
Of waking sleep.

The irate bees
Seemed just like fleas
As they made their escape
In two's and three's.

There was a fierce lady named Quade,
Who beat her sweet mate with her braid,
  Till the wretch came afraid
  And decided to trade
That braid-wielding lady named Quade.

There was a great hater named Slade,
Who delivered each day a tirade;
  Till his neighbors were sated,
  Had him seized and deflated,
And were free of that hater named Slade.

These men are sheep who nightly sleep in graves,

But ne'er may stay, nor even dream.

They daily wake—each day three-quarters slain . . .

Too dazed to be, they only seem.

I say I hate thee, Kate . . .

And with a deep and glowering glee,

Make keenest courtesy

Seem to bid thee: die for me!

Exercise nine—Improvisation in Communication through the Ybuzz Focus

The object of this exercise is to communicate with another person through pure sound, in this case the vibrant EE of the Ybuzz and the vibrant A of the +Ybuzz.

step 1. Select a partner and sit facing him.

step 2. Conduct a conversation, communicating solely through inflections of the Ybuzz and +Ybuzz, without verbal content or actual words. Try to threaten with the dark quality of the lower ranges of the Ybuzz. Try to insinuate and conspire. Use the contained energy of the Ybuzz tonal action to be as persuasive and communicative as possible.

Comment: Within the limited range and the limited number of vowels of the Ybuzz and +Ybuzz, try to find all the emotions you can. Try to find and feel the emotions that rise out of the tonal sensations of the Ybuzz. Try to vary the two vowel sounds with pitch and intensity.

CHAPTER VIII

The Connecting Links
and the R-Derivative

*B*EFORE WE TAKE the next step in tonal action, there are two more types of vowels to be taken up. In the past two chapters, we have covered the seven structural action vowels, #1, #21, #3, #4, #5, #51, and #6; the two tonal action vowels, the Ybuzz and +Ybuzz; and two diphthongs that combine structural and tonal action, 3y and 6y. With the neutral vowels and the R-derivative, the repertoire of vowel sounds will be complete.

The neutral vowels are important because they occur in our speech so often. Like the tiny circles of gold or silver wire that hold the jewels of a necklace together, they may play a less colorful role than the other vowels and the consonants, but they must be there or our speech will fall apart.

These vowels are much like the schwa vowel in the International Phonetic Alphabet (IPA), which represents sounds like the A in *alone*. The Lessac system, however, uses four different symbols instead of the single schwa of the IPA. These are a particular boon to foreign students and will be useful to all, a bit later on, in the achievement of crisper, cleaner, more beautiful consonant articulation.

The four neutrals are: N¹, O͝O as in *took;* N², Ĭ as in *tick;* N³, Ĕ as in *tech;* N⁴, Ŭ as in *tuck*. In the IPA, the N⁴ is represented by two different symbols: the catch-all schwa for the vowel sound in the first syllable of *above* and another symbol for the vowel in the second syllable. In the Lessac system, both of these are considered N⁴, the only difference being that the second syllable is stressed and the first is not.

These vowels can be considered neutral for a number of reasons:

1. They are formed with a neutral facial posture—the inverted megaphone shape reduced to its minimum, much as it is for the Ybuzz vowels.

2. Except in singing or in speech with a deliberately sustained emphasis, they are all short, staccato, grunt-like sounds.
3. When a neutral vowel comes between two consonants, it represents the shortest possible distance between the two—in practice, such a syllable becomes thoroughly neutralized and sounds more like a consonant than a vowel exercise.
4. Although a stressed neutral syllable always calls for a specific neutral vowel sound, these vowels often color each other, and in most unstressed syllables they are so phonetically inconsequential as to be interchangeable, which further neutralizes the quality of the vowel.
5. They may be thought of as weak forms, at one time more closely related to vowels with a much stronger phonetic coloring: Thus the N^1 in *full* might have related to the #1 in *fool;* the N^2 in *fill* to the Ybuzz in *feel;* the N^3 in *wren* to the #6 in *ran;* and the N^4 in *come* to the #5 in *calm.*

In pronouncing these vowels, the error to be avoided is not shortening them, but rather expanding them until they begin to sound like what we might call the parent vowels. The awareness of this concept is of particular benefit to foreign-speaking students, but it will help all of us to cleaner articulation if we will remember always the principle of treating these short staccato sounds as the shortest possible distance between any two consonants. It will contribute not only to vowel facility and skillful consonant articulation, but also to naturalness and fluency of speech, to the principle of liaison in speech, and to rhythmic variety and contrasts.

Stress and Unstress

The neutrals make up approximately 65 per cent of the vowel sounds in formal communication, and the average is much higher in informal conversation. They appear in stressed, semistressed, and unstressed syllables, and in weakened conversational forms of stronger vowels as well.

There are varying degrees and combinations of syllabic stress:
1. Except for the weak forms, there is the inevitable stress of monosyllabic words, such as *wood* or *dull.*
2. There are words that have one stressed syllable and one or more unstressed syllables, such as *gov'ern-ment, ex'it,* or *in-dic'a-tive.*
3. There are words with more than one stressed syllable—a primary and a secondary stress—along with one or more unstressed syllables, such as *con,fla-gra'tion, in,con-sis'tent,* or *et,ce'te-ra.*
4. There are double words that carry equal stress on both syllables, such as *love-sick, cup-ful, kid-stuff, bul-finch,* or *sit-in.*

5. There are words or syllables that acquire a partial or semistress from the skillful and effective use of structural, tonal, or consonant action. Conversely, during very relaxed conversation or through carelessness or exhaustion, words and syllables will be corrupted, and will lose their stress.

I personally feel that the whole question of comparative and relative stress of the neutrals is overstressed itself. It would appear to me that if a neutral syllable or word requires additional strength or emphasis for whatever reason, it will quite naturally be spoken with greater stress and accent. The neutral vowel in the word *rid,* for example, while stressed, is not essentially different from the neutral vowel in the word *hybrid.*

The correct neutral vowel must be used in a stressed syllable, but even here the technique of moving from consonant to consonant with maximum dispatch, as if you thought the vowel without actually saying it, is your best guarantee that you will develop the proper skill with the neutrals and that the vowel will remain uncorrupted. Thus: the N^1 *good* should be thought of as g--d; the N^2 *fill* as f-ll; the N^3 *them* as th-m; and the N^4 *custom* as c-st-m.

The Interchangeable Vowels

In unstressed syllables, if the consonants are right, the neutral sound will usually be right, regardless of the vowel used or the spelling of the syllable. With good consonant action, many words will sound perfectly natural with any of several neutral vowels: the word *people* can be pronounced peop-N^1-le, peop-N^2-le, or peop-N^4-le; while *government* can be governm-N^4-nt, governm-N^1-nt, governm-N^2-nt, or governm-N^3-nt. The point is that with skillful use of consonant action in the unstressed or weak forms, concern over the choice is unnecessary: Use the one that comes naturally. In some instances, one vowel or another may seem an economical choice: The letter E in the unstressed *re-* prefix, as in *repeat,* is preferably N^2, as in *rid;* the *-ess* suffix, as in *duchess,* may take N^3 but will also take N^2. In others, such as the suffixes *-tion* and *-ful,* an economical choice does not seem very essential.

Problems with foreign or regional accents can often be reduced by coloring one neutral with another. Foreign students, who veer toward the stronger vowels, should color the N^2 of *fill* with the N^3 of *fellow,* and the N^3 with the N^2. This will prevent the first word from sounding like the Ybuzz *feel* and the second like the #6 *fallow.* In the same way, N^1 and N^4 can borrow color from one another to prevent *took* from sounding like the #1 *tool* and *tuck* like the #5 *tahk.* Southerners, on the whole —— tend to use N^2 and N^3 interchangeably in stressed syllables. They can avoid this by thinking of N² as closely related to the Ybuzz and N³ to the #6 stretch vowel as it might be said with a neutral facial posture and no significant space between the side teeth. These are devices rather than rules.

Neutral Vowels in Weak Forms

A distinctive feature of spoken English is the use of many common words in either a strong form or one or more weak forms, depending upon the amount of emphasis or lack of emphasis. The weak forms occur, of course, only in unstressed positions in sentences. The words most commonly weakened in informal speech are the connecting words that link nouns, adjectives, verbs, and adverbs into meaningful sentences: articles, such as *an* and *the,* prepositions, such as *at, for,* and *of;* conjunctions, such as *and* and *or;* and pronouns, such as *them* and *him.* Contractions, such as *they're, they'll, we're, you'd, I'm, he's,* are also weak form, and a few verbs and other parts of speech may sometimes be weakened.

Although the N⁴ substitutes for the strong vowel in most of the weak forms, the other neutrals are also used in some. Where the weakening process seems to have eliminated the vowel altogether, the very shortest N⁴ is still present. Many are so indefinite that designation of a specific neutral is unnecessary indicating they are actually interchangeable.

Most weakened forms are acceptable in informal conversation, but there is a group that is not. I mention it, however, to point to a process that becomes irreversible if proper standards are not maintained energetically. Through carelessness, ignorance, or laziness, entire syllables are lost, and *different* becomes *diff'rent, February* becomes *Feb'yary, practically* becomes *practic'ly, usually* become *us'ally, casually* becomes *cas'ally, evening* becomes *ev'ning,* and *library* becomes *li'bry.*

Unstressed R Endings

Certain unstressed final syllables ending in R always take an indefinite neutral vowel. These R-colored vowel or vowel-colored R endings include *ar, er, or, ur, ure, ir,* and *yr.* As with any R that follows a vowel and precedes a consonant, you may sound the consonant R as strongly as you like if, in the rest of the word, you use structural action well and avoid nasality, throatiness, pressed or pinched lips, and tight jaw. I urge deemphasis of the R only to the extent that it tends to disturb or abuse our standard of euphony. Even the Midwesterner need not eliminate his R if he observes this euphonic standard of voice and speech.

These unstressed R endings fall into three groups:
1. Words ending in *er, ar,* and *or* take N⁴: *er*—sever, mother, feather,

deliver, tower; *ar*—vulgar, Caesar, dollar, altar, molar; *or*—actor, doctor, honor, dictator, proctor.

2. Words ending in *ur* and *ure* take either N⁴ or N¹: *ur*—murmur, femur, augur; *ure*—nature, pleasure, moisture, fixture, seizure.

3. Words ending in *ir* and *yr* take either N⁴ or N²: *ir*—tapir, fakir, elixir; *yr*—satyr, martyr, zephyr.

The Neutral Diphthongs

There are four diphthongs that include neutral vowel sounds. N¹, N², and N³ each provide the first sound for one diphthong, and the #3 stretch vowel begins the fourth. The second sound is always N⁴ and is indicated by a small n. Thus we have N¹n, as in *poor*; N²n, as in *peer*; N³n, as in *pear*; and 3n as in *pour*.

These diphthongs are always followed by an R, and this R, as with any final R, is always pronounced distinctly when it can be phrased directly into another word that starts with a vowel; otherwise, it should be somewhat deemphasized. The danger in pronouncing these neutral diphthongs with a very strong R before a consonant, or especially before a pause, is that they tend to become two syllables: *poor* become *poo-wer*, *peer* becomes *pee-yer*, *pear* becomes *pay-yer*, and *pour* becomes *poh-wer*. They should always be monosyllables.

Neutral Exercises and Word Lists

Exercise one—Neutral Spelling

A demonstration of the variations in the spelling of the neutral vowel sounds. Run through these with dispatch, in a series of four quick beats, very much like a brisk 4/4 tune.

N¹ (o͝o)= could	look	took	full	vo͝ory	wo͝ory	hook
N² (ĭ) = kid	live	tick	fill	viry	wiry	hick
N³ (ĕ) = ked	lev	tech	fell	very	wery	heck
N⁴ (ŭ) = cud	love	tuck	fuhl	vuhry	worry	huck

N¹ =	jo͝ost	pull	ro͝og	stood	do͝od	mo͝ony
N² =	gist	pill	rig	stid	did	minny
N³ =	jest	pell	reg	stead	dead	many
N⁴ =	just	puhl	rug	stud	dud	money

Exercise two—Neutral Word Lists

In words of more than one syllable, all primary and secondary stress syllables are marked.

N[1]—used in stressed syllables of many words spelled with U, OO, O, and OU

bush	butch'er	foot	stood	could
bull	pul'pit	good	wom'an	would
full	cush'ion	look	wolves	should

N[2]—used in stressed syllables of many words spelled with I and Y and some spelled with U and UI

crib	lift	in.di-vid'u-al	built	busi'ness	myth
live	sick	in'te-gral	guild	bus'y	syn'er-gy
bridge	kiss	in'fi-nite	build	mys'ter-y	i-dyl'lic
hill	be-gin'	con-vince'	build'ing	sym'pa-thy	phys'i-cist

N[3]—used in the stressed syllables of many words spelled with E, A, EA, U, IE, and some spelled with EI, AE, EO, AI.

bed	ver'y	en-deav'or	cem'e-ter.y	aes-thet'ic
left	dead	health	an'y-thing	leop'ard
stem	breath	an'y	mil.i-tar'i-ly	bur'y
bes'tial	meas'ure	man'y	said	friend
col-lect'	deaf	sec're-tar.y	says	heif'er

N[4]—used in the stressed syllables of many words spelled with U, O, and OU, and some spelled with OE and OO

buzz	judge	much	un'cle	hun'gry	suc-cumb'	doz'en
once	oth'er	a-bove'	slov'en-ly	come	noth'ing	does
tough	young	e-nough'	south'ern	coun'try	cou'ple	blood

Comment: Foreign students should remember to color N[1] and N[4] with one another, and N[2] and N[3] with one another, not only in these words but in the sentences in the next exercise.

Exercise three—Neutral Sentences

The specific neutral vowel to be practiced is always underlined twice; all other neutrals are underlined once. Remember to practice these neutrals as the shortest distance between two consonants.

> *N[1]*

The good-looking cook took a good look at the butcher with

the crooked foot, who stood near the wooden pulpit, his hand on the Good Book, his face full of sugary looks.

2. The rookie crook, who forsook the cook he mistook for a "bull," couldn't pull the bullet out of his foot with the rusty hook, so he took the cushion from the wooden nook and pushed it near his foot.

Comment: Do not think of this vowel sound as a short $\overline{OO}$, but as a very short $\breve{OO}$.

N^2

1. Mister Smith and his six assistants didn't finish their visit in this city till after weeks of spirited and indignant quibbling with Mister Milligan.

2. The written permit admitted him to the political ritual in spite of the indignant guard.

3. Despite her timidity and morbidity, she impressed me with her intrepidity, her natural dignity and thought rapidity; yet Bill was dismayed at her frigidity and seeming inability to smile.

Comment: Do not think of this vowel sound as a short Ybuzz, but as a short $\breve{I}$.

N^3

1. The very best and efficient men of the regiment bellied themselves toward the edge of the precipice and were getting ready to frustrate the bestial efforts of the enemy.

2. Tell Emma to let Dennis's best friends enjoy themselves whenever they come even if they raise merry hell.

3. Fred Perry sent his secretary to collect the September rent from the restless and ever-murmuring tenants.

Comment: Do not allow this vowel sound to become too much like the #6 stretch vowel.

N^4

1. Aside from the customary stuff about the public good, the tough young southerner once again stood head and shoulders above the slovenly official judge.

2. Once nothing but hungry destruction succeeded, the blood of dozens of other countries was the unutterable by-product.

Comment: This is the key neutral sound, especially for the foreign student.

Exercise four—Diphthong Word Lists

Pronounce words like cure, lure, and pure as if a consonant Y followed the initial consonant—kyure, lyure, and pyure.

N^1n = poor	tour	cure	lure	pure
N^2n = peer	tear	seer	leer	cheer
N^3n = pear	tear	care	lair	chair
3n = pour	tore	core	lore	chore

N^1n = manure	dour	boor	Ruhr	sure
N^2n = near	dear	bier	rear	sheer
N^3n = ne'er	dare	bare	rare	share
3n = nor	door	boar	roar	shore

Exercise five—Diphthong Sentences

N^1n

During the soup du jour course, the two boors were successfully lured into taking the tour through the Ruhr valley after being reassured regarding the poor accommodations.

N^2n

The sincere speaker appeared to be in tearful fear of his beer-drinking hearers, but by sheer luck the searing jeers turned to clear cheers.

N^3n

Mary handled the various wares at the Fair with great care while her Airedale was perched precariously on the staircase.

3n

During the war, more and more people looked up at the roaring, soaring airplanes with apprehension, thinking back to the scores or more of years ago when they had thrilled to the same sight.

Exercise six—Neutral Frequency

This paragraph shows how often the neutrals can occur in general communication. Use it as an exercise for neutrals and consonants.

Wouldn't it be a wonderful experiment if this intrinsically physical but non-listening method could be initiated in six or seven different sections of this country. It would appear inevitable that with one year's training, the students—the Texans, the Midwesterners, the Californians, the Southerners, the Alaskans, the New Yorkers—when getting together, would recognize upon this confrontation, an intrinsic similarity and effectiveness in the form and facility of their speech and voice functioning, yet each group would retain its own particular local indigenous charms. Everyone involved in this experiment, bringing with him different opinions and interests as well as conditioning, would nevertheless find it significantly more comfortable and pleasurable to engage successfully in the kind of serious intercommunication that could lead to a better, more fulfilling common understanding.

The R-Derivative

As the name implies, the R-derivative is a vowel that derives from the consonant R and retains part of the color and placement of the R. The relationship between the two is a subtle one: When the firm contact between the undersides of the tongue and the insides of the upper back teeth—the necessary tongue position for a legitimate consonant R—is loosened to the point where the trombone-like vibration of the R is weakened or lost, the resulting sound, which moves freely through the mouth without friction, is the R-derivative vowel, as in *early, absurd, divert, worth, murmured, sir, urbane, kernel, work, journal, myrtle, cistern,* and *bird.* Though the vowel has many different spellings, its pronunciation is always the same, and it is always followed by the R itself.

To form the R-derivative, begin with a clear consonant R, as in *read,* and sustain it. Then form the full inverted megaphone stretch with a lip opening as close to that for the #3 vowel as possible. Continue the sound and think the R, but slip the tip of the tongue down to the inside of the lower teeth which loosens the tongue contact from the side teeth. You should now have the sound of the R-derivative, a sound like a nebulous R or a vocalized preparation for the R.

The Role of the R

The British tend to pronounce words such as *early* and *bird* with a sustained R-derivative and no consonant R at all; many Americans hit the consonant R and eliminate the preceding vowel. Preferably these words should be pronounced with a well-formed R-derivative vowel, followed by as much consonant R as you choose. The degree of R-coloration is optional, but a genuine consonant R should never be substituted for the R-derivative vowel. A temporary exception to this rule, for foreign students only, will also be discussed in the section on accent elimination in the appendix.

There can be some degree of choice in the pronunciation of any final R or any R preceded by a vowel and followed by another consonant. I usually recommend that these be deemphasized because the R in this position has a backward influence on the voice: It tends to force a part of the word back into the throat, with poor tone, tension, and loss of clarity as a result. But if you use sufficient structural action to relax tension in the tongue and jaw and sufficient tonal action to direct the vibration forward on the hard palate, you can use as much or as little R as you please and the vocal quality will never suffer.

R-Derivative Exercises and Word Lists

Exercise one—R-Derivative Word List

Especially in practice, exaggerate the facial posture, with a lip opening close to that for the #3 vowel. The feeling should be primarily structural, plus a sense-memory recall of a dilute R vibration. As long as you use a strong stretch form, you need never be concerned with the degree of R pronunciation. The vowel is not underlined in words of one syllable.

bird	sermon	worm	surly	rehearse
Thursday	perch	worse	surgeon	dearth
birch	verve	absurd	gurgle	search
shirk	Gertrude	cur	durst	earnest
girdle	universal	turgid	refurbish	colonel
girl	servile	unworthy	unfurl	myrrh
virtue	world	usurp	nurture	Myrna
berth	work	hurdle	adjourn	serpent

Exercise two—R-Derivative Sentences

1. The curly-haired working girl burst into an unrehearsed flir-

tation in order to divert the determined attention of a certain third person.

2. The dirty worm squirmed nervously and furtively when the early bird returned.

3. The pert nurse had the nerve to flirt with the perturbed surgeon.

4. The sum of thirty dollars spurred the surly clerk on to finish the irksome work for the foreign firm by the third day.

Exercise three—Weak Form Drill

Both the strong vowel form used in primary stress and the neutral used in the weak form are shown in this sample list of words. Practice both forms and note the effect of each on meaning and naturalness.

Word	Strong form	Weak form	Weak form phrases
an	#6 stretch	N^4	Have 'n apple
the	Ybuzz/N^4	N^2 before a vowel	Cover th' earth
		N^4 before a consonant	Cover th' world
at	#6 stretch	N^2 or N^4	Look 't th' book
for	#3 stretch	N^4	I did it fuh fun
			I did it f'r Emma
from	#4 stretch	N^4	I come fr'm
of	#4 stretch	N^4	river 'v mud
upon	#4 stretch	N^4	depending up'n circumstances
to	#1 stretch	N^1 or N^4	I intend t' go
are	#5 stretch	N^4	The boys 'r in
			The boys uh' there
was	#4 stretch	N^1 or N^4	He w's right
were	R-derivative	N^4	They wuh' very kind
			They wuhr in
have	#6 stretch	N^4	What've you done?
has	#6 stretch	N^4	This's been proved
do	#1 stretch	N^4 or N^1	How d' you do it?
shall	#6 stretch	N^4 or N^1	How sh'll it be?
will	N^2	N^2, N^4, or N^1	The church'll be full

can	#6 stretch	N^2 or N^4	He c'n go
and	#6 stretch	N^1, N^2, or N^4	You 'n I
			You 'nd I
them	N^3	N^4	Look 't th'm
him	N^2	N^4	Look 't 'm
her	R-derivative	N^4	Take it to 'ur

Comment: Foreign students should not practice the weak form independently. They must experience the etymological process of phonetic change while doing it, and should therefore use the strong form in these phrases, constantly accelerating the speed of pronunciation while at the same time deemphasizing volume and stress.

The Vowels in Retrospect

You have now covered all of the English vowels—the solo instrument that will be supported by the consonant orchestra—and have learned to form them by nonauditory tono-sensory control. They fall into six specific categories.

1. The stretch vowels—based on maximum structural action

   #1 as in *ooze, you,* or *smooth*
   #3 as in *all, norm,* or *laud*
   #4 as in *odd, bond,* or *doll*
   #5 as in *alms, gnarl,* or *father*
   #6 as in *add, nasty,* or *back*

2. The stretch diphthongs

   #21 as in *ode, no,* or *foam*
   #51 as in *ounce, now,* or *outhouse*
   3y as in *boil* or *boy*
   6y as in *wild* or *aisle*

3. The Ybuzz vowels—based on vibratory tonal action

   Ybuzz as in *easy* or *seethe*
   +Ybuzz as in *aim* or *made*

4. The R-derivative—based on diffused R vibration with the tongue disengaged, plus a #3 stretch position

R-derivative as in *worm, early,* or *urn*

5. The neutral vowels—based on neutral facial posture and short, staccato. grunt-like sounds.

N^1 as in *took*
N^2 as in *tick*
N^3 as in *tech*
N^4 as in *tuck*

6. The neutral diphthongs

N^1n as in *poor*
N^2n as in *peer*
N^3n as in *pear*
$3n$ as in *pour*

Phonetic Analysis of the Vowels

In the selections that follow, all of the vowels produced by structural and tonal action are indicated by their appropriate symbols. The neutrals are not numbered, but indicated simply as N. The ℛ represents the R-derivative vowel.

I APPEAL TO ANY WHITE MAN TO SAY IF EVER HE ENTERED
LOGAN'S CABIN HUNGRY, AND HE GAVE HIM NOT MEAT; IF
EVER HE CAME COLD AND NAKED, AND HE CLOTHED HIM
NOT. DURING THE COURSE OF THE LAST LONG AND BLOODY
WAR LOGAN REMAINED IDLE IN HIS CABIN, AN ADVOCATE
FOR PEACE. SUCH WAS MY LOVE FOR THE WHITES THAT MY
COUNTRYMEN POINTED AT ME AS THEY PASSED, AND SAID:
"LOGAN IS THE FRIEND OF WHITE MEN." I HAD EVEN
THOUGHT TO HAVE LIVED WITH YOU, BUT FOR THE INJURIES
OF ONE MAN. COLONEL CRESAP, THE LAST SPRING, IN COLD
BLOOD AND UNPROVOKED, MURDERED ALL THE RELATIONS

OF LOGAN, NOT SPARING EVEN MY WOMEN AND CHILDREN. THERE RUNS NOT A DROP OF MY BLOOD IN THE VEINS OF ANY LIVING CREATURE.

THIS CALLED ON ME FOR REVENGE. I HAVE SOUGHT IT. I HAVE KILLED MANY. I HAVE GLUTTED MY VENGEANCE. FOR MY COUNTRY, I REJOICE AT THE BEAMS OF PEACE. BUT DO NOT THINK THAT MINE IS THE JOY OF FEAR. LOGAN NEVER FELT FEAR. LOGAN WILL NOT TURN ON HIS HEEL TO SAVE HIS LIFE. WHO IS THERE TO MOURN FOR LOGAN? NOT ONE!

—LOGAN

I JOIN WITH YOU MOST CORDIALLY IN REJOICING AT THE RETURN OF PEACE. I HOPE IT WILL BE LASTING AND THAT MANKIND WILL AT LENGTH, AS THEY CALL THEMSELVES REASONABLE CREATURES, HAVE REASON ENOUGH TO SETTLE THEIR DIFFERENCES WITHOUT CUTTING THROATS; FOR IN MY OPINION, THERE NEVER WAS A GOOD WAR OR A BAD PEACE. WHAT PAST ADDITIONS TO THE CONVENIENCES AND COMFORTS OF LIFE MIGHT MANKIND HAVE ACQUIRED, IF THE MONEY SPENT IN WARS HAD BEEN EMPLOYED IN WORKS OF UTILITY! WHAT AN EXTENSION OF AGRICULTURE, EVEN TO THE TOPS OF THE MOUNTAINS, WHAT RIVERS RENDERED NAVIGABLE, OR JOINED BY CANALS; WHAT BRIDGES, AQUE-DUCTS, NEW ROADS, AND OTHER PUBLIC WORKS, EDIFICES

AND IMPROVEMENTS, RENDERING ENGLAND A COMPLETE PARADISE, MIGHT NOT HAVE BEEN OBTAINED BY SPENDING THOSE MILLIONS IN DOING GOOD, WHICH IN THE LAST WAR HAVE BEEN SPENT IN DOING MISCHIEF—IN BRINGING MISERY INTO THOUSANDS OF FAMILIES AND DESTROYING THE LIVES OF MANY WORKING PEOPLE, WHO MIGHT HAVE PERFORMED THE USEFUL LABORS.

—BENJAMIN FRANKLIN

THE CORNER STONE OF THE REPUBLIC LIES IN OUR TREATING EACH MAN ON HIS WORTH AS A MAN, PAYING NO HEED TO HIS CREED, HIS BIRTHPLACE, OR HIS OCCUPATION, ASKING NOT WHETHER HE IS RICH OR POOR, WHETHER HE LABORS WITH HIS HEAD OR HAND; ASKING ONLY WHETHER HE ACTS DECENTLY AND HONORABLY IN THE VARIOUS RELATIONS OF HIS LIFE, WHETHER HE BEHAVES WELL TO HIS FAMILY, TO HIS NEIGHBORS, TO THE STATE.

CHAPTER IX

Tonal Action II—
The Call

WE HAVE FINISHED with the vowels. Unlike structural action and our first excursion into tonal action—the Ybuzz—the call technique will introduce no specific phonetic sounds; nevertheless, this further extension of tonal action is an important step in building the voice before we go on to the subtler articulation of the consonants.

With the Ybuzz you have learned to experience the feeling of tonal action in approximately the lowest eight half pitches of the vocal range. The particular result of these Ybuzz sensations is a vital, pleasant, rich vocal quality in normal conversational speech. The call goes beyond the Ybuzz in tonal action and is designed to expand and develop the range, pitch, volume, production, and quality of practically the entire speaking voice, most of the female singing voice, and approximately two thirds of the male singing voice.

While the Ybuzz is practiced with reduced structural action and a minimal space between the teeth, the call technique makes use of the full inverted-megaphone stretch and the widest space between the teeth. The Ybuzz is specifically identified with the spoken vowel sounds EE andEY; the call encompasses all vowel sounds except the EE. In practicing the call technique, however, the vowel sounds may be treated with a considerable degree of latitude—an approximation is all that is necessary. You may feel various shades and gradations of the vowel sound OO or O or AW or AH during a call, depending upon your pitch, and you may identify the result as the OO or O or AW or AH vowel, but it will certainly differ from the sounds of these vowels in normal conversational speech. The call is always primarily governed by a specific vibratory sensation—a fully concentrated tonal feeling—designed to expand the technical and emotional ranges of the voice, where the subtler qualities of vowel articulation are secondary. In their mutually complementary ways, both the Ybuzz and the call are designed to explore the resonant qualities of your voice and to put these qualities at the service of your speech, of your singing, of your acting, of your everyday functioning.

The Origin of the Call

In Hebrew, the word *Kall* literally means the voice, and from biblical times to the present, callers throughout the world, both secular and religious, have produced beautiful and exciting vocal tones, sometimes consciously, sometimes quite unaware.

It is said that in the days when the Temple stood in Jerusalem, an official known as the Caller would make early morning announcements in tones so hauntingly beautiful that women would pause in their morning chores to listen and, so it is reported, sometimes to faint from ecstasy. In later days street vendors called their strawberries or melons, cockles and mussels, or hot-cross buns in melodies that have inspired composers, serious and popular alike. The soldiers' call for "Wa-a-a-ater boy" that Kipling turned to poetry, the "All abo-o-oard" of the train conductor, the golfer's "Fo-o-ore," the traffic cop's "Pu-ul o-o-over," the engineer's "O-oka-a-ay, let 'er go-o-o-o-o," the stage manager's "Pla-a-aces ple-e-e-ease," the lumberjack's "Ti-i-imbe-e-e-er," or just anyone's unusually hearty "Hello-o-o the-ere" are all examples of calls used today and every day. The peddler and the newsboy often develop perfect call techniques out of the necessity for calling attention to themselves and their wares over the roar of the city without harming their throats or ruining their voices.

Conscious or not, in ritual or in everyday use, the good call is never a strident scream or a hoarse yell or merely a loud shout. The call is an exhilarating, resilient, resonant tone, esthetic enough to form the basis of the opera singer's recitative as well as at least sixty per cent of his singing, efficient enough to provide the actor's verbal accent and interpretive vocal emphasis; the call is the bridge in tonal production between the conversational speaking voice and the singing voice; the call is the heightened vocal quality necessary for highly emotional speech.

The call as well as the Ybuzz, fed by a skillful vibrato, is the basis for the singer's most artistic techniques in all but the highest, or so-called covered, male tones. Practically the entire range of the female voice can be developed by the call, but only the lower two thirds of the male voice benefits specifically from this technique. The top third—short of the falsetto voice—is classified by most teachers as the *covered* or *closed* tones. These tones are developed by what I have referred to in Chapter V as the backward or soft-palate yawn. The call takes place in what can be referred to as the *open* or hard-palate range and is assisted by the forward or hard-palate yawn.

Control of the Call

In speech, the call sensation may be felt in varying degrees whenever a more vigorous emphasis or a stronger accent is required. The feeling comes most often when the stressed syllable includes a #1, #21. #3, +Ybuzz, R-derivative, or neutral—usually N^1, N^2, or N^3—vowel.

To understand either the Ybuzz or the call thoroughly, you must remember that tonal action is the control of a vibratory current of sound in a state of constant movement, radiation, and transmission, propogating in the bones of the face and head. Like a beam of light or a stream of water, the vocal sound current may be concentrated or diffused. The concentrated tone—the full call or Ybuzz action—occurs mainly in formal delivery or when addressing a large audience; the diffused or dilute tone, in informal conversation. These changes, however, are no more than variations on a single principle: that every vowel is a voiced tone incorporating the elements of pitch, volume, and quality, and that every tone is to be felt as a vibration in that solid bony mass consisting primarily of hard palate, nasal bone, sinuses, and forehead. The feeling is to be experienced as an organic, intrinsic, private sensation—private, that is, in the same way that a blush or a swallow or a stomach rumble is a private sensation. The only difference is that tonal action is an intentional habit pattern, intelligently utilized, not an involuntary act, and its basis is physical vibration and resonance rather than chemistry and physiology.

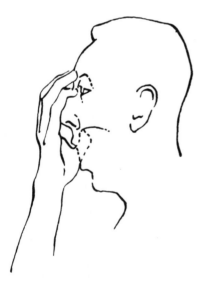

Figure 52. The vocal nozzle in the palm of your hand.

In animated speech, the speaker with a well-focused voice often falls quite naturally into the use of the call, particularly for the purpose of emphasis, stress, or accent. In that sense, the call is a part of the natural speech pattern, but generally speaking, in normally inflected, intimate or informal speech, the tonal focus of the voice is felt, not as a compact, dark, intensely contrasted vibration, but as a somewhat lighter, more diffused resonance. The important point is that both the fully concentrated call focus and the partly concentrated or diffused tonal action of conversation originate from the same instrument, are activated by the same process, move in the same direction, and transmit from the same bony resonators — with good tonal action you can move easily and naturally from one level of pitch and intensity to the other or make use of any of the gradations between.

If you place your thumb on the hard palate and your four fingers around the bridge of your nose, touching the forehead, you hold in the palm of your hand what we might call the vocal nozzle (fig. 52). It intensifies, controls, and transmits the sound stream, just as the nozzle of a water hose controls the water and narrows it into a concentrated stream of high kinetic energy or disperses it in a fine spray (fig. 53). Without a nozzle, water from the hose splashes to the ground with no focus and no useable kinetic energy. Without use of the vocal nozzle, tone becomes

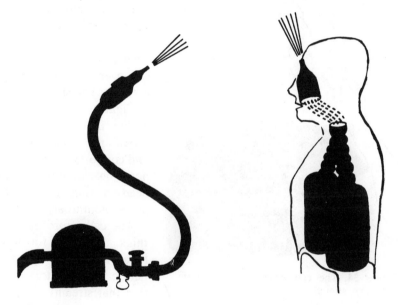

Figure 53. The vocal nozzle controls sound as the nozzle on a hose controls water.

localized in less favorable areas, spreads and weakens or becomes a surge of uncontrollable and unpleasant force and pressure. Vocal sound waves misdirected or forced to the pharynx, throat, or lips are comparable to water escaping through holes in the hoseline, weakening the current at the nozzle.

To Develop the Call

Take a position at one end of the largest room available. Cup one hand around your mouth and pretend to call to someone about a city block away, using the word *Hello* but abridging it to h'LLO. The LO is really the part of the word that carries the main tonal action. Don't try to sustain the call at first, but make it rather short; it should feel exhilarating and free.

Now repeat the call, but prepare for it with the full inverted-megaphone stretch. This will give you a pleasant yawn sensation in the cheek muscles—not the kind of yawn that screws up the face and directs the voice toward the soft palate and throat, but the kind of yawn stretch that you feel comfortably while sounding the vowel O (fig. 54). As

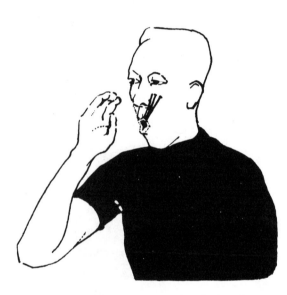

you call out h'LLO with this facial posture, feel the vocal sensation and direct it to the hard palate and to the nosebone—not the soft palate. Repeat the h'LLO call over and over, making it cleaner and sharper. Make it lighter in volume but darker in color. The tone should be coursing easily and comfortably through the bony nozzle into the forehead, a singing and completely nonthroaty sensation.

The call improves as you think the yawn for it can be achieved only by coordinating the vibratory sensa-

Figure 54. The call position is based on the yawn stretch.

tion that streams simultaneously through all parts of the bony nozzle with the properly coordinated facial posture. You must avoid the slightest suggestion of force or feeling of breath. Check periodically for escaping breath by holding the back of your hand close to the lips.

The Pitch of the Call

If the call is to feel right, the receiving area or focus pocket on the hard palate must be completely filled. As with the Ybuzz the size of the pocket will change as the pitch changes and the vibratory sensation will concentrate toward the gum ridge which is always part of the pocket, or expand toward the back of the hard palate. But whether large or small, the pocket must be comfortably filled, not overloaded or underloaded with tone. Never think of the voice as being propelled or splashed into the mask of the face. Under this pressure the vibrations are forced out through the mouth or, if the attack is harsh enough, back into the throat. Instead, they should seep or course through the bony mass—not *invading* the mask but *pervading* it.

If the pitch of the call is lowered or raised a mere half step, the perception of the change, as in the Ybuzz, is subtle and the reduction or increase of the focus pocket extremely slight. When you lower the pitch by a larger interval, however, you will find that the tonal sensation recedes more substantially from the rear of the hard palate to occupy a smaller focus pocket toward the area of the gum ridge. *At the same time,* although the facial posture remains fully forward with maximum space between the teeth, the retrenchment of the focus pocket conditions a relative reduction in the lip opening and a subtle change in the vowel sound from a resonant O for example, to a smaller, more contained O and ultimately to

OO. As you raise the pitch, the process occurs in reverse: The pocket expands toward the center or rear of the hard palate and toward the sides of the upper teeth without retreating from the forward area near the gum ridge, while the size of the lip opening increases simultaneously and the vowel changes again from OO to a larger OO to an O to a larger O, to AW and ultimately to AH (fig. 55).

Through all these changes, the call itself retains the same tonal consistency and character. *It remains unchanged in tonal texture, quality, concentrated focus, stentorian brilliance, and relaxed energy.* The sensation of the proper call technique is felt *in a state of equilibrium, constantly spinning through the hard palate, nasal bone, and forehead.* The only change with changing pitch is in the size of the focus pocket and the lip opening. As with our other action-sensations, even the deaf and tone-deaf can feel and control these changes.

Figure 55. Both focal pocket and lip opening change as pitch is raised or lowered.

Call Exercises

In practicing the call exercises, you must not dissociate yourself from the sensation; you must not attempt to stand aside as a casual, or even an interested, observer—this is tantamount to listening to yourself from the outside or by feedback. Never think that *it* doesn't work as though you were the innocent victim of *its* intransigence. The instrument is not on the outside, organically isolated—*you are* the instrument. You must think, concentrate, learn to perceive new feelings, and program these feelings into your computer brain. Do not let the call action thrust the chin forward and up: Keep the crown of the head high and the chin level down.

Exercise one—The Short Spontaneous Call

step 1. Do several short h'LLO calls. Do them spontaneously as if you were actually calling someone about a block away.

step 2. Now take the call up and down the scale on as many different pitches as you comfortably can.

Comment: If you have difficulty in changing pitch, try sliding down a bit from the Call in step 1 and try to sense this action as a pitch change. Observe the effect of changing pitches on the focus pocket on the hard palate and note that at the lower pitches you will be moving toward a small O or OO and at the higher pitches toward a larger O or AW.

Exercise two—Call Sustention

Performing the call as a series of tonal impulses or beats is excellent preparation for the sustained call on a single pitch. The exercise, written out, would be:

> h'LLO
> h'LLO-O
> h'LLO-O-O
> h'LLO-O-O-O
> h'LLO-O-O-O-O
> h'LLO-O-O-O-O-O etc.

step 1. Begin with a short call.

step 2. Now do a second call, adding another O on tne same general pitch level, linked to the first but produced with an additional tonal impetus in a gentle but firm pulsation.

step 3. Continue repeating the call, each time adding another O until you have linked together as many as a dozen. Don't close the lip opening before each new impulse; keep a series of O's, not a series of "woes." Without actually raising the pitch, you should feel the sustention becoming progressively sharper and the vibrato increasing in the bony areas of the face. Essentially this also constitutes a fine, clear singing tone.

step 4. Repeat the call with a series of linked O's, but this time lessen the tonal attack before each impulse so that you approach a dynamic sustention on a single pitch. End each call with a tiny, natural falling inflection.

Exercise three—Muscle Shaking (see fig. 51)

step 1. Practice the sustained call while shaking the hands briskly but gently and loosely up and down or sideways. Try it first with one hand as in a speaking gesture; then with two hands as though shaking maracas in a rapid but gentle rhythm.

step 2. Observe how the loosening of the body, including the neck and face, encourages the call to pulsate into the bony area. Remember this vibrato as a sense memory and program it into your brain.

step 3. Continue the call and try to continue the vibrato effect without shaking the hands.

step 4. If the vibrato seems to get lost, feed it periodically by shaking the hand.

Comment: Muscle shaking is a natural way of inducing relaxation and will offset muscle stress, a tendency to be over-careful, or a declining facial posture. When the body shaking exercise is clearly understood, it lends itself to all sorts of improvisation. Do Exercise 3 on as many different pitches as possible until you can sustain comfortably on every pitch in your hard palate range.

Exercise four—The Yodel Call

step 1. Do a sustained h'LLO call.

step 2. While sustaining the O, and on the same pitch, shade into a suggestion of EY—an expansion and enlargement of the first sound of the +Ybuzz diphthong: h'LLO-EY-O-EY-O-EY-O-EY-O as though slowly preparing to perform a yodel.

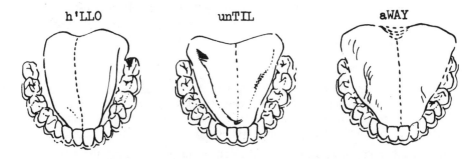

Figure 56. The tongue widens as the call goes from O to EY.

Comment: Neither the megaphone stretch nor the lip opening should change during this exercise. Only the tongue will accommodate the vowel change by spreading or widening momentarily for the EY (fig. 56) which will take on a little of the quality of the German Ö or the R-derivative without the R, in the higher pitches. When this exercise is done more and more rapidly it approximates a yodel effect.

Exercise five—Vowel Changes

step 1. Do a sustained h'LLO call.

step 2. Repeat the same call and on the same pitch using the words aWAY, unTIL, and unEARTH.

step 3. Practice the call on each of these words as you did with h'LLO in Exercises 1 to 3.

Comment: Treat the first syllable in aWAY, unTIL, unEARTH the same as you did the h'LLO—almost throw it away and concentrate the call action on the second syllable. Remember that the call is no respecter of specific vowel sounds and keep the inverted megaphone shape and the lip opening exactly the same for each vowel. Do not let quality, texture, timbre, or tonal focus change. Accommodate the different vowels by means of mental compensation and, where necessary, some tongue adjustment, rather than by a change in structural form or lip opening.

Exercise six—Siren Drill

In practicing this exercise, begin with shorter glides, or glissandos, over a small part of your range; as you gain confidence and skill, increase the length of the glide until you cover your entire call range as if you were imitating a siren. During the siren exercise keep the call in constant contact with the hard palate; something like a train keeping contact with the rails— don't jump the rails.

step 1. Do a sustained h'LLO call.

step 2. Slide the call down in pitch, feeling the tonal action on the hard palate as a reduction of the focus pocket toward the area of the gum ridge and feeling, too, a gradual reduction in the lip opening with a concomitant change in vowel sound.

step 3. After the down-glide, slide the call up in pitch, feeling the tonal action, lip opening, and vowel change in reverse.

step 4. Slide the call in a series of short down and up glides.

step 5. Do the same siren exercise on aWAY, unTIL, and unEARTH.

Comment: As you slide the call up or down, never for an instant let the concentrated vibrations leave the hard palate pocket to spread into a dilute

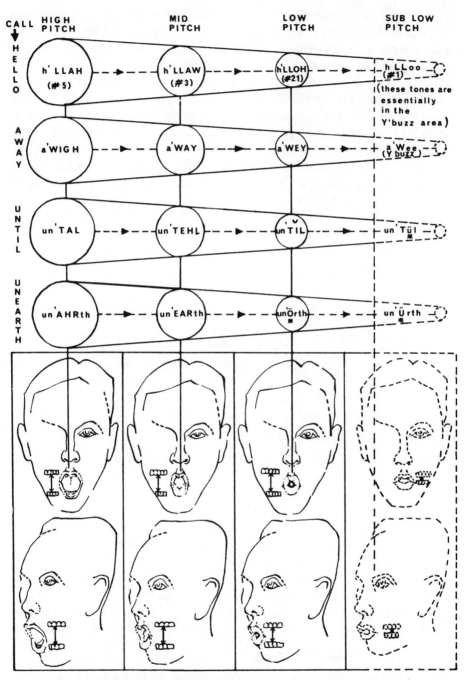

Figure 57. Focus pocket, lip opening, space cushion between the teeth, and vowel changes are all coordinated with pitch changes from the high call down to the Ybuzz range.

tone. At no time should you listen to the vowel or permit it to determine the course of the siren glide, but remain flexible enough to permit the vowel sound to change naturally and imperceptibly: from stretch vowel #5 through #4, #3, and #21 to #1 in h'LLO; from 6y through the German Ö and the +Y to the Ybuzz in aWAY; from #6 to N^3 and N^2 to the French U—very much like the Ybuzz—in unTIL; and from #5 through the R-derivative to N^2n in unEARTH. In the very lowest pitches the space between the teeth and the inverted-megaphone stretch as a whole will be reduced to accommodate the very small focus pocket until the focus pocket and the lip opening are so small that the tone glides into a Ybuzz area. In the aWAY, unTIL and unEARTH calls this last stage shifts into an actual Ybuzz sound (fig. 57). It is not important that the words sound completely intelligible to you for several reasons: (1) We are preoccupied here with voice building; (2) the vowels, when used dynamically, are constantly subject to modification; and (3) the consonants are primarily responsible for intelligibility anyway.

Exercise seven—The Barking Call

step 1. Do a series of short, staccato, disconnected calls on YO-YO-YO-YO-YO. Do not sustain the Y's—here they are treated as fairly short consonants. Do not use too high a pitch on these calls. They should feel something like short, clean blasts or perhaps the barking of a fairly large dog.

step 2. Do the same type of call on YEY-YEY-YEY-YEY-YEY.

step 3. Do both calls more rapidly.

step 4. Repeat steps 1, 2 and 3 using the consonant R instead of Y.

Exercise eight—The Call on Consonant L

Certain so called syllabic consonants are both a challenge to, and reinforcement of, the call technique. With the consonant L the challenge is to direct and keep feeding the dark tonal call focus into the forehead area and maintain it there while the tongue holds its contact with the hard palate; then as the tongue disengages and moves back, the voice flows freely through the palate again, and the answering vowel profits from this reinforcement and springs forth as a full-fledged call—clear, beautiful, and stimulating.

step 1. Do a sustained h'LLO call on a medium pitch.

step 2. While sustaining the O move the tongue up to the L position—the tip touching the gum ridge—without weakening or diluting the call sensation.

step 3. Alternate between L and O while concentrating on retention of the intensified call sensation: h'LLO-O-O→L-L-L-L-O-O-O→L-L-L-L-O-O-O→

L-L-L-LO-O-O→L-L-L-L-O-O-O, etc.

step 4. Repeat the exercise on various pitches.

step 5. Repeat steps 1 to 4 on aWAY-AY→L-L-L-L-AY-AY-AY→L-L-L-L-
AY-AY-AY—→L-L-L-L-AY-AY-AY—→L-L-L-L-AY-AY-AY, etc.

step 6. Repeat steps 1 to 4 on: unTI-I-I→L-L-L-L-I-I-I→L-L-L-L-I-I-I→
L-L-L-L-I-I-I→L-L-L-L-I-I-I, etc.

step 7. Repeat steps 1 to 4 on: unFUℛ-ℛ-ℛ→L-L-L-L-Uℛ-ℛ-ℛ→L-L-L-L-Uℛ-
ℛ-ℛ→L-L-L-L-UR-ℛ-ℛ→L L-L-L-Uℛ-ℛ-ℛ, etc.

Comment: The ℛ represents the R-derivative vowel.

Exercise nine—The Call on Consonant R

As with the call on L, the challenge here is to consolidate the call sensation
in the nasal bone and forehead and to feel the reinforcement of the call
technique as the tongue disengages and permits the sound waves to flow
freely through the hard palate again.

step 1. Do a sustained h'LLO call on a medium pitch.

step 2. While sustaining the O, move the tongue to the R position—the sides
touching the inside corners of the upper back teeth and the tip curled
up—without weakening or diluting the call sensation. Concentrate on
directing a clear, strong R vibration into the upper nasal bone and
even more strongly into the forehead.

step 3. Alternate between R and O, thinking the word *roar* and concentrating on
retention of the intensified call sensation: h'LLO-O-O→R-R-R-R-O-
O-O—→R-R-R-R-O-O-O→R-R-R-R-O-O-O→R-R-R-R-O-O-O, etc.

step 4. Repeat steps 1 to 3, thinking the word *rare* in step 3, on: aWAY-AY-AY→
R-R-R-R-AY-AY-AY→R-R-R-R-AY-AY-AY→R-R-R-R-AY-AY-
AY, etc.

step 5. Repeat steps 1 to 3 thinking the word *rear* in step 3, on: unTI-I-I→
R-R-R-R-I-I-I→R-R-R-R-I-I-I→R-R-R-R-I-I-I→R-R-R-R-I-I-I, etc.

step 6. Repeat steps 1 to 3, using the R-derivative vowel, on: deFEℛ-ℛ-ℛ— R-R-
R-R-Eℛ-ℛ-ℛ→R-R-R-R-Eℛ-ℛ-ℛ→R-R-R-R-Eℛ-ℛ ℛ, etc.

Comment: Since the consonant R is essentially a backward, throaty sound,
this exercise can also serve to direct the R resonance toward the bony nozzle,
particularly the forehead area. The ℛ represents the R-derivative vowel.

Exercise ten—The Siren Call on Consonant R

step 1. Sound the consonant R with a strong vibration in the nasal bone and forehead.

step 2. Keeping the tongue in the R position, begin on a medium pitch and siren up with the call technique to a larger lip opening and as high a pitch as you comfortably can.

step 3. Siren back to the starting pitch, maintaining the call sensation in the nasal bone and forehead.

step 4. From a medium pitch, siren down on the call technique to a small lip opening and as low a pitch as you comfortably can.

step 5. Siren back to the starting pitch.

Comment: Be sure to keep the tongue in the R position through this exercise.

Exercise eleven—Call Phrases

Pretend you are in the fields, in the desert, on the ocean, or in a city street calling to someone far away.

step 1. On a comfortable medium high pitch, do a sustained call on each word of each phrase.

step 2. Repeat the phrases on several pitches, including the low ones.

1. Those old boats don't float!
2. Fill this kit with bills!
3. They may take trains late today!
4. Let Nell's friends rest well!
5. The good-looking cook took a good look.
6. Ahoy there!
7. All boats in!
8. They came home!
9. This is good!
10. Where were you?
11. You may go.
12. Take him away!
13. Okeh, let 'im go!

Comment: The very lowest pitches will help lay the foundation for good, rich, intensive focus in everyday normal speech, and the low to medium pitches will help bring out the desired effects in emphasized and accented words.

Exercise twelve—Improvisation in Communication through Tonal Action

The object of this exercise is to communicate with another person through pure sound; in this case the concentrated vibrations of tonal action applied to all the vowels.

step 1. Select a partner and sit facing him.

step 2. Conduct an animated discussion or debate, using no verbal content or actual words, but trying to communicate through all the resonant variations of the Ybuzz and call focus. Try to get through to your partner, to persuade him, to overwhelm him. Become angry, then fearful. Try to impose your will with the energy of concentrated tonal action.

Comment: In tonal action, you can use all possible combinations of pure sound from the lowest purring of the Ybuzz to the stentorian roar of the full high call. Use these tones exactly as you would use inflections on words. Use all the vowels, the whole range of your voice, and every level of intensity.

Exercise thirteen—Selective Call

Try this exercise after you have developed a reasonably high degree of call skill, using the phrase: "You just don't know what we've been through."

step 1. Practice this phrase as in Exercise 11.

step 2. Now select the words you care to emphasize and practice the phrase with full call only on these words.

step 3. Now practice the phrase with full call on one word at a time, beginning with the first word (you), then second (just), then third (don't) and so on. Each time the sentence takes on a different meaning and interpretation.

step 4. Now read the sentence with strong call emphasis on every word and note the interpretive intensity and the degree of personal involvement.

Exercise fourteen—The Virtuoso Call Exercise

This exercise requires not only proficiency but consummate artistry in the skillful manipulation and feeling of tonal action.

step 1. Read a text of your own choice from any book or newspaper, using a full stentorian, comfortably sustained high-pitched call focus on every syllable: Nevertheless, maintain a normal pattern of strong and weak stresses by sustaining some stronger syllables longer, and some weaker syllables less, to preserve the meaning of the text, even though it seems to be delivered in slow motion. Make every word clearly intelligible by paying strict attention to the consonants.

step 2. Lower the pitch slightly after every phrase or every six or seven words until you reach the lowest pitch on which you can maintain a genuine call focus while still using the full stretch with maximum space between the teeth. Remember to heed the consonants to maintain intelligibility.

step 3. While still producing the full call focus, compensate for the next one or two lower pitches by reducing the space between the teeth a bit until you find yourself maintaining the beginning of a +Ybuzz-like concentration of tone. Be particularly careful to pay attention to the consonants. Do this to the point of wanting to roll the R's like the British or Russians or Irish do. You should now be functioning in a combination Ybuzz and +Ybuzz area.

step 4. Now shorten the duration of these low-pitched but still fully concentrated vocal tones and gradually add the appropriate, though subtle, up and down inflections of the speech communication. Since you are still using a small lip opening and a very small focus pocket to hold onto as concentrated a tone as possible on every syllable, most of the vowels will sound strangely unfamiliar; this, plus the rolling of the R's, will produce a kind of dialect—a heavy and rather peculiar version of a combined Welsh-Scotch-Irish brogue.

step 5. Now, gradually, but deliberately, revert to a maximum use of the inverted megaphone stretch while retaining the richest possible tonal resonance and the darkest tonal color. You will find that your reading will quickly acquire expulsive undistorted speech quality. When this point has been reached begin to read more rapidly until you have achieved normal, smooth, conversational utterance while still using the structural form and while still feeling the maximum degree of rich, dark tonal action in the palate, nose, and forehead. This is your legitimate and new speaking voice.

Comment: In the early part of the exercise, ignore the vowel sounds—very few of them will be compatible with normal speech—and concentrate on adding a little duration to the stressed syllables, on phrasing, and particularly on clear-cut consonant diction to make the words completely recognizable and intelligible. If your words are understood despite the call treatment of the vowels, you can be satisfied for the time being that your consonant action is adequate and that you are preserving the meaning of the text. The use of a rolled R, especially on the low pitches, will help maintain a good call focus and make your consonant action more lively. By step 5, you will be employing full structural action plus the strongest carry-over of tonal action that will permit a normal, nondistorted vowel pronunciation and speech quality. You will also have gained by this time new and permanent habit patterns in the use of structural and tonal action. The difference between the use of structural action here and in the structural action sentences and reading selections in Chapter VI is purely a matter of voice—the addition of maximum tonal action. In Chapter VI we concentrated on form *only*, experiencing the changed voice quality as an incidental by-product; here we finally add the structural action with fully intentioned maintenance of maximum tonal focus as a carry-over from the rest of the exercise. As a matter of clarification let me differentiate the terms +Ybuzz-like focus, low call, and dilute tone. The first is the most concentrated focus in the Ybuzz and +Ybuzz range with only a small space between the side teeth; the second is the fully concentrated call focus on a low pitch but with full inverted-megaphone stretch and almost maximum space between the side teeth; the third is nonconcentrated focus with variable use of the structural form. Anytime the call or Ybuzz spreads or weakens a bit, it becomes a dilute tone.

Exercise fifteen—Diluting the Call Concentration

This exercise will familiarize you with good tonal action that is not a call but the dilute or diffused focus that is used in eighty to ninety per cent of conversational speech and fifty to sixty per cent of speech from the stage. It is comparable to what you achieved in the last step of Exercise 14.

step 1. Begin with a h'LLO call on a comfortably low to low-medium pitch; then, while holding on to the richest, most vibrant resonance in the bony nozzle, open your lips very gradually until you reach the #5 position.

step 2. Alternate between the low medium call and the #5 vowel.

step 3. Do steps 1 and 2, starting with an aWAY call and diluting to 6y.

step 4. Do steps 1 and 2, starting with an unTIL call and diluting to a #6.

step 5. Do steps 1 and 2, starting with an unFURL call and diluting to a #5.

Comment: Note that you move from concentrated to dilute focus, to concentrated, and back again to dilute without once moving out of the tonal action current. Remember that the concentrated call focus and the diffused focus are opposite ends of the spectrum of tonal action, and they differ primarily in degree of density or concentration.

Exercise sixteen—The Alphabet Poem

Recite the alphabet as a poem in your most creatively expressive style, with all the romantic lyricism that the Spanish or the Russians put into the reading of their poetry. Play all the Ybuzz and +Ybuzz effects in the alphabet and carry them over into the call refrain that follows each line. This refrain should be recited or sung as inventively and as imaginatively as possible. Use all the call variations for different effects, and play it as you feel it; the format used in the poem is only a suggestion.

> A, B . . . . C, D . . .
>> EY-O, EY-O, EY-O-O, EY-O
>
> E, F G . . .
>> EY-O-O. EY-O, EY-O, EY-O
>>> . . . . H, I . . . . J, K
>>> EY-O, EY-O, EY-O, EY-O
>>> L M N O-O P
>>>> EY-O-O-O . . . EY-O-O-O
>>>> EY-O, EY-O
>
> QR . . . . ST
>> EY-Y-O, EY-Y-O. EY-O-O, EY-O
>
> U and V
>> EY-O-O-O-O . . . EY-O-O-O-O
>> EY-O, EY-O
>>> . . . . . double U and XYZ
>>> EY-O-O-O, EY-Y . . . EY-Y . . . EY-O-O-O

Exercise seventeen—Reading Selections

Read these passages with imagination and freedom of choice, using, on any of the words you choose, the most concentrated call focus compatible with an intelligent handling of meaning.

1. No, my friends, that will never be the verdict of our people. This nation will always be able to legislate for its own people on every question without waiting for the aid or consent of any other nation on earth.

2. If we be conquered, let men conquer us, and not these bastard Bretons, whom our fathers have in their own land beaten, bobbed, and thumped. Fight, gentlemen of England! Fight, bold yeomen! Draw, archers, draw your arrows to the head! Spur your proud horses forward, and ride in blood.

3. If you say just one more word, so help me, I'll kill you! . . . You get it through your head, we don't want you around here—we don't want you *or* your lousy favors—we want you to take off and stay the hell away!

Comment: Don't be careful—don't be careless. With what you know now, you can afford to be carefree. Use the calls to reflect a meaning that comes from inside you, not from the sound of the word.

Exercise eighteen—Character Calls

Play each of these roles with a clear, comfortable, sustained resonant call. Find your own pitch and your own motivation.

1. *Train conductor:* All aboard—Tacoma . . . Emporia . . . Tuscahoma . . . Roanoke . . . Daytonsburgh . . . Baltimore . . . Philadelphia . . . Williamsburg . . . Buffalo . . . Dover . . . New Brunswick . . . and all points north—A-a-a-all abo-o-o-o-o-a-rd

2. *Street vendor:* Apple . . . Potato . . . Watermelon . . . (Pronounced: Epaw . . . Pohtehtoh . . . wawtahmelohn . . .)

3. *Captain of a sailing schooner:* Ahoy there *Marco Polo*—Can we help you?

4. *Construction worker:* Okay, Joe . . . Let 'er go-o-o-o-o-o-o-o! Okay, Bill . . . take 'em away-ay-ay-ay-ay-ay!

5. *Man in crowsnest:* Ship ahoy! Four points off starboard bow!

6. *Drill sergeant:* Company halt! About face! Present arms! Parade rest!

7. *Messenger at arms over PA:* Now hear this! . . . Marlow, Radioman third class . . . Report to the brig—on the double!

8. *Fight announcer:* Ladies and gentlemen . . . Presenting the feature bout of the evening . . . In this corner, weighing two hundred and four pounds, from Puerto Rico, Antonio Morello!

9. *Newshawk:* Read all about it—War Declared! Get your paper —wad'ya read?

10. *Peddler:* Jumbo potatoes—fifteen pounds for a quarter . . . Get your ice-cream cone—give your tongue a sleigh-ride.

11. *Anybody:* Don't you ever dare do that to me again!

12. *Foreman:* Okay, down there, let's go! Get your big fat butts movin' and load that timber—keep 'em rollin'!

13. *Fan:* Hold that line! . . . Hold that line! . . . We want a touchdown! We want a touchdown!

14. *Stage manager:* Places everybody! . . . Let's go! . . . Places!

Comment: Be careful not to lose the call focus on the words like *we* and *you* in No. 3. As you practice, range from the full high-pitched call to a medium pitch, to a low pitch, to a Ybuzz and finally back to the high-pitched call.

Exercise nineteen—The Call Becomes Singing

step 1. Call "water boy" as a short command.

step 2. Call "water boy" as a command but sustain it longer, as if with earnest concern.

step 3. Call "water boy" as a command and sustain it longer, as if with comfortable and pleasant anticipation and therefore with greater melody.

step 4. Call "water boy" but with the melody of the traditional song . . . or with a melody which you supply.

Comment: Singing is sustained speaking. Anytime you voice a well executed call and sustain it on various pitches, you are singing—you are making beautiful, artistic tones. Of course, a professional singer needs more advanced training and study in related subjects, but with a well controlled call and Ybuzz technique you are capable of achieving many vocal effects and nuances with your singing voice that even many trained singers find difficult.

CHAPTER X

Consonant Action

*C*ONSONANTS are the interpreters that convey the meaning of speech—they make the spoken word intelligible.

Consonants are the instruments that provide musical accompaniment to speech—they produce rhythmic patterns, melodies, and sustained tonal colors.

Consonants provide contrasts and variations—to the single, sustained note of the vowels, they bring percussion and sound effects.

Consonants can be a new energy experience if you form them within the Lessac concept of concentration upon the feeling and taste of speech.

As a class, consonants are distinct from that other general classification of speech sounds, the vowels. Where the vowels are all voiced and all produced alike as pure and unobstructed, frictionless sounds, the consonants may be voiced or unvoiced and are all produced differently, using the techniques of obstruction, impedance, interruption. and friction.

Consonants form the skeletal structure of words and are responsible for intelligibility. In such pairs of words as *seeds* and *siege* or *laws* and *loss,* it is the correct consonant sound that conveys the correct word. Although the phonetic specificity of the vowels is, to a considerable degree, expendable, consonants must always remain phonetically constant. If the consonant is properly felt, the word will remain intact and the meaning clear, regardless of the phonetic distortion of the vowel, but when consonants are changed or lost, the whole word is changed or lost. Without a properly executed T, the word *wrote* may very well be heard as *rode, rogue, roan, roam, rope, robe, role, rove, rose, roast,* or *roach*— if it is heard as a word at all. Your speech will improve almost at once if you remember and abide by the rule that while there is some tolerance for error in producing vowels, there is practically no tolerance for error in producing consonants.

To this intellectual concept of the consonants,

I want to add an esthetic concept. At best, they have always been given a rather prosaic role in verbal communication; the vowels have always been considered the esthetic, and the consonants the workaday, parts of speech. But consonants bring more than intelligibility to speech; they provide a multiplicity of musical values and instrumental qualities, built-in tempo and speed controls, and a wide variety of contrasts and variations. Each consonant has its own characteristic sound, its own timbre, its own quality: Some are lingering legato sounds; some are crisp staccato. The pleasure to be gotten from good consonant action comes to a large extent from playing and experimenting with these action-sensations as instrumental qualities, and much of the variety and beauty of speech comes from the results of these experiments. If you use consonants for comprehensibility alone, you have not begun to exploit their possibilities! This concept of consonant action suggests a reversal of the relative positions of vowels and consonants in singing and speech: In singing, the vowels make the principal artistic contribution; the consonants a utilitarian one. But in general speech, the consonants carry most of the melody and rhythm, while the vowels serve primarily for emphasis.

Consonant Control

The first step in the Lessac approach is to classify each consonant as an instrument of the orchestra—melodic, percussive, or sound effect. We think of some consonants as strings, brass, or woodwinds because their timbres and their legato tones add melody to speech; some are drums or cymbals because their sharp, percussive beats add rhythm; others are whistles and wind machines because of the special qualities they add.

The next step is to learn the action of each simulated musical instrument and the sensation of that action—then to apply this action-sensation to voice and speech. Consonant action, the third in our trinity of actions, is an energy, joining structural energy and tonal energy to make up the totality of physical voice and speech dynamics. Just as the energy of structural action is based on the physical sensation of muscular sense-memory, and the energy of tonal action on vibratory sense-memory, so the energy of consonant action is based on feeling the timbres, the resonances, and the rhythmic characteristics of the instruments in the consonant orchestra.

The technique of feeling the consonants is guided by the principles that guide the musician when he plays *his* instrument, for we will simulate his techniques with *our* instrument, the human voice. Whether he plays a drum, a string, a woodwind, a brass, or a sound effect, the musician never forces, never pounds, never scrapes, never squeezes, never pushes, never tightens. The action for each consonant will be described, but what you must concentrate on in consonant control is not *where* to move the lips or teeth or tongue, or *which* to move, but *how* to feel the sensation of those actions lightly, softly, smoothly—in easy balance but positively. The drum tap of the T or K will be a superior tap if the tap is lightweight and quiet. The sustained S is a superior S the softer, the higher, the sharper, and the lighter it is. The sustained V is the most satisfying to experience and to hear when the rich vibration is made without the slightest escape of breath. Play your consonants the way a musician plays his instrument; if you bear down heavily, if your lips, tongue, and jaw are tight, if you force breath through the mouthpiece, if you permit extraneous sounds or noises to escape from the instrument, you are a poor musician—you play your instrument badly.

The instrumental approach is most important when a consonant precedes another consonant or is the final sound before a pause or semi-pause. The consonant before a vowel requires less attention because the vowel that follows maintains a vocal line and keeps the sound of the whole syllable moving forward. Of course, when you learn to play and feel a consonant musically, it will function better before a vowel as well; nevertheless, you really have to go out of your way not to pronounce the T in *take*, the L in *live*, the initial D in *demand;* but the K in *take*, the V in *live*, and the N and the final D in *demand* are all easily lost or corrupted.

This corruption is the source of sloppy speech, *and precisely there, where sloppy speech begins, is where the technique of consonant action is most effective.* At the point where poorly conditioned speech habits cause most people to slip into enervation, carelessness, and bad diction, you will learn to experience a new energy, *to feel a new speech sense almost like taste,* to explore an expanded area of concentration, and to develop a new sense of values. When you fully exploit the execution of a word for consonant action, you will add meaning, emphasis, and emotional content to your speech.

The Consonant Orchestra

In figure 58, you will find the entire range of musical consonants classified—a full complement of strings, drums, cymbals, and woodwinds, and a fair representation of sound effects and brass. You will learn to play the instruments properly in the work section, but here let me introduce them generally and make an exploratory survey, beginning with the string section:

I hear and feel the consonant N as a violin because

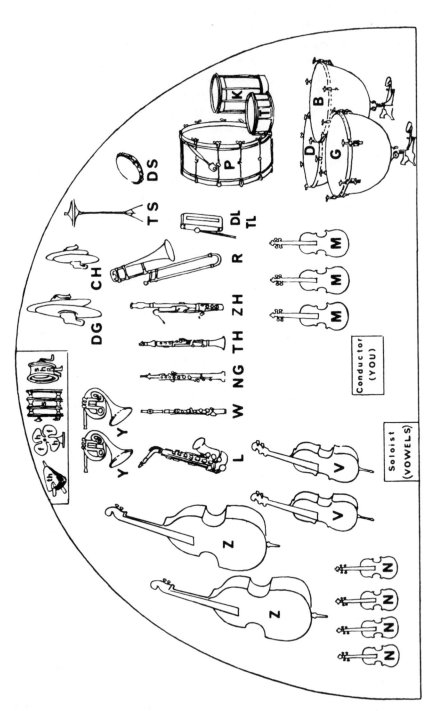

Figure 58. The consonant orchestra.

of its clear, fine-spun resonance, which can be sustained throughout the vocal range. The N is often used effectively by choruses for melodic moods; it is the clearest melodic consonant. Try singing it on any pitch in your vocal range. Sustain it on the word *demand* or *minstrel* or *found*—feel the sensation of resonance and think of it as the N violin.

The viola is a larger violin with a deeper, darker resonance. The consonant counterpart of this sound is the gentle hum of the M, through lightly touching lips. Try singing it on a number of pitches, and sustain it on the words *symptom, amnesty,* and *lamp.*

Among the other sustainable voiced consonants, you will find that the vibrant V sounds remarkably like the cello. Sing a melody on the V and sustain it on words like *themselves, proved, involve,* and *verve.*

The natural counterpart of the bass fiddle in our consonant orchestra is the Z. Try its deep vibrations on a number of pitches, then sing a melody on the Z and sustain it on *wisdom, zones, schism,* and *amazed.*

The percussion is also an important section of the orchestra—the drums, the tympani, and the cymbals. In speech, the B, the D, and the hard G are the three tympani or kettle drums. These voiced consonants have three unvoiced counterparts, the P, T, and K, whose voiceless, staccato, clicking sounds are the tapping of the bass drum, the snare drum, and the tom-tom. As you experiment with these drumbeat consonants in words like *robe, robed, reed, rag, dragged, drop, dropped, feet, lake,* and *lacked,* you will feel the clear, clean, incisive tapping sensations of the percussive consonants.

The last group in the percussion section is the cymbals: the ordinary crash cymbals represented by the CH, the Chinese cymbals represented by the DG, the "high hat" or afterbeat cymbal represented by the TS, and the tap of the tambourine represented by the DZ. The concept of these last two combinations as specific consonant sounds is new to the English language; yet they are as distinct from the individual T and S and the individual D and Z as are the CH and DG from the T and SH or the D and ZH. In many other languages, the TS is designated by a separate orthographic symbol. Experiment with the consonant cymbals in words like *match, witchcraft, wedge, judgment, scientists, contracts, adopts, deeds, dividends, builds.*

A third section, more used, perhaps, in our consonant orchestra than in the symphony orchestra, is the sound effects. Our whistles and wind machines are the S, the F, the SH, the H, and the unvoiced TH. All of these consonants are unvoiced or breath sounds; properly played, these sound effects will contribute elements of incisiveness, crispness, and clarity to your speech. Try them on words like *desk, incestuous, theft, pushed, which, moisture,* and *breath.*

The woodwind section includes the bassoon, whose deep bass is represented in the consonant orchestra by the ZH as in *mirage;* the oboe, represented by the NG, as in *twang,* a word that describes the nasal quality of NG; the flute, represented by the W, a vowel-like consonant that appears phonetically only before a vowel, as in *wind;* the saxophone, represented by the L, as in *old, welcome,* and *Lionel;* and the clarinet, represented by the voiced TH, as in *clothe* or *breathe.* In the marching or concert band, the clarinet usually takes over the melodies assigned in the symphony orchestra to the violins, violas, or cellos, and in speech, the clarinet TH and the cello V have remarkably similar vibratory sensations.

Consonant Chart

Voiced	*Unvoiced*
These consonants are phonated with vocal cord vibration and cannot be whispered.	These consonants are made without vocal cord vibration and cannot be voiced.

— *Cognates* —

as in *babe* ——————— B	P ——————— as in *Pope*
as in *dead* ——————— D	T ——————— as in *tight*
as in *agog* ——————— G	K ——————— as in *cook*
as in *noon* ——————— N	
as in *mime* ——————— M	
as in *verve* ——————— V	F ——————— as in *fife*
as in *zones* ——————— Z	S ——————— as in *safes*
as in *breathe* ———————TH	TH ——————— as in *breath*
as in *pleasure* ———————ZH	SH ——————— as in *wish*
as in *sing* ———————NG	
as in *lisle* ——————— L	
as in *window* ——————— W	
as in *beyond* ——————— Y	
as in *rewrite* ——————— R	
	H ——————— as in *high*
as in *judge* ———————DG	CH ——————— as in *church*
as in *intends* ———————DZ	TS ——————— as in *physicists*

We use only two brass instruments in our consonant orchestra: The trombone is represented by the consonant R, which is played emphatically when followed by a vowel, as in *railroad,* and muted or deemphasized before another consonant, as in *murky* or *lark.* The French horn is represented by the Y, another vowel-like consonant—our familiar Ybuzz as a vowel; a consonant only before a vowel, as in *yonder.*

I have not included in the consonant orchestra, nor in the consonant chart, the Q, X, C, or WH. The Q is always sounded as either K or KW; the X as KS, GZ, or Z; and the C as S, K, CH, or SH. When properly pronounced, WH is an HW, the first an unvoiced, the second a voiced consonant; it is not, as some phoneticians claim, the unvoiced counterpart of the W. That consonant is no more affected by the H sound before it in *when* than by the K sound before it in *queen.*

You will notice in the consonant chart that nine consonants have counterparts or cognates—that is, they are paired. There is no articulatory or mechanical difference in the way the two members of a pair are executed or produced; if you can execute one properly, you can execute the other equally well. The only difference is that one uses voice, the other, breath. The unvoiced consonants, since they are made without phonation of the vocal cords, are the only speech sounds that are produced entirely within the oral cavity and appear to make their way out through the lips. They are made with the glottis open and can only be whispered. But even these *whispered* sounds are made without breathiness, for the S, F, SH, and unvoiced TH are executed best when absolutely *no* breath stream can be felt coming through the lips; even the P, T, and K can be made without conscious use of breath, but admittedly this requires consumate skill and virtuoso control. If you try to voice the whispered consonants, they will turn into their voiced counterparts, or in the case of H, which has no voiced counterpart, disappear. All other sounds ride wholly or in part on the voice and move in the path of tonal action. The voiced consonants cannot be whispered and will turn into their unvoiced counterparts if you try, or into a breathy sigh if they have no unvoiced counterparts.

Exercises in Consonant Action

Listen to as many of the instruments as possible—there are recordings available that demonstrate the instruments of the orchestra. Play some of the instruments if you can, associating their sound with their consonant counterparts. In the initial description of the consonant orchestra, I grouped the consonants by the sections of the orchestra. These classifications will be broken somewhat in the more detailed description of how the consonants are formed and felt, in order to put the pairs of cognate consonants together and also to permit a more logical progression where one sound is based on another. In practicing the words and poems, use the best structural action for the vowels, but don't linger on them; move with dispatch from one consonant to the next, touching lightly on the vowel between. In the poems, sustainable consonants will be underlined twice and percussive consonants once; in each section, however, only those consonant instruments already practiced will carry markings. Although linking, phrasing, and rhythmic variations will not be discussed until the end of the chapter, begin connecting the words of the poems into groups and phrases throughout the exercises. Some consonants will carry no markings where you will expect to find them; this has to do with the rhythmic variations, which will be discussed later. During consonant practice, check periodically to make sure that you use no extraneous breath by placing the back of your hand to your lips.

The N Violin

Cognate: none

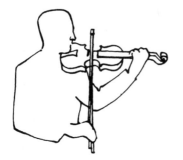

Conventional Classification: nasal consonant made with tongue blade to upper gum ridge

The sound of the N, which simulates the violin, is the most versatile and musical consonant sound; it can be sung throughout the entire vocal range. Though the N is completely nasal and not a practical instrument for voice placement, it is nevertheless a most resonant, forward consonant, which furnishes much of the musical, articulatory timbre and melody of speech. Played simultaneously with the M viola, it creates the most beautiful consonantal hum.

To feel the action of the N as a violin: With lips slightly apart and with a small space between the teeth, gently bring the upper surface of the tongue to the roof of the mouth at the hard palate; then loosen the tongue, leaving only the rim in contact with the gum ridge all around the upper teeth. You will use a similar position for the D drumbeat, but instead of releasing the tongue for the drumbeat, sing on the N, allowing the sound to flow through the bony resonating areas and escape through the nose.

Play this consonant instrument gently and tunefully without pressing the tongue or forcing the breath through the nose. The violin will not sing if the violinist presses hard with his bow.

You will feel a gentle vibration along the rim of the tongue.

Practice feeling the N violin as a sustained vibratory sensation where it occurs as the last sound in a word or before another consonant.

town	none	govern	open	women	lantern
undone	insane	unseen	return	monsoon	mountain
condone	incline	unlearn	Indian	unison	envision

Carry the singing of the N violin over to the poem, and remember to connect words into phrases.

I can today envision none
     but one
whose taint has sent my sun
into a plunging,
       lone
          descent . . .
And even winter's moon is down.

Note: Do all the poem-selections two ways: 1) for their musical value (sing the consonants for melody—rhythm—beat—style), 2) to punctuate and intensify the statement as emphatic prose (feel the consonants so as to reveal the sophisticated or unexpected word or'thought meaning.)

The M Viola

Cognate: none

Conventional classification: nasal labial consonant

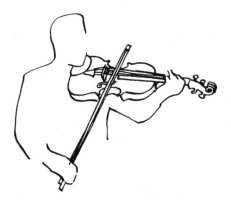

The humming of the M, which simulates the viola, is one of the wordless songs that people sing all over the world, whatever their language.

To feel the action of the M as a viola, simply allow your lips to meet very gently and hum. Leave a slight space cushion between the upper and lower teeth, like that for the Ybuzz, and let the tongue relax on the floor of the mouth.

Play this consonant instrument without pressing the lips together or tightening any of the muscles around the mouth. The lips, whatever form they take, should always be so relaxed that they feel almost puffy.

You will feel a gentle vibration or a keen tingle in the fleshy part of the lips—so much so, sometimes, that you will want to brush your hands over your lips to control the tingle that remains after the M has ended.

Practice feeling the M viola as a sustained vibratory sensation when it occurs at the end of a word or before another consonant, and continue to play the N violin wherever it occurs in these positions.

dim	maim	sum	fume	alarm	supreme
symptom	anthem	minim	atom	them	amphitheatre
embalm	become	momentum	tame	complain	humdrum

Carry the feeling of the consonants over to the poem, and remember to link words into phrases.

> Mem'ries are compliments supreme . . .
>> and yet,
> Embalmed and dimmed,
> they trample . . .
> Maim the moment's
> tamed simplicity
>> and become
> a humdrum hymn,
> an anthem
>> wheezed in a ruined apse,
> To a damned . . .
> contemning Past.

The V Cello

Cognate: F sound effect

Conventional classification: voiced fricative-labiodental consonant made with upper teeth to lower lip

The full, buzzing vibration of the V simulates the cello, an instrument that makes some of the most beautiful music in the entire orchestra.

To feel the action of the V as a cello, allow the lower rim of the upper teeth to touch the mucous membrane gently about an eighth of an inch below the inside of the lower lip, and sing a buzzing melody. The upper lip is not involved and is completely separated from the lower.

Play this consonant instrument without blowing or forcing the breath. Any sensation of breath at all will transform the resonant cello vibration into the sound effect F.

You will feel a gentle, dark, buzzing vibration or sharp tingle on the lower lip.

Practice feeling the V cello as a sustained vibratory sensation where it occurs at the end of a word or before another consonant, and continue to play the N violin and the M viola wherever they occur in these positions.

give	improve	connive	tentative	everyone	positive
love	contrive	behave	conceive	sensitive	gravestone
lively	caveman	lovelorn	driveway	approve	divebomb

Carry the feeling of the consonants over to the poem, and remember to link words into phrases.

A lively lovelight lives but to connive . . .

Gets hives

from wives.

The lovelorn drive love to the grave, to thrive

on chives . . .

not wives.

The F Sound Effect

Cognate: V cello

Conventional classification: unvoiced fricative-labio-dental consonant made with upper teeth to lower lip

In the sound effect F, the dark vibrations of the V cello are stilled to the whisper of a fan.

To feel the action of the F as a sound effect, play the V cello; then turn off the voice and continue in a whisper. The unvoiced, whispered V is a perfect F.

Play this sound effect without blowing or forcing or tightening the lip. Check with the back of your hand very close to your lips to make certain that no breath stream or even a trace of mild warm air escapes.

You will feel a gentle, smooth, airless sensation that sounds something like the gentle rustle of a quiet electric fan.

Practice feeling the F sound effect as a sustained voiceless sensation where it occurs at the end of a word or before another consonant, and continue to play the N violin, the M viola, and the V cello wherever they occur in these positions.

laugh	triumph	enough	graphmaker	cough	muffler
nymph	halfway	after	laughter	cliffdweller	fjord

Carry the feeling of these consonants over to the poem, and remember to link words into phrases.

The graphmaker laughed a laugh

of triu_mph_ . . .

for ha_l_fway cross his cle_ft_ i_n_ two,

a wood ny_mph_ cou_ghed_,

a_n_d so_f_t,

lau_gh_ter

tarried a_f_ter.

The Z Bass Fiddle

Cognate: S sound effect

Conventional classification: voiced sibilant-fricative consonant made with tongue to gum ridge

Still darker than the vibrations of the V cello is the resonant buzz of the Z bass fiddle, the voiced counterpart of the S, which was first discussed in the breathing exercises in Chapter IV.

To feel the action of the Z as a bass fiddle, form the S as you have already learned, with the side teeth gently touching and the tongue toward the roof of the mouth. The sound is emitted through a tiny aperture between tongue and teeth, either centered at the tip or slightly to the side. If this opening is centered, then both sides of the tongue-rim gently touch the upper gum ridge; if to the side, then the forward portion of the opposite side of the tongue, including the tip, is in gentle contact with the hard palate. With the tongue in the S position, add voice as if you were singing, until the Z vibrates in the very small tongue aperture behind the upper teeth.

Play this consonant instrument with no breathiness and no pushing; let it sing lightly, gently, easily, and vibrantly with the deep resonance

of a bass fiddle. Any breath at all will contaminate the resonance
of this instrument with the S sound effect.

You will feel a smooth but strong resonant vibration in the teeth as well as
in the front of the tongue.

Practice feeling the Z bass fiddle as a sustained vibratory sensation where it
occurs at the end of a word or before another consonant, and continue to play the other consonant instruments.

daze	breeze	prize	Joe's	blazes	cheers
is	was	has	his	hers	ours
yours	theirs	these	those	whose	transpose
confuse	wisdom	amaze	emphasize	because	sympathize

In English, S is pronounced as the Z bass fiddle when: (1) a final S
phonetically follows a voiced consonant, as in *wins* or *sales;* (2) a
final S is added to a word that ends with a vowel sound, to form the
possessive or plural, as in *pianos* or *Joe's;* (3) a medial S follows *re-,
de-,* or *pre-* and precedes another vowel, as in *result, desist,* or *presume;*
there are some exceptions to medial S, especially when the *re-, de-,* or
pre- are not prefixes or are hyphenated prefixes. There are also a
number of other instances of S pronounced as Z, but these usages
cannot be classified into rules.

Practice feeling the sustained vibrations of the double strings:

violin plus bass:	returns	zones	interns
viola plus bass:	consumes	systems	condemns
cello plus bass:	unnerves	conserves	disproves

Carry the feeling of the consonants over to the poem, and remember to link
words into phrases.

> These interzones
>   whose sizzling days
> have seized the tears
>   from worlds ablaze
> are scenes
> with Ceres,
>   lone and crazed,
> or fears

o𝑓 seer𝑠

who dream amazed.

The S Sound Effect

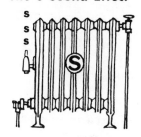

Cognate: Z bass fiddle

Conventional classification: unvoiced sibilant-fricative consonant made with tongue to gum ridge

The S sound effect is a light, high-pitched sensation, like the gentle escape of steam from a radiator, that induces an incisive quality in words where it precedes other consonants.

To feel the action of the S as a sound effect, play the Z bass fiddle, then turn off the voice and continue in a whisper. The unvoiced, whispered Z is a perfect S.

Play this sound effect softly, sharply, steadily, and smoothly. If you con-contrate on this action and keep the teeth gently occluded and the tongue toward the roof of the mouth, you will always produce a satisfactory S, whether the sound comes through a central tongue aperture or a slightly lateral one.

You will feel a steady, sharp sensation, too soft to be a whistle, between the teeth—but no breath or air coming through your lips when the S is properly executed.

Practice feeling the sustained S sound effect where it occurs at the end of a word or before another consonant, and continue to play the other consonant instruments.

force	basis	entrance	kiss	monstrous	incestuous
moisture	robustious	question	dance	blaspheme	emphasis

Carry the feeling of the consonants over to the poem, and remember to link words into phrases.

> Whistling cross the blistering past,
> She wrestled
>
> with a kiss . . .
>
> At last

She danced with questions on her lips;
Moisture
             glistened softly,
                          passed too close
and psst! . . .
A moment on her fingertips.

The B Tympani Drumbeat

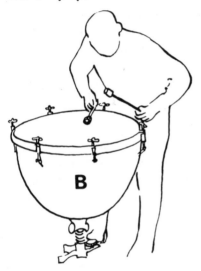

Cognate: P drumbeat

Conventional classification: voiced labial stop or plosive consonant

The voiced tap of the B tympani or kettle drum is played with a light springing apart of the lips.

To feel the action of this percussion consonant, close the lips gently together with a feeling of cushiony softness, then let them spring lightly apart. With a momentary vocal resonance that stops with the end of the spring, the result will be a delicate but clearly voiced B drumbeat.

Play this drumbeat on the springing away from contact—*not* by pressing the lips together and exploding the sound through the built-up breath pressure, an action that produces a forced, breathy noise and tightness and tension in the jaw and lip muscles.

You will feel a gentle, voiced pulsation on the lips like a delicate, crisp tap— an energy but no effort.

Practice feeling the springing action of the B drumbeat where it occurs at the end of a word or before another consonant, and continue to play the other consonant instruments.

stab	job	bribe	hubbub	suburb	microbe
imbibe	abhorrence	absence	probably	disrobe	subvene
absorb	abdomen	ablaze	cobweb	cobbler	hobnob

Carry the feeling of the consonants over to the poem, and remember to link
words into phrases.

> The hubbub in the suburb
>> was just a microbe in a cobweb
>>> compared
> to the hubbub of the hobnobs
>> bobbing on the job,
>> imbibing and cavorting,
>> and probably subscribing to sin.

The P Bassdrum Drumbeat

Cognate: B tympani

Conventional classification: unvoiced labial stop or plosive consonant

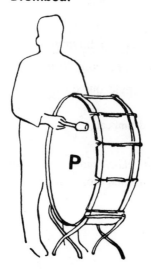

The whispered tap of the P bassdrum is played with a light springing apart of the lips.

To feel the action of this percussion consonant, close the lips gently, as for the B, then let them spring lightly apart. In a whisper, the B will become a perfect P.

Play this drumbeat on the springing away and deliberately make, not a P, but what you *feel* as a B in a whisper, without the slightest puff of air, and you will never be explosive on microphone nor shoot an offensive spray of saliva at a nearby listener.

You will feel a gentle pulsation on the lips like a delicate, crisp tap—an energy but no effort.

Practice feeling a gentle but precisely executed tap as you whisper the B to make the P drumbeat where it occurs at the end of a word or before another consonant, and continue to play the other consonant instruments.

trap	stop	clamp	escape	asleep	periscope
capsize	lapse	optimum	captain	tip-top	shipshape
stump	flip-flop	stopgap	gape	lollipop	strap

Carry the feeling of the consonants over to the poem, and remember to link words into phrases.

Oh tip-top lollipop,

flip flop your sticky stump!

O pop tap poppylop,   Up down periscope,
Captain of my ship—   Strap-stop the trap
Capsize, flopsize,   my tilly top lillypop
Lapsing into sleep.   pop lipped pollyplop

will pipple our escape.

The D Tympani Drumbeat

Cognate: T drumbeat

Conventional classification: voiced tongue-front palatal stop consonant

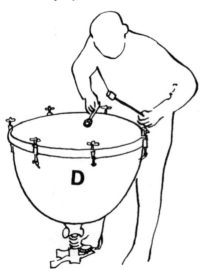

The voiced D tympani beat is also played with a light springing action, this time of the tongue.

To feel the action of this percussive consonant, place your tongue on the upper gum ridge as you did to play the N violin; then as the brief vocal resonance comes through, let the tongue spring away to play the D drumbeat.

Play this drumbeat on the springing of the tongue away from the soft cushiony contact with the upper gum ridge, *not* by pressing the tongue hard against the palate.

You will feel a gentle pulsation in the tongue.

Practice feeling the bouncing action of the D drumbeat where it occurs at the end of a word or before another consonant, and continue to play the other consonant instruments.

woodman	advertise	handmade	adverse	madcap	sandpiper
amplitude	unsound	unplanned	livelihood	said	conceived
verbalized	identified	alarmed	stockade	ceded	blended

Carry the feeling of the consonants over to the poem, and remember to link words into phrases.

The madcap woodsman

advertised,

identified

his livelihood:

He mended handmade wood windwipers

and inadvertently lost his head—

he said:

Because of the life I've led,

a cad like me is sure to wed.

It is said I am mod

and a little bit odd

cause I add to my wad

and it makes me so glad

To think of myself as a mod man

quite

mad.

The T Snare Drum Drumbeat   *Cognate:* D tympani

Conventional classification: unvoiced tongue-front palatal stop consonant

The light T tap of the snare drum is played with the same springing action of the tongue as the beat of the D tympani.

To feel the action of this percussive consonant, place the tongue in the position for the D; a whisper during the springing of the tongue, with no vocal resonance, will form the light, percussive tap of the T.

Play this drumbeat with a light springing action of the tongue, *not* with pressure against the palate, and with a light and airless whisper.

You will feel a gentle pulsation in the tongue.

Practice feeling the whispered D to make the clean, gently sharp tap of the T where it occurs at the end of a word or before another consonant. A final D after an unvoiced consonant and silent E is also unvoiced, that is, it becomes a T, as in *strapped*. Continue to play the other consonant instruments.

street	net	omnipotent	habit	rebate	quartet
abutment	depart	incandescent	inundate	concrete	glanced
Antwerp	hatpin	incitement	Baptist	admit	dropped

Carry the feeling of the consonants over to the poem, and remember to link words into phrases.

> O omnipresent, omnipotent sophist,
>
> titillating to excitement
>
> and parting crowds:
>
> I dreamed a quartet of battered women,

brandishing hatpins but wearing no hat,
had chased you down the streets of Antwerp—
and net-barbed
and wet-garbed
dropped you into a tin of wet concrete,
which was sweet . . .
if not neat.

The G Tympani Drumbeat

Cognate: K drumbeat

Conventional classification: v o i c e d
tongue-back plosive consonant

The deeper tympani drumbeat of
the hard G is played delicately with
the soft palate and the back of the
tongue, an action a little more difficult and a bit more subtle than
the other percussive consonants for
a nation of teeth gritters and jaw
clampers.

To feel this percussive consonant, place the back of the tongue in gentle
contact with the soft palate, while the tip of the tongue rests in-
actively inside, at the lower front teeth. With the mouth half open,
let the tongue spring away from the soft palate as you voice the
beat of the G tympani.

Play this drumbeat on the springing action in the back of the oral cavity,
without tightening, pressing, or pushing.

You will feel a delicate yet crisp tap and a gentle, voiced pulsation of the
back of the tongue and the soft palate.

Practice feeling the light bounce of the tongue away from the soft palate
where the G drumbeat occurs at the end of a word or before

another consonant, and continue to play the other consonant instruments.

dig	beg	fog	fatigue	league	catalog
suggest	ignorant	intrigue	pigment	Dogberry	recognized
straggler	vaguely	augment	quagmire	zig-zag	synagogue

Carry the feeling of the consonants over to the poem, and remember to link words into phrases.

> Vaguely, I recognized the ignorant straggler who dug her way
> > Zig Zag
> > through fog and quagmire
> > . . . . . I suggested to her . . . .
> > > Augment your bag
> > > and do not lag,
> > > nor straggle
> > > nor dig
> > > nor zig
> > > nor zag
> > > through the fog and mire of quag
> > > and minds that sag . . . . . Hag!

The K Tom-Tom Drumbeat

Cognate: G tympani

Conventional classification: unvoiced tongue-back plosive consonant

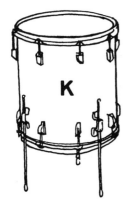

Darker than the other unvoiced percussion instruments but still crisp, the tom-tom click of the K, like its cognate drumbeat G, comes from the soft palate.

To feel this percussive consonant, place the tongue in the G position; an unvoiced whisper as the tongue springs away from the soft palate will produce the soft, clicking beat of the K.

Play this drumbeat on the springing action without tightening, pressing, pushing, or breathiness.

You will feel a delicate, yet crisp tap and a gentle pulsation of the back of the tongue and the soft palate.

Practice feeling the G drumbeat on a whisper to make the clear, soft click of the K where it occurs at the end of a word or before another consonant, and continue to play the other consonant instruments.

make	plaque	panic	shellac	success	unmask
crack	Cockney	checkmate	accessory	monarch	dejected
ache	unique	eccentric	crackpot	milkwood	Antarctic

Carry the feeling of the consonants over to the poem, and remember to link words into phrases.

> The panicked Cockney
> checkmated
> the dejected monarch,
> who ached at this success . . .
> thought himself attacked
> (knew himself shellacked)
> and wondered
> most eccentric'ly:
> If he could take . . .
> and break . . .
> this crackpot Cockney
> with exile in Antarctica.

Double Drumbeats

A characteristic of the percussion section of the consonant orchestra is the frequent doubling of the drum beats—the PT, the KT, the BD, and the GD—and a characteristic of sloppy speech is the frequency with which one or both of the beats is dropped. They need not be difficult—just feel the double tap-tap—but it is not enough to imagine that you *heard* both of these sounds; the only assurance that you have *produced* both is the specific sensation of each as a separate event; the two can be executed with surprising drumbeat rapidity. A correct tongue or lip position in preparation for these consonant drumbeats is not enough—without the specific drumbeat sensation any well-intentioned drumbeat preparation is useless. But no matter how light or how gentle the taps, if you feel them, your listener will hear them.

Practice feeling both drumbeats, and continue to play the other consonant instruments.

PT double drumbeat:

apt	wept	accept	looped	hoped	stopped
chipped	stamped	escaped	concept	clasped	adapt

KT double drumbeat:

act	effect	inflict	obstruct	subject	enactment
sacked	picked	wrecked	stacked	tracked	docked
joked	raked	booked	peeked	flaked	streaked

BD double drumbeat:

stabbed	robbed	robed	bribed	rubbed	sobbed

GD double drumbeat:

flogged	rigged	hugged	lagged	tugged	wagged

Carry the feeling of the consonants over to the poem, and remember to link words into phrases.

> His home was wrecked—
>   sacked, raked, and blacked
>   again.
> He'll accept and he'll adapt.
>   But he wept then . . .
> Flogged, stabbed, stamped, and raked,
> He hoped and hugged a dream,
>   sobbed and wept,
>   character cleft,
>   bereft,
>   and left.

The TH Clarinet

Cognate: TH sound effect

Conventional classification: voiced tongue-point-to-teeth fricative consonant

The warm, vibrant sound of the voiced TH simulates the clarinet, a woodwind instrument with a quality much like that of the V cello. Although this sound creates difficulty for many people, when executed correctly the TH clarinet is very easy to play.

To feel the action of the TH as clarinet, slip the rim of the tongue between the upper and lower teeth—perhaps even more than necessary at first, the sides of the tongue filling the side spaces between the teeth; then sing, feeling a buzz or motor-purring vibration throughout the front rim of the tongue.

Play this consonant instrument gently, without biting down on the tongue and without forcing any breath. Do not practice the weaker form with the tongue against or behind the upper teeth. When you know the strong form well and are familiar with its use, the weakening process will take place quite naturally and inevitably when the tempo or the informality of the speech situation calls for such action.

You will feel a tingling vibration on the rim of the tongue outside the teeth.

Practice feeling the TH clarinet as a warm vibration on various pitches where it occurs at the end of a word or before another consonant, and continue to play the other consonant instruments.

breathe	unsheathe	soothe	bathe	loathe	writhe
smooths	seethed	breathed	breathes	clothes	loathsome
withdraw	withstand	therewith	truths	tithe	toothed

Carry the feeling of the consonants over to the poem, and remember to link words into phrases.

"Foresoothe me, do!"

the loathsome, snaggletoothed werewolf proclaimed,

as he seethed beneath the unsheathed knife—

tithes extracted from his hide.

"I cannot breathe smoothly for I have toothed two writhing worms

. . . . and have need to soothe my wounds."

The TH Sound Effect

Cognate: TH clarinet

Conventional classification: unvoiced tongue-point-to-teeth fricative consonant

The thin, bellows-like friction stream of the TH sound effect is a dry and gentle whispered counterpart of the warm vibrations of its cognate, the TH clarinet.

To feel the action of the TH as sound effect, play the consonant as clarinet, then turn off the voice and continue in a whisper.

Play this sound effect lightly and softly, without even the slightest pressure of air, which will turn the thin whisper into a heavy, throttled hiss.

You will feel a steady but airless sensation of escaping breath stream.

Practice feeling the TH sound effect as a light, thin whisper where it occurs at the end of a word or before another consonant, and continue to play the other consonant instruments. Be particularly careful to play the consonants that occur before the TH.

breath	earth	birthday	myth	teeth	booth
breathless	months	truth	tenths	toothsome	sixths
forthwith	fifths	threnody	thwart	breadth	width

Carry the feeling of the consonants over to the poem, and remember to link words into phrases.

The breathless months move slowly over earth

as the fourth threnody brings to truth

the myth of time:

Thwarted thoughts

and lost desires

on the last long breath of that sixth year.

The SH Sound Effect   *Cognate:* ZH bassoon

Conventional classification: unvoiced tongue-blade sibilant consonant

The distant wind-like sound of the SH is the universal call for silence.

To feel the action of the SH as sound effect, bring the side teeth gently together in the natural bite and shush quietly. The tongue will take its natural position during this action without any effort on your part.

Play this sound effect softly, sharply, and smoothly. Check with the back of your hand for complete absence of air; keep the wind in the distance.

You will feel a high-pitched wind sensation, almost like a whistle, but no rush of air.

Practice feeling the SH sound effect as a soft, sharp shushing where it occurs at the end of a word or before another consonant, and continue to play other consonant instruments.

hush	dish	mesh	push	harsh	flashlight
wishful	Oshkosh	clash	harshly	fishnet	bashfully
bashed	brushed	hash	shrike	schtick	cashregister

Carry the feeling of the consonants over to the poem, and remember to link the words into phrases.

Hush!

You push too harshly.

Never rush me . . .

Ahhh! wi<u>sh</u>ful thinking,

for eve<u>n a</u>s you bru<u>sh</u> your hair

so feveri<u>sh</u>ly . . .

each strok<u>e a</u> cla<u>sh</u> . . .

you pu<u>sh</u> too har<u>sh</u>ly . . .

Hu<u>sh</u>!

The ZH Bassoon

Cognate: SH sound effect

Conventional classification: voiced tongue-blade sibilant consonant

The deep rumbling of the ZH simulates the bassoon and adds voice to the hush of the SH. Though the sound has no alphabet identification, it is a sound we use.

To feel the action of the ZH as bassoon, make the whispering SH and add vocal resonance.

Play this consonant instrument vibrantly, without forcing any breath into the sound. When the tonal vibration begins, all suggestion of the SH sound effect must vanish.

You will feel the thin wind of the SH overridden by the deep rumbling vibrations of the ZH, resonating against the teeth and at the tip of the tongue.

Practice feeling only the tonal vibrations of the ZH bassoon where it occurs at the end of a word or before another consonant, with no hint of the wind of the SH sound effect, and continue to play the other consonant instruments.

garage	beige	massage	garaged	corsage	mirage
entourage	badinage	menage	rouge	Taj Mahal	massaged

Carry the feeling of the consonants over to the poem, and remember to link the words into phrases.

I massaged my eyes

as the motley menage

(my entourage)

as in a mirage . . .

a dreamlike collage . . .

disappeared in a Taj

Mahal.

I garaged my camel and went for a drink.

The L Saxophone

Cognate: none

Conventional classification: tongue-tip-to-gum-ridge liquid consonant

The L saxophone is a self-effacing instrument, although it asserts itself somewhat more when it precedes a vowel than when it precedes a consonant.

To feel the action of the L as saxophone, place the tip of the tongue on the upper front gum ridge and let the vocal resonance come through without any sense of pressure.

Play this consonant instrument with a light touch—as little tongue touching the gum ridge as possible. If you have difficulty with the position, place the whole rim of the tongue on the upper gum ridge, as for the N violin, then loosen all of it except for the tip at the front gum ridge—what you have left is the L.

You will feel a gentle, vowel-like resonance, only slightly impeded by the tongue position.

Practice feeling the light touch of the L saxophone, and continue to play the other consonant instruments.

doll	fall	prevail	protocol	kneel	conceal
film	elm	help	revolve	willed	delve
gold	fooled	dolphins	sylphlike	asphalt	milkwood

Carry the feeling of the consonants over to the poem, and remember to link
words into phrases.

> The sylphlike dolphin spring
>
> willed its way
>
> through the filmy wold . . .
>
> A milky thing,
>
> veiled whimsy and fooled gold,
>
> concealed in slow, cold, mournful,
>
> lilted times to come.

The NG Oboe

Cognate: none

Conventional classification: voiced tongue-back, velar nasal continuant

The twangy, nasal tone of the NG simulates the oboe, an instrument sometimes said to have an oriental tonal quality. The NG is a single, sustained, vibrated nasal sound in which neither the N violin nor the G tympani beat plays any part.

To feel the action of the NG as oboe, sing with the back of the tongue in
contact with the soft palate, while the tip touches gently inside
the lower front teeth.

Play this consonant instrument without effort or tension for a sustained nasal
vibration coming through the nose.

You will feel a twangy, nasal resonance.

The use of the NG oboe is more complex than that of some other consonant
instruments. It must not, to begin with, be confused with the N
violin followed by a G pronounced as a DG Chinese cymbal, as
in *hinge.* The substitution of the N for the NG in participle endings

is a common error, and there is common confusion about the correct use of the G or K drumbeat following the NG.

Practice the final NG as the oboe alone, with no suggestion of the bouncing action of the drumbeat as the tongue leaves the soft palate at the end of the word.

hang	belong	strong	young	sing	tongue
seeing	hitting	being	batting	reading	loving

Exceptions: In words ending in NK, the N represents an NG oboe, followed by a K tympani drumbeat.

ink	flank	monk	drunk	honk	brink

Practice the medial NG as the oboe alone *(not* followed by a G tympani beat) when the portion of the word it ends has a meaning in common with the whole word.

singing	pingpong	dungheap	swinger	things	hanged

Exceptions: In the comparative and superlative forms of the words shown below, the oboe is followed by a G drumbeat.

stronger	strongest	younger	youngest	longer	longest

Practice the medial NG as an oboe that *is* followed by a G or K drumbeat when the portion of the word it ends is meaningless in terms of the whole word. In this category are many words spelled with an N, carrying the oboe resonance, followed by a K or by the C, CH, or Q variants of K.

anger	England	strength	malingering	Rangoon	tangle
bongo	finger	shrinking	relinquish	Inca	anchorage
uncle	cankerous	ankle	delinquent	unctuous	defunct

Exceptions: In some proper names and a few other words in this category, the oboe is *not* followed by a drumbeat.

Birmingham Washington Buckingham Nottingham Bingham gingham

Practice these words and decide whether the oboe is followed by a drumbeat. and continue to play the other consonant instruments.

tangling	linger	English	language	strangle	length
kingly	singer	strength	wrongful	hunger	hanger
gangs	singles	languish	Long Island	bringing	warmonger
jungle	singsong	stringier	springing	clangor	elongate
singular	sanguine	wringing	triangular	lengthy	Congo

Carry the feeling of the consonants over to the poem, and remember to link words into phrases. Wherever the NG oboe is followed by a drumbeat, an extra underline will be added under the NG or its equivalent. as in *hunger*.

Strangle that hunger for kingly things

that linger . . .

Sanguine.

A tangled strength with wrongful anger,

hanging,

shrinking young, and

Unctuous.

Make languished tongues once loving

again sing

again ring.

The DG Chinese Cymbal

Cognate: CH crash cymbal

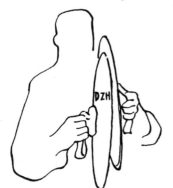

Conventional classification: v o i c e d tongue-point-plus-tongue-blade sibilant consonant

The muted clang of a Chinese cymbal is simulated by the soft, sliding resonance of the DG, a combination of the D drumbeat and the ZH bassoon into a single consonant sound.

To feel the action of the DG as a Chinese cymbal, place the tongue on the upper gum ridge for the D drumbeat, then let the tip peel downward to let the ZH resonance come through before the tongue springs away to end the sound.

Play this consonant instrument smoothly and do not let a whisper of the SH dull the ZH resonance at the end nor let the sound dissipate into a slushy sustention of the ZH. The DG Chinese cymbal must be played with a light, quick, energetic staccato treatment of the ZH as the final sound.

You will feel a phonated, sliding, percussive sensation flowing from the hard palate into the gum ridge.

Practice feeling the staccato resonance of the DG Chinese cymbal where it occurs at the end of a word or before another consonant, and continue to play the other consonant instruments.

edge	rage	George	image	abridgment
largely	besiege	judgment	engagement	acknowledgment
engaged	pledged	abridged	averaged	encouraged

Carry the feeling of the consonants over to the poem, and remember to link the words into phrases.

> His rage edged slowly
>
> and images engaged his mind:
>
> A besieged judgment
>
> Pledged a moment, wedged a way,
>
> and made a ledge to stand on,
>
> To nudge all pain away.

The CH Crash Cymbal

Cognate: DG Chinese cymbal

Conventional classification: unvoiced tongue-point-plus-tongue-blade sibilant consonant

In the crisp clash of the CH crash cymbal, the voiced D and ZH of the DG Chinese cymbal become the whispered T drumbeat and SH sound effect blended into a single sound.

To feel the action of the CH as a crash cymbal, place the tongue firmly on the upper gum ridge for the T drumbeat and crash through gently but sharply with the SH.

Play this consonant instrument crisply, with no sustention of the SH, depending on a feeling of staccato action rather than breath and ending lightly, quickly, energetically.

You will feel a sharp, crisp, percussive sensation between the tip of the
tongue and the gum ridge.

Practice feeling the crisp staccato of the CH crash cymbal where it occurs
at the end of a word or before another consonant, and continue
to play the other consonant instruments.

etch	march	church	catch	bewitch
witchcraft	watchman	patchwork	matchmaker	churchman
matched	fetched	itched	switched	watched

Carry the feeling of the consonants over to the poem, and remember to link
words into phrases.

<blockquote>
A ma<u>tch</u>maker i<u>tch</u>ed to ca<u>tch</u> a bewi<u>tch</u>ing lady

for the wa<u>tch</u>man of the chur<u>ch</u> . . .

But wi<u>tch</u>cra<u>f</u>t entered and wa<u>tch</u>ed

the pa<u>tch</u>work of fate

and le<u>f</u>t the man at the chur<u>ch</u>

. . . in the lur<u>ch</u>.
</blockquote>

The DZ Tambourine

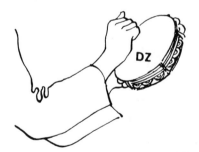

Cognate: TS after-beat cymbal

Conventional classification: v o i c e d tongue-
point-plus-tongue-blade sibilant consonant

The delicate percussive action of the DZ
is like a single light tap on the tambourine.

To feel the percussive action, press the tongue against the upper gum ridge
for the D drumbeat and peel tne tip down a bit as the vibrant Z
comes through just before the whole tongue springs away.

Play the DZ in a light staccato fashion, ending quickly and energetically
without sustention of the Z.

You will feel a momentary buzz between the tongue and the gum ridge.

Practice feeling the staccato buzz of the DZ tambourine, and continue to

play the other consonant instruments. Where the N violin precedes
the DZ tambourine, be doubly careful not to turn it into an N
followed by a Z bass fiddle, as in *Ben's* instead of *bends* and *fines*
instead of *finds*.

bids	deeds	towards	roads	aids
ends	finds	husbands	commands	swords
fields	holds	builds	scalds	demands

Carry the feeling of the consonants over to the poem, and remember to link
words into phrases.

> The sword's command
>
> ends husbands' rights
>
> . . . and wrongs!
>
> Leaves all demands
>
> in foreign hands
>
> and sounds a marching song;
>
> Bends former friends
>
> towards bitter ends
>
> Among the sands of time.

The TS After-Beat Cymbal   *Cognate:* DZ tambourine

Conventional classification: unvoiced tongue-
point-plus-tongue-blade sibilant consonant

The crisp whisper of the TS ends a number
of words, like the after-beat, or high-hat,
cymbal often used in popular orchestras.

To feel the percussive action, press the tongue against the upper gum ridge
for the T drumbeat, then crash through gently with a sharp, soft
S sound effect.

Play the TS crisply, lightly, and energetically, with only the slightest staccato
incisiveness on the S.

You will feel the beginning of a percussive hiss, or crisp, cricket-like sound,
between the tip of the tongue and the teeth.

Practice feeling the staccato incisiveness of the TS after-beat cymbal, and
continue to play the other consonant instruments. The consonant
action is a bit complicated when the after-beat cymbal comes after
another consonant at the end of a word; be sure to feel the proper
action-sensation of the K and P drumbeats, the S and F sound
effects, and the N violin whenever they precede the final TS.

bets	hates	limits	debates	casts	artists
contrasts	effects	gifts	thefts	lifts	sifts
adopts	adapts	attempts	exempts	acts	scientists
instincts	precincts	districts	patients	entrants	physicists

Carry the feeling of the consonants over to the poem, and remember to link
words into phrases.

> Don't leave your last effects
>   as gifts . . .
> They are thefts
> from one whose limits were hates
>   and constant debates . . .
> whose cosmic scientist's instincts,
>   tracking through the pasts
>   of ancient Picts and Kelts,
> drew welts.
> Yet still alive, casts sighs aside . . .
>   attempts . . .
>   forgets . . .
>   events once sung on a hollow drum
> Time drifts—

R<u>ifts</u>

<u>in a</u> passio<u>n</u> to co<u>me</u>!

The H Sound Effect

Cognate: none

Conventional classification: glottal consonant

Like the barest whisper of wind, the H sound effect hints at the vowel to come. By itself, it sounds like a gentle sigh we exhale on. It is sounded as a consonant only when it precedes a vowel or vowel-like consonant. Phonetically it does not exist when final or followed by any consonant other than W or Y.

To feel this sound effect, sigh almost inaudibly in a whisper, while the lips take the form of the sound that follows.

Play the H gently without force or pressure or excess breath.

You will feel nothing more than a slight hesitation before the vowel.

Practice feeling the brief hesitation gently and airlessly, and continue to play the other consonant instruments.

* when	hue	which	overwhelm	whistle	behold
hewn	what	whipped	whisper	heuristic	hero
whet	whiffle	whisk	whack	whelped	hippy

Carry the feeling of the consonants over to the poem, and remember to link words into phrases.

> Whe<u>n</u> rough-hew<u>n</u> you
> half-<u>whistled into</u> li<u>fe</u>,
> You ge<u>n</u>tled hue<u>s</u>
> a<u>nd whispered</u> clue<u>s</u>
> a<u>nd whetted</u> eyes
> in a <u>whim</u>sy di<u>sguise</u>—
> Half hints so rife
> ha<u>lf</u>-hi<u>de</u> your <u>hew</u>.

* In this group all "wh" words are pronounced as "hw"

The W Flute

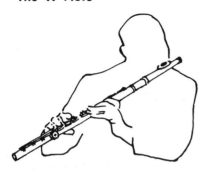

Cognate: none

Conventional classification: labiovelar or lip-back consonant

The W flute is a lovely hint of vowel-like sound that begins where the #1 stretch vowel ends. It exists only in the brief space that connects the O͞O sound with any vowel that immediately follows the W; it cannot be sustained without reverting to an O͞O. Almost a vowel, it can be considered a consonant because the lip opening is so reduced as to impede and confine the vowel sound for an instant. As a phonetic sound it is never final and never followed by another consonant.

To feel the flute-like action, bring the lips to the smallest possible aperture and precede the following vowel with a tiny resonance.

Play the flute lightly and quickly, remembering that the W exists only between the O͞O and the next vowel—O͞O - ā (way).
    w

You will feel the full forward stretch for the #1 vowel and then reduce the lip opening still further, to create the slightest impedance of the O͞O as it moves to the following vowel sound.

Practice feeling the smallest possible lip opening before the vowel, which is the only position in which W appears as a consonant, and continue to play the other consonant instruments.

    wind   away   wormwood   wander   wigwam   Wellington

Practice linking words that end in the stretch vowels #1, #21, or #51 into initial vowels in the following words, with the W between as the link.

    to excel   you are   no intrusion   now everyone
       w   w   w   w

The reading selection for the W flute will be combined with that for the Y French horn.

The Y French Horn

Cognate: none

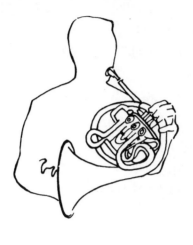

Conventional classification: tongue-front consonant

The Y French horn is nothing more than a touch of Ybuzz before another vowel. Like the W flute, it exists only in the connecting space between vowels, in this case the EE and whatever vowel follows, and it cannot be sustained without reverting to a Ybuzz. In the process of liaison, the tongue crowds forward to impede and confine the vowel sound just enough to create consonant action. As a phonetic sound it is never final and never followed by another consonant.

To feel the Y consonant action, move swiftly into the following vowel after the slightest Ybuzz tonal action.

Play the Y French horn crisply and without forcing the resonance, remembering that the Y exists only between the Ybuzz and the next vowel—ēē - ōō (you).

You will feel the Ybuzz quickly cut off as it slides into the following vowel.

Practice feeling the slightest possible Ybuzz resonance before the vowel, which is the only position in which the Y appears as a consonant, and continue to play the other consonant instruments.

> you   yonder   beyond   piano   yardarm   peony

Practice linking words that end in the Ybuzz, +Ybuzz, 3y, or 6y into initial vowels in the following words, with the consonant Y between as the link.

> he insists   every altitude   goodbye audience
>
> today is the day   destroy everyone   to die in peace

Carry the feeling of the consonants over to the poem, and remember to link
words into phrases.

> Yonder lies the wormwood tree,
>
> beyond the yellow wishing well,
>
> away from winter's majesty
>
> and the winding willow's sanctity.

> A winsome thing, this thing beyond,
>
> a yearning thing of past reprieve . . .
>
> Yet someday think of yesterday
>
> and turn away from wormwood wand.

The R Trombone

Cognate: none

Conventional classification: tongue-point consonant

The strongly vibrating R trombone creates
a substantial, legitimate consonant sound
when it precedes a vowel, but it creates a
danger as well: Because of the nature of
its articulation and placement, it tends to
pull entire words backward into the throat whenever it appears as final consonant or before a consonant. The only protection is good structural and
tonal action in the preceding vowel.

To feel the action, hug the inside of the upper back teeth or gums with the
posterior underedges of the tongue, while the tip of the tongue
curls upward.

Play the R trombone as fully as you like as long as you use enough structural
action to dilute the potential tension and enough tonal action to
pull the throaty vibration forward onto the hard palate.

You will feel, in the full-fledged American R, essentially a confined vibration in the throat area that should be deemphasized whenever the
sound is not absolutely necessary.

Practice playing the R trombone cleanly and completely before a vowel, either in a single word or at the beginning of another word, because the vowel will absorb the strong vibration as the lips maintain a forward direction, and continue to play the other consonant instruments.

Rarify	reread	arrange	terrestrial	hurry	drive
terrorist	torrent	library	tear off	aristocrat	Tipperary

Carry the feeling of the consonants over to the poem, and remember to link words into phrases.

> Rondos written round my mind,
>
> Roses rousted out of bed;
>
> Torrid torrents in a hurry
>
> roar pronouncements never read:
>
> I am sorry to remember . . .
>
> draw a cross through memories . . .
>
> and render dead
>
> the words unsaid
>
> in . . . rondos
>
> ringing
>
> round
>
> my head.

Practice deemphasizing the R trombone as much as possible when it appears before a pause or before another consonant, by concentrating on the full, positive structural form applied to the preceding vowel. In other words, in the precise positions where other consonant instruments can be fully played, the R trombone should be underplayed. Continue to play the other consonant instruments.

bored	form	endured	pure	dour	father
barred	farm	endeared	pier	dear	canard
bird	firm	endorsed	pare	dare	zephyr
beard	deferred	entered	pore	door	nature

Carry the feeling of the consonants over to the poem, and remember to link words into phrases.

Rolling more than naturally,
I love your form; a zephyr wind
endured of time,
a poor martyr to frivolity;
endorsed, endeared, and possibly
a firm door barred,
a dear bird flown . . .
a moment all my own.

The DL and TL Woodblocks   *Cognates*

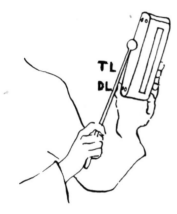

Conventional classification: voiced and un-voiced tongue-tip to gum-ridge consonants

The woodblock clicks of the DL and TL complete the percussion section of the consonant orchestra. These consonant actions are difficult for many speakers, who find it awkward to bounce the D or T drumbeat off the gum ridge and return there immediately for the L saxophone, so another kind of percussive action is generally used.

To feel the woodblock click, press the tongue into the drumbeat position on the upper gum ridge, then let the sides of the tongue bounce away with a click, while the tip remains in position for the sustained L that follows. Voiced, this action produces DL; unvoiced, TL.

Play the percussive action with emphasis on getting to the L saxophone as quickly as possible, and the woodblock click will substitute for the drumbeat automatically. To disengage the tongue completely between the drumbeat and the L saxophone in words like *bottle* is not necessarily incorrect if the emphasis remains on reaching the L, and the vowel between is kept neutral and short.

You will feel the typical drumbeat pulsation damped in the tip of the tongue as the woodblock click slides into the L.

Practice feeling the quickness of the D click before the sustained L saxophone at the end of a word.

| meddle | medal | paddle | idle | idol | hurdle |
| needle | cradle | bridle | waddle | coddle | puddle |

Practice feeling the D click even when the L is not sustained because a vowel sound follows.

paddling	ladling	cuddling	straddling	puddling	idling
friendless	maudlin	handling	swindling	windlass	kindling
boldly	mildly	worldly	coldly	wildly	baldly
blindly	friendly	kindly	blandly	fondly	worldliness

Practice feeling the unvoiced click of the TL woodblock in the same way.

little	cattle	bottle	Beatles	settle	fatal
evidently	saintly	succinctly	elegantly	exactly	arrogantly
perfectly	correctly	distinctly	ardently	lately	insistently
teetotaler	settling	settler	listless	rattling	gauntlet
outlet	frontlet	dauntless	restless	fistless	gentlest

You are the idol of my cradle . . .

mildly maudlin, yes,

but all the same,

wildly idle

in its handling;

so fondly worldly . . .

a hurdle for your name.

The gentlest little thing

you give me

is a saintly outlet.

You will run the gauntlet,

settling

. . . not exactly fatal

. . . not lovely all the same.

Miscellaneous Word Lists

Practice playing all the instrumental consonants with deliberateness and skill.

first	firsts	patience	tennis	serendipity
second	seconds	patients	tens	etymological
third	thirds	petitions	tends	ejectamenta
fourth	fourths	entrance	tense	synergistic
fifth	fifths	entrants	tents	extraterritorialism
sixth	sixths	thieves	tenths	rather
seventh	sevenths	Thebes	whirls	recalcitrance
eighth	eighths	fines	worlds	recapitulative
ninth	ninths	finds	whirly	recapitulance
tenth	tenths	Ben's	worldly	reconnoiterer
eleventh	elevenths	bends	wouldst	reconnaissance
twelfth	twelfths	bashes	couldst	January
thirteenth	thirteenths	batches	shouldst	February
fourteenth	fourteenths	tracks	wouldn't	sanguineousness
fifteenth	fifteenths	tracts	couldn't	satiate
sixteenth	sixteenths	acts	shouldn't	characteristic
seventeenth	seventeenths	axe	didn't	palimpsest
eighteenth	eighteenths	asks	hadn't	Wednesday
nineteenth	nineteenths	Rubicon	liaison	amanuensis
twentieth	twentieths	rubicund	sapient	amateurism

Improvisation in Communication through Consonant Action

Now that you have learned to play, and play with, all the instruments of the consonant orchestra, test their ability to communicate even without verbal content or actual words. Choose a partner and try to create a communication between the two of you, using only the various consonant sounds. Be incisive, bitter, conspiratorial, domineering, threatening, whining, pleading, demanding. The wide range of melodic, percussive, and sound effect qualities in the consonants gives you a great deal of material to work with. Use the melodies, the sound effects, and the percussion as you would inflections on words. Don't hesitate to use the vowel-like qualities of the W flute and the Y French horn to widen the range of expressive possibilities.

Consonant Action in Connected Speech

As I have already indicated in the instructions before each of the consonant poems, connected speech is essential when you speak in phrases and sentences; you must not treat each word as a separate entity, unrelated to the words on either side of it, which means that you cannot treat each, or any, consonant as a single entity, unrelated to the consonants on either side of it. If you feel the double drumbeats in *take time* in the same way that you feel them in the single word *practice*, you are beginning to link properly. If, in the phrase "you've known this," you play the V cello, the N violin, and the S sound effect without separating the words, you will be connecting skillfully while feeling the melody and the effect of the sustained instruments. If, in the phrase "shocked, frantic, and cowed," you feel the K and T drumbeats in *shocked,* the N violin and the K drumbeat in *frantic,* the N violin and the D tympani in *and,* and the D tympani in *cowed,* without any separation or gaps anywhere—as if the phrase were one long word—you will be connecting, linking, and phrasing, while at the same time experiencing new ingredients in articulation and new tastes in speech.

The practice of running words together by dropping final consonants or those before other consonants is undesirable, but when you have learned to feel every consonant as a separate instrument, nothing is lost and much is added by connecting one word to another. Because every word in a phrase or sentence is sharply delineated by the rhythms, nuances, and dynamics of the consonants—without the separation of pauses—you can speak and read as rapidly as you wish without ever speaking *too* rapidly. The only valid objection to speed in speech is that words are unintelligible and understanding is thereby lost; but if the consonants are *not* lost—if you feel them and your listener hears them—intelligibility is preserved, and you cannot, physically, talk too fast. Speaking at a seemingly rapid tempo then becomes the exciting exercise of a creative skill of great significance to the actor or professional speaker.

So practice running one word into another with intention. You can accept the challenge because you are armed with this special technique of consonant action. Practice:

antiquated people	as	antiquate dpeople
cultivate anything	as	cultiva tanything
characteristic themes	as	characteristi kthemes
married women	as	marrie dwomen

Do them slowly at first, then pick up speed until the phrase sounds perfectly natural. Do the same with longer sentences:

For Steve there remained but one alternative.

For Ste vthe remain dbu twu nalternative.

The good-looking cook took a good look.

The goo dlooki ngcoo ktoo kagoo dlook.

These sentences may appear confusing in print, but practice them rhythmically, without separation, and you will soon feel a lovely sense of connectedness, and after a few repetitions, the words and sentences will sound natural, clear, clean, sharp, attractive, and effective.

Remember then that a final consonant should always be carried over, or linked, to the initial letter of the next word, except before a pause. The pause may be for breath or for one of a number of exceptions to the rule: All rules are suspended whenever special emphasis or tempo or interpretation requires an unorthodox treatment. But correct linking, done skillfully, is the key to natural, smooth speech. When you feel the nonpercussive consonants as sustained melodies and sound effects, and the percussive sounds are short and staccato enough . . . when you learn not to dwell on the vowels but to hop to the consonants with dispatch . . . when you learn to scan a line quickly while sustaining a melody or sound effect, to find the next double-underlined consonant, and feel free to quicken the tempo between . . . you will have begun to enjoy the benefits and qualities that can accrue from the use of consonant action.

The exact technique of linking depends upon the letters involved: Any final consonant may be linked directly into any vowel at the beginning of the next word. When a final consonant is followed by an initial consonant, however, the combinations fall into two categories, which must be treated somewhat differently:

1. Nonrelated consonants are formed by actions sufficiently different that they can each be played fully and linked directly, without loss of individual instrumental character and without any break in the flow, rhythm, or tempo of connected speech.

2. Related consonants are formed at the same, or nearly the same, contact point in the mouth and cannot be played individually without a break between.

In the second category, there are several types of relationship: Identicals and most cognates always fall into this category; here, compound consonant sounds are treated as identicals or cognates of other consonants on the basis of their initial sounds—since DG is phonetically a combination of D and ZH, it is treated, for the purpose of linking, as an identical with D and a cognate of T, while CH, a combination of T and SH, is an identical with T and a cognate of D; on the other hand, DG and CH are not treated here as cognates of one another, since the final sound of one is not a cognate of the initial sound of the other. In addition, there are semirelated consonants—the D or T followed by SH, TH, S, Z, or N; and B or P followed by M. When the order of these semirelated consonants is reversed, the relationship disappears—they become nonrelated consonants and can be linked directly. But whatever the relationship, all related consonants are treated in the same way: The first is prepared—that is, the tongue or lips take the position for that consonant—but only the second is executed as a full-fledged consonant sound. The preparation keeps the result from being a mere dropping of the final consonant.

Direct linking: Practice linking final consonants directly into vowels, as in *far above* or *take over;* continue to play the other consonants.

1. grab it	9. that's enough	17. breathe in
2. stop up	10. leads on	18. birth of a nation
3. bad actor	11. run off	19. massage it
4. get out	12. home owner	20. wash up
5. drag along	13. give away	21. sail away
6. back away	14. enough of it	22. over all
7. arrange everything	15. because of it	23. strong executive
8. catch on	16. missed out on it	24. this is it

Play and link: Practice playing final consonants fully and linking them to fully played nonrelated consonants, as in *neck tie* or *love knot;* continue to play the other consonants. Percussive consonants are underlined once, sustainable consonants twice.

1. sob sister	16. smooth surface	31. take time
2. keep this	17. wisdom tooth	32. big deal
3. stand back	18. barrage balloon	33. can't be
4. what for	19. wash clean	34. canned goods
5. big money	20. hill country	35. watch Germany
6. stack pack	21. night report	36. it's good
7. don't you	22. predict whether	37. exciting game
8. match cover	23. judge carefully	38. that's bad business
9. that's mine	24. room temperature	39. word list
10. gone forever	25. back with	40. drop kick in football
11. told him	26. hot wind	41. red car
12. leave soon	27. judge severely	42. mysterious witch
13. staff party	28. those ships	43. dark neighborhood
14. has been	29. this sheep	44. ask not why
15. loose talk	30. last row	45. understand patience

Prepare and link: Practice preparing for the action of the final consonant and executing the related initial consonant that follows, whether it be identical, cognate, or semirelated, as in *hot dog.*

Identical	*Cognate*	*Semirelated*
1. stab back	1. bribe paid	1. stab me
2. help pack	2. keep back	2. help me
3. good deal	3. bad time	3. good news
4. don't talk	4. sit down	4. that seems
5. big guns	5. dog collar	5. good smoke
6. stick close	6. dark gray	6. red zone
7. even now	7. five friends	7. cute zebra
8. some men	8. seems so	8. patent nonsense
9. have vitality	9. bequeath theatres	9. mist shrouded
10. life force	10. quoth thus	10. dead ship
11. fence sags	11. not George	11. broad theme
12. cloth thrown out	12. did change	12. asked them
13. bad judge	13. this zone	13. did that
14. not Charlie	14. hated tsetse fly	14. won't throw it

As you already know, consonant action can contribute much, not only to the intensity and quality, but to the meaning and interpretation of speech and to subtle interpretive changes. You have also seen the subtle changes that can be rung on a single sentence by sustaining the call on different words. In Chapters XI and XII, you will fully explore and exploit the rhythms, dynamics, and nuances of consonant energy as well as the qualities of the other energies. Here, let us experiment briefly with a few rhythmic consonant variations for change of meaning.

Feeling rhythmic variations: Practice these sentences, playing all the consonant instruments marked, with special emphasis and sustention on those underlined twice, and linking as indicated. Let each reading call up an image that pours life into the meaning of the words; feel the consonant action-sensation and the personal involvement with the meaning at the same time, and let them grow from, and reinforce, one another.

1. They said it.
2. They defend it.

3. They defend him.

4. I'll defend him.   I'll defend him.

5. I'll defend them.   I'll defend them.

6. They'll defend him no matter what I do.

Sample Paragraph for Testing Consonants

The old resident of the neighborhood bitterly condemned the characteristic tirades and unchristian behavior displayed by government, business, and police representatives. He asked why the city permits a situation that tends to reach the lower depths for tens of thousands of the city's inhabitants; why it adopts improvements for privileged groups, yet the long-promised urban renewal program, five-sixths curtailed and no longer ambitious, is still being blocked or ignored by bureaucratic policy and cowardly subterfuge. Why, he asked, hadn't that materialized? He succinctly dismissed the "good will" myths so sanctimoniously projected by local social scientists. We looked around the dilapidated, yet once picturesque, neighborhood, destroyed by bullets, bottles of Molotov cocktails, bricks, and fire—it is no mirage. The effects of the holocaust throughout the city's precincts are overwhelming; the destruction includes the length and breadth of the shopping districts. I want to try to understand this tragedy. Who controls the not-so-mysterious witchcraft that overnight turns into hospital patients those who yesterday stood for patience and reason? The Negro population is as tense as a tightened fiddle string—nine tenths of them would rather live in dog-tents than in the rat-infested holes that pass for apartments in the city.

Reading Exercise Applying Consonant Action

BUT IN A LARGER SENSE, WE CANNOT DEDICATE, WE CANNOT CONSECRATE, WE CANNOT HALLOW THIS GROUND. THE BRAVE MEN LIVING AND DEAD, WHO STRUGGLED HERE, HAVE CONSECRATED IT FAR ABOVE OUR POOR POWER TO ADD OR DETRACT. THE WORLD WILL LITTLE NOTE, NOR LONG REMEMBER WHAT WE SAY HERE, BUT IT CAN NEVER FORGET WHAT THEY DID HERE. IT IS FOR US, THE LIVING,

RATHER, TO BE DEDICATED HERE TO THE UNFINISHED WORK,
WHICH THEY WHO FOUGHT HERE HAVE THUS FAR SO NOBLY
ADVANCED. IT IS RATHER FOR US TO BE HERE DEDICATED
TO THE GREAT TASK REMAINING BEFORE US—THAT FROM
THESE HONORED DEAD WE TAKE INCREASED DEVOTION, TO
THAT CAUSE, FOR WHICH THEY GAVE THE LAST FULL MEAS-
URE OF DEVOTION; THAT WE HERE HIGHLY RESOLVE, THAT
THESE DEAD SHALL NOT HAVE DIED IN VAIN; THAT THIS
NATION, UNDER GOD, SHALL HAVE A NEW BIRTH OF FREE-
DOM, AND THAT GOVERNMENT OF THE PEOPLE, BY THE
PEOPLE, AND FOR THE PEOPLE, SHALL NOT PERISH FROM
THE EARTH.

Guide for Consonant Action

single underline, as in *tapped*	percussion, tap the sound
double underline, as in *delves*	sustain the sound
linking curve, as in *but in a*	direct linking from final consonant to initial vowel
linking curve plus slash, as in *cannot dominate*	related consonants; prepare the first, execute the second
single underline plus linking arrow, as in *cannot consecrate*	play and link to the next consonant
linking curve plus W, as in *you insist*	W connective
linking curve plus Y, as in *the earth*	Y connective
slash only, as in *dazed* or *calm*	letter is silent

Part Three: The Uses of a Good Voice

NO ACTION STANDS ALONE. It comes from somewhere as an expression of something; it creates an answering action and becomes, along with that response, a part of something else. A beautiful voice remains a sound . . . articulated speech a rhythm . . . until you put them to use. As you have developed these qualities through mastery of the trinity of energies, you have experienced them as an integral part of your own individuality—as an extension of yourself, deeply rooted in yourself. You have learned *use* along with development—all that remains is refinement, the transformation of skill into artistry and artistry into virtuosity. In the five chapters of Part Three, we will consider the deeply searching role of voice and speech in the communicating personality. Though several of the chapters are directed specifically to the actor, they do not bypass the interests of other readers. Acting is basically communication, and the techniques of the actor, properly used, can be as useful off stage as they are on stage. And since off stage includes those who are severely handicapped in their use of voice and speech, we will consider briefly the application of the principles and techniques of the Lessac system to their problems as well.

CHAPTER XI

Vocal Life I—

Exploration

*I*N THE EIGHTEENTH CENTURY, when every lady carried a fan, she could communicate a hundred different messages with it—by the way she held it, where she held it, whether it was open or closed or somewhere between. But the action-sensation of voice and speech is not, and must not be considered, an isolated device for communication in that sense. When the trinity of energies is used for meaningful expression of ideas and emotions, it becomes a true vocal life inextricably intertwined with emotional life and physical life. Thus vocal life is an essential support of this new trinity, just as structural action, tonal action, and consonant action are each essential supports of vocal life.

You have been developing vocal life from your very first step in achieving structural action. Now it must be consolidated; it must become habit, but not a set of mechanical or automatic habits superimposed upon the other aspects of expression. Such habits, involuntary and unresponsive to intelligent direction, do provide control, but a rigid control that walls-in communication and confines it to a fixated, conditioned response. The control we seek is a flexible guide—the habit of fusing the actions of the part with the function of the whole. We are talking about the habit of experiencing the physical sensations of voice and speech with relaxed energy and the habit of awareness and recognition of these sensations—*never* the habit of performing these actions *without* awareness. This kind of control, this kind of habit, permits a real response and the most effective response, geared specifically to the needs of the moment, not a conditioned reflex geared only to its own preconditioning.

Everyone who would use his voice and speech most effectively, but in particular the actor, must avoid not only this mechanical approach to vocal life but the very idea that vocal life is exclusively, or primarily, a stage technique. The energy inherent in vocal life can be invaluable in preparing a role, in rehearsing, and in performance, but voice and speech onstage should differ in no essential way from voice and speech offstage. Vocal life is not a wrapping used to make a shiny and attractive package out of the actor's emotional life; rather it should be considered an intrinsic part of the structure of which emotional life and physical life are also parts. Vocal life is at the same time both cause and effect: Emotional life and physical life extend into, and are informed by, the fullest capacities of the vocal instrument. The action becomes an interaction, a perpetual "round dance" among the trinity of emotional-physical-vocal life. First one and then another action leads but the other two are always there to lend support, just as the earlier trinity of structural, tonal, and consonant energies is in constantly shifting balance in vocal life. The emotions expressed may be influenced, controlled, or even created by the vocal quality, or the gesture that expresses them; a strong gesture may also strengthen the vocal quality, and a softer voice may bring subtlety to the gesture.

Vocal life cannot be put on, and if it cannot be put on, it cannot be taken off. As a part of the higher or deeper trinity, it is as much an inner energy as emotion, as much a function of the body as gesture. If vocal life is to be an organic experience you must feel it; you must feel it as an activity within yourself; and you must feel an involvement in this activity.

You have already been cautioned against listening to yourself, using the ear as a guide to tonal quality, but neither can you create an organic vocal life by thinking the sound first. Either listening or thinking will deemphasize the true role of vocal life or even block out a genuine, productive vocal life altogether. Control cannot be imposed before or after the fact, by thought or by listening, but can only grow out of the moment, the result of your intrinsic feeling of the action, if real vocal life is to emerge. In this way, vocal life acts in synergy with emotional life and physical life, and each of these energies enhances the others, to create a single spontaneous effect greater than the sum of the parts that make it up.

The perceptual insight into vocal life, then, is part of the same physical and psychological apparatus involved in the perception and control of emotional and physical behavior. When vocal life takes its proper place in this trinity, it both expresses and helps to create emotional life; it becomes a discriminating force that explores the possibilities and determines the degree and kind of the actor's emotional life on stage. Just as you can be moved emotionally by a piece of music, so can you find new feelings, new images, and new meanings in the dynamics of your own

voice and speech when you experience the music and the life of the consonants, the vowels, and the resonance.

The Creative Aspect of Vocal Life

That vocal life can be a creative as well as an
expressive energy can easily be demonstrated by applying in turn, to a
speech or scene, each of the three energies that make up vocal life. In the
work section of this chapter you will find a number of dramatic soliloquies
and readings. Read each selection through, placing the emphasis first on
structural action, then on consonant action, then on the call focus. Exaggerate; play with the sounds; emphasize one energy but never quite let
the others go. If you explore the text freely with your voice, without fear
of sounding silly or wrong, the result will sometimes be unorthodox, sometimes even a little eccentric, but you will find in these experiments unexpected
new meanings and interpretations. You will be exploring the full poten-
tialities of your voice, acquiring a physical sense memory of its range that
will enable you to utilize it to its fullest capacity.

In this approach, remember that you are not after
vocal music for the sake of vocal music, *not sound imitating emotion, but
sound inspiring and creating emotion.* You must use each energy with a
complete awareness of, and a complete involvement in, the emotional
nuances created by the sound. Never use your voice by rote; let it be part
of a searching process—a search for sounds, moods, rhythms, emotions,
and meanings; a search for *new* patterns, and the facile breaking of old
ones. If you feel the energy of vocal life—feel it inside yourself, a part
of yourself—the words, the tones, and the emotions will be an organic
whole. Thus the exercise will remain creative and never degenerate into
routine elocution.

Begin, if you like, by reading the selection once
for literal meaning, but don't let this meaning become the guide to your
vocal expression; simply paraphrase it mentally. If the literal meaning tends
to impose itself too strongly, you may do better to begin the exercise without
a too-careful preliminary reading. Using this exercise on totally unfamiliar
material after a superficial scanning can do no harm and may produce new
insights into the text.

Read the selection with structural energy leading.
With the full inverted megaphone stretch, you will find yourself singing
on the vowels, bringing out all their poetry, intonations, and inflections;
at the same time the use of the dilute or spread tonal energy can produce
feelings of quiet confidence and projection, gregariousness, and expulsive
emphasis, a warm enthusiasm, a rounded gentle precison. Vowels which

get their shape from facial posture, based on structural action, are genial and sympathetic in sound — a way of speaking to a child — and can also be outgoing enough for the special lyric qualities of certain kinds of poetry, and story telling. With structural action leading you will sometimes find a reminiscent quality entering—the communication of memories.

In the music of structural action, you sing the simple melody of the vowel without being constrained to fill it up with the call focus. The melodic line and the tone lie within the range of soft, warm, and even rich pastel colors, but colors of lower intensity than the stronger, brighter, or darker hues of concentrated tonal action. The use of structural action induces a warm relaxed feeling. The tempo of structural action is more fluid and seems slower than that of consonant action because the vowels are played for a longer duration and given fuller emphasis. Structural action has a variety of range, pitch, duration: When used alone—without consonant energy to stir it up and without tonal energy to carry it off on flights of excitement and force—it turns into the expository lecture or declamatory speech which may, by itself, sometimes seem a bit conservative or formal or over deliberate; but by itself, it can also soar on wings of spoken song and poetic fancy. Always remember that structural action is the "mold" substance in speech . . . the substance on which the other actions act and travel.

Read the selection with consonant energy leading. You will find yourself experimenting with a new kind of rhythm, speed, and melody—an interplay between dynamic tempos tapped out by the percussive consonants, the sustained legato of the melodic consonants, and a clear, cutting sibilance provided by the sound effect consonants. You can experience an intimate intensity, a quiet excitement, a subdued persuasiveness. A light, tripping, percussive use of the consonant energy can also lead your vocal characterization to an impish, mischievous lyricism. You can find quick comic rhythms, whispered conspiracies, light social insincerities, as well as crisp incisiveness, cynicism, and anger as you begin to cut and bite with the consonants. But most important, if you play with the consonants, you will find your own inspirations—you will find in the random results many potential subtleties of characterization spanning the range from sudden whimsy to tragic bitterness.

Neither the practical nor the esthetic importance of the consonants in our speech can be over stressed. In *Building a Character* Stanislavski traces the beginning of his interest in consonants to an aphorism in S. M. Volkonski's *The Expressive Word*: "If vowels are a river and consonants are the banks, it is necessary to reinforce the latter lest there be floods." The image is good as far as it goes, but it can go further. The consonants are not only the banks that control, but the river bed itself

—the rocks and sandbars, the deeps and sudden drops that create eddies, change the direction of the stream, let it run quietly, race it through rapids, and plunge it into waterfalls. The river bed determines the character of the stream and in a large measure, consonants not only determine the intelligibility of speech, as has already been pointed out, but control emotional meanings as well. Good consonant action, more than anything else, really makes the difference between the vital energy of vocal life and the rolling sonorities of an old-fashioned kind of stage speech on the one hand, and the slovenly mumble of those who make a god of naturalism on the other. But good consonant action means even more than precision. If the actor thinks that he creates with the vowels and with the tonal action and merely maintains intelligibility and precision with the consonants, he is wasting a large part of his resources for he overlooks the creativity of the consonants. The entire orchestral concept of consonant action opens up a musical approach to the consonants that can give them greater importance than they have been given in the past. This is true in the sung as well as the spoken word. The consonant need not be considered an interruption of the singing of the vowels, something to be suppressed as much as possible —but rather a whimsical or dramatic intensification of the emotional content of the song as well as a clarification of the meaning to be conveyed by the vowels that are sung. It should be emphasized that in the song or aria, generally, it is the vowel that sings while the consonant speaks; whereas in speech, always, the consonant both sings *and speaks.*

Read the selection with tonal energy leading. The call is the explosive speech situation, enthusiastic, exhilarating . . . the voice of command. You are on the offensive with full range of volume and pitch for exuberance, anger, or hysteria. You can roar; you can laugh; you can cry. You may feel a wild dionysian freedom surging through you as well as through the words; you may feel rising despair, the keening of women on the Irish coast. On the other hand, there is a definitive emphasis and confident security in the calmer, more cultivated call, especially in the low and middle pitch range, along with the sharply concentrated Ybuzz and +Ybuzz. There is mystery too, in the quiet call: Light, high, and ghost-like, it searches; it questions; it reaches out. What can be whimsy or conspiracy in the consonants, and legato melody in structural action may become something like an antic Slavic passion in the call.

Concentrated tonal action brings out the greatest strength, the greatest tonal variety and contrast. It stretches sound and focuses it: At the same time it contributes to the feeling of great energy in relaxation and is a most relaxed use of maximum vocal energy. Without it, either concentrated power or the voice itself is sacrificed.

Read the selection with a combination of the three

energies. Continue to use the intellect freely in its capacity to search, question, wonder, and probe—not yet to mold, form, or choose; do this despite the fact that the meaning is by now illuminated by new perceptions and ideas from the rhythms, tones and sound effects that you have explored in the first three exercises. You should find yourself wandering at random down the three paths of the three energies; they will intersect and one will lead you back to another. As you become totally involved with the moment-to-moment reality, let that energy lead that you feel first; let the interpretation and the use of the energies remain free and unstructured; let yourself wander—with awareness—through ignorance, finding new insights as you go; let the vocal life express and inspire the emotional life at the same time.

As you gain confidence with these exercises, you will begin to realize how truly the trinity of actions is a totality—one energy leading easily into or blending with another. When tonal action leads, the structural form is also constant; when structural action leads, a great many accented syllables fall into a natural call focus for emphasis; and consonant action plays in and out between the other actions, adding percussion and melody, color and vitality, rhythm and intelligibility. This is the time for exploring still greater variations and uncovering still more ideas, which begin to fashion the actor's choices and provide the materials with which the director can create.

An Exploration of a Technique

Let these exercises and the sensations you experience, lead you where they will, remembering always to stay with them, to be aware, to be involved. You may want to repeat each section several times, to explore all the potentials and exploit all the variations of each energy. Play with each new approach to the text, letting bizarre and eccentric effects take over, even at first to the exclusion of meaning and interpretation. As long as you retain your involvement and let the consonant energy and the feeling of the sound coursing through the bone interact with the emotional perceptions they evoke, new meanings and new interpretations will continue to evolve out of this exercise: For it is still an exercise in creatively exploring, discovering, inventing and exploiting sound. Concentrate on letting an understanding of the text grow out of the vocal life rather than letting the tonal quality be predetermined by an intellectually perceived meaning in the text.

Do not be afraid to be wrong. Perhaps the most devastating thing that can be said about an actor is: "He never made a real mistake." If you never make a mistake, if you never go wrong or too far out, if you never violate the rules of taste, order, and form, you will never begin to investigate the range of possibilities within a role or, more importantly, within yourself. The careful actor becomes the "adequate" actor, who is really a bad actor by omission. He stays carefully within the bounds of his own capabilities, within the bounds of the right way to do things, never venturing beyond to see whether there may not be more exciting possibilities, as well as dangers, there. He cannot be criticised for what he does, but he can easily be overlooked; any character he plays on stage leads a pallid half life for lack of what he does not do. To be bad by commission, however, is a learning process. The great actor transcends concepts of the right or the wrong way. The new and the exciting lie outside the accepted boundaries. I suspect that an actor who has never been discouragingly bad, at least alone with himself, will never be really excitingly good. The teacher as well as the student must be aware of the value of being wrong and the importance of letting the student explore freely without the constricting concept of a "right way."

Searching for Opposites

As you let your vocal life freely explore the text and your own emotional life, many different sides of a character, many unexpected glimpses into his depths, will begin to evolve. You may find cruelty in Hamlet and kindness in Iago, petulance in Juliet and beauty in Mistress Quickly. *Don't look just for reinforcement of emotion that seems implicit in the text.* Look for possible contradictions; the quick comic rhythm where the meaning is sinister, the tone of a caress in an expression of hatred. A search for opposites can uncover and help create subtle nuances that escape the actor when he approaches them directly. When you cannot quite find the precise quality of a word or speech or scene, the opposite of what you think that quality is may come more easily. Work on this opposite; then proceed to *its* opposite, which may surprise you by being more appropriate than your original conception. Sometimes you may even come upon a quality you had never thought to look for. When opposites seem equally valid, you have a better grasp of the real contradictions of a character. Look at a seagull, admire its beauty; then catch the scavenger quality as it dives for fish in the sea. Notice the miniscule grotesquerie of the pecking of the large beak; then watch again the majesty of its flight, and you have a better idea of what a seagull really is . . . something more than a graceful V against the sky.

The search for opposites is particularly adapted to breaking preconceived patterns. If, in reading a strongly rhythmic text, such as Elizabethan blank verse, you find it difficult to free yourself from the internal rhythm of the meter, you might try an opposing rhythm. If the accent is on the second beat, explore the effects of accenting every third beat, or every first beat. Play with it like the musician who explores the quality of a fox-trot melody by experimenting with it as a waltz or rhumba. One energy can also break the emotional pattern of another: try supressing the intense emotion of a call with sharp consonant action, or taming the call with a more confident surface of structural action.

Uncovering the Subtext

When the same actor reads the same speeches repeatedly with consonant, structural, or tonal energy, thereby creating a different psychological atmosphere, different moods, different vocal music, different patterns each time, the exercise may well illuminate the *subtext* of the lines, the subconscious of the character, and, interestingly enough, possibly the subconscious of the actor. What may be happening is that as you explore all the possible ways of saying something, you are at the same time becoming more acutely aware of possible ways of feeling. Now, when you synthesize the energies and put together the insights you have gotten from each, you will create original and valid total characterizations that contain the complexity and the inevitability of life on a larger scale.

This exploration of the text of a role with each of the energies of vocal life is not just an early training exercise; it can be a useful approach throughout an actor's career. With experience, you will learn to shortcut some steps mentally, but this basic use of the energies with true involvement will always uncover unsuspected truths. Not only is it useful for getting a thorough grounding in a role early in rehearsal, but a quick return to it now and then will break undesirable patterns that may accumulate in rehearsal or performance. It may add new insights and restore vitality when your playing has gone stale through custom—although custom should never have that effect if you maintain your involvement with the two trinities—structural-tonal-consonant and vocal-physical-emotional.

The creative function of vocal life may even make sense out of nonsense. One of the most popularly misunderstood lines in Shakespeare is Juliet's cry: "Romeo, Romeo, wherefore art thou Romeo?" The question is "Why?" but for years unsophistocated audiences, scores of comedians, at least one famous actress, and a brilliantly budding young director have misconstrued it as "where?" Yet an actress with this misconception might gain an intimation of the true meaning if she practices her vocal variations with real involvement and real awareness of what is happening as each of the energies probes the text. With this intimation in mind, an intelligent study of the text will reveal the rest. Actors as well as audiences sometimes ask "what does it all mean?" when they approach one of the plays of the Theatre of the Absurd. Here, especially, no intellectual probing of the text will necessarily provide an answer because the meaning is in the emotion and finally in the actor himself—as well as in the audience. Only through the internal experience of vocal life probing emotional life, can the actor hope to perceive such meaning for himself and externalize it for the audience.

If you have involved yourself in these exercises, you will not "speak lines" that hang naked in space; you will not speak words that are useless, empty receptacles—you will have something to say, and it will stand out against a background of perceptions. Your vocal life will be so intrinsic a part of you that you will be only indistinctly aware of its dynamics, knowing that meaning and purpose come not from the word symbol, but from inside you.

Practice Material for Developing Vocal Life

Throughout these exercises, remember that essentially you are still working with a trinity of actions even though a particular action is in the lead. Be free and inventive with each action, never losing sight of the fact that you are uttering not words but meanings and feelings. Four of the selections—the speeches of Richard II, Hamlet, Queen Margaret, and Ophelia—will be used with each energy. You will find different rhythms, different nuances, different sides of the character in each reading. The markings in the margins are only guidelines or indications; you may choose to use them in the beginning, but there are many more to be found from your own exploration.

The short bit of creative analysis of a few lines from the speech of Richard II is included here only as a brief example of the potent contribution each reading and each action can make to "in depth" interpretation and understanding. We have intentionally refrained from expanding such evaluation and discussion because we do not want to *tell* you what you will find, and by doing so, perhaps compromise your own experimenting and your own discoveries. The last thing we want at this stage is to pre-determine or pre-suggest any part of the interpretation, the music, the effects of the exercise. Even when you become a virtuoso artist or a master teacher of this technique you must never permit your artistic talents to exploit a speech or a line or even a word until you have experimented with it and thoroughly explored it with the trinity of vocal actions. Only when you have successfully experienced and perceived *speech as acting* and *voice as acting,* are you ready to prepare for the performance of the still higher trinity of vocal, emotional and physical life on stage.

Exercise one—Communicate through the Vowels (Structural Action)

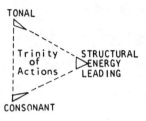

TONAL

Trinity
of
Actions

STRUCTURAL
ENERGY
LEADING

CONSONANT

The Role of the Trinity: Though structural action leads, you must feel at all times the resonant sensation of tonal action in its spread dilute form. Welcome the periodic call focus which drops in for special emphatic accents on such vowels as #1, #21, Ybuzz, and +Ybuzz; and remember that though the esthetic role of the consonants is played down in this exercise, good consonant action is always necessary for intelligibility.

The gentle music of the vowels produced by structural action is innately calm and self-contained; yet structural action need not be confined to the expression of these qualities. The literal meanings of words and phrases may clash with their calm expression to create unexpected emotional edges and corners. Observe the manner of Richard II when he addresses Bolingbroke and the nobles who have joined the rebellion against him. The words are full of bitterness and anger, but a full and predominant use of structural action softens the anger to chiding and the bitterness to self pity. The contrast between the manner and the words can even give a color of deliberate irony to the speech, but in the end the bitterness turned to self pity undercuts the irony and makes that irony ineffectual. See how the smoothness of the vocal expression can almost turn lines 6 and 7 into an absurdly reasonable request; how it provides a subtext to line 14 that turns "my master, God omnipotent" into "God, my special friend, my loving father, who protects me with that love." The full expression of structural action imposed on the underlying emotion gives an unreal air to the entire speech.

KING RICHARD:

note: Structural emphasis on a word turns the unbelievable into its opposite ... brings out irony and sarcasm in first 14 lines — turn lines 6 + 7 into an absurdly

We are amazed; and thus long have we stood

To watch the fearful bending of thy knee,   2

Because we thought ourself thy lawful king: 3

And if we be, how dare thy joints forget   4

To pay their awful duty to our presence?   5

If we be not, show us the hand of God   6

That hath dismiss'd us from our stewardship;   7

For well we know, no hand of blood and bone   8 *reasonable request—*

Try a deliberate stretch form on first 3 words, line 11—

On line 14, structural action emphasizes special possessive relationship between Richard and God.

Continue with your own markings— be inventive—both in your practice+ thoughts— Avoid the mechanical... Remember—not one single utterance is a valid exercise if it does not inspire or reflect an image... or a feeling of "as if" or subtext.

Can gripe the sacred handle of our sceptre,   9

Unless he do profane, steal, or usurp.   10

And though you think that all, as you have done,   11

Have torn their souls by turning them from us,   12

And we are barren and bereft of friends;   13

Yet know, my master, God omnipotent,   14

Is mustering in his clouds on our behalf,   15

Armies of pestilence, and they shall strike   16

Your children yet unborn and unbegot,   17

That lift your vassal hands against my head,   18

And threat the glory of my precious crown.   19

Tell Bolingbroke—for yond methinks he stands—   20

That every stride he makes upon my land   21

Is dangerous treason: he is come to open   22

The purple testament of bleeding war;   23

But ere the crown he looks for live in peace,   24

Ten thousand bloody crowns of mothers' sons   25

Shall ill become the flower of England's face,   26

Change the complexion of her maid-pale peace   27

To scarlet indignation, and bedew   28

Her pastures' grass with faithful English blood.   29

* * * * * * * *

Try to see how the last nine lines offer

Not all the water in the rough rude sea   30

Can wash the balm off from an annointed king;   31

The breath of worldly men cannot depose   32 *beautiful opportunity for lyrical variability...*

The deputy elected by the Lord: 33

For every man that Bolingbroke hath press'd 34

To lift shrewd steel against our golden crown, 35

God for his Richard hath in heavenly pay 3c

A glorious angel: then, if angels fight, 37

Weak men must fall, for heaven still guards the 38
right.

RICHARD II
Act III, ssc. 2 and 3

Suggestion for exploration: first select the most likely accent words containing stretch vowels... and emphasize these.... Then search for opposites by emphasizing the least likely accent words, and treat them as if they were the most significantly meaningful.... Then combine the two... explore the different rhythms, melodies & meanings

OPHELIA: O, what a noble mind is here o'erthrown!

The courtier's, soldier's, scholar's eye, tongue, 2
sword,

The expectancy and rose of the fair state, 3

The glass of fashion, and the mould of form, 4

The observ'd of all observers—quite, quite down! 5

And I of ladies most deject and wretched, 6

That suck'd the honey of his music'd vows; 7

Now see that noble and most sovereign reason, 8

Like sweet bells jangled out of tune, and harsh, 9

That unmatch'd form, and feature of blown youth, 10

Blasted with ecstacy: O, woe is me, 11

To have seen what I have seen, see what I see! 12

HAMLET
Act III, sc. 1

HAMLET: O, what a rogue and peasant slave am I!

Don't worry about following strict meter— the accents, melody, inflections, interpretive dynamics + nuances fully explored, will lend themselves to a correct and interesting meter of its own— Do not be timid in your exploration!

In this reading restrain the tendency to employ full "call" focus... Concentrate on the imagery created by the structural action sensations... You can be sharp and strong without using a "call"...

An occasional "call" is fine, but here, we want to explore the experiences, images, periences, images)

Is it not monstrous that this player here,   2

But in a fiction, in a dream of passion,   3

Could force his soul so to his own conceit   4

That from her working all his visage wan'd;   5

Tears in his eyes, distraction in's aspect,   6

A broken voice, and his whole function suiting   7

With forms to his conceit? And all for nothing!   8

For Hecuba?   9

What's Hecuba to him or he to Hecuba   10

That he should weep for her? What would he do,   11

Had he the motive and the cue for passion   12

That I have? He would drown the stage with tears,   13

And cleave the general ear with horrid speech;   14

Make mad the guilty and appall the free;   15

Confound the ignorant, and amaze, indeed,   16

The very faculties of eyes and ears.   17

Yet I,   18

A dull and muddy-mettled rascal, peak,   19

Like John-a-dreams, unpregnant of my cause,   20

And can say nothing; no, not for a king   21

Upon whose property and most dear life   22

A damn'd defeat was made. Am I a coward?   23

Who calls me villain? breaks my pate across?   24

Plucks off my beard and blows it in my face?   25 *ideas, moods and motivations which are the climate of structural action.*

Tweaks me by the nose? gives me the lie i' the   26
   throat,

As deep as to the lungs? Who does me this?   27

Ha!   28

'Swounds, I should take it, for it cannot be   29

But I am pigeon-liver'd, and lack gall   30

To make oppression bitter; or ere this   31

Continue, of course, with your own markings—

I should have fatted all the region kites   32

With this slave's offal:—Bloody, bawdy villain!   33

Remorseless, treacherous, lecherous, kindless   34
   villain!

O, vengeance!   35

HAMLET
Act II, sc. 2

QUEEN MARGARET: What! Were you snarling all before I came,

On each reading vary the intensity, inflections, sustentions, etc. Accent, slide up or down, be lyrical, be sarcastic, astonished, questioning, angry. . . . the choice is yours — but never make the same choice

Ready to catch each other by the throat,   2

And turn you all your hatred now on me?   3

Did York's dread curse prevail so much with heaven   4

That Henry's death, my lovely Edward's death,   5

Their kingdom's loss, my woeful banishment,   6

Could all but answer for that peevish brat?   7

Can curses pierce the clouds and enter heaven?   8

Why, then, give way, dull clouds, to my quick   9
   curses!

. . . . stay, dog, for thou shalt hear me.   10

twice. For example:
Sustained question-
ing on YOU (line 3),
followed by breath,
pause, then full
structural action
on ALL .... or try
sustaining all
followed with a
full structural
emphasis on YOUR.

note what happens
on next line if
SO is emphasized
with a short but
vigorous downward
slide —

If a "Call" comes
don't stifle it — —
If structural em-
phasis appears to
make the reading
sound pragmatic
or prosaic, let it!

If heaven have any grievous plague in store   11

Exceeding those that I can wish upon thee,   12

O, let them keep it till thy sins be ripe,   13

And then hurl down their indignation   14

On thee, the troubler of the poor world's peace!   15

The worm of conscience still begnaw thy soul!   16

Thy friends suspect for traitors while thou livest, 17

And take deep traitors for thy dearest friends!   18

No sleep close up that deadly eye of thine,   19

Unless it be whilst some tormenting dream   20

Affrights thee with a hell of ugly devils!   21

Thou elvish-mark'd, abortive, rooting hog!   22

Thou that wast seal'd in thy nativity   23

The slave of nature and the son of hell!   24

Thou slander of thy mother's heavy womb!   25

Thou loathed issue of thy father's loins!   26

Thou rag of honour! thou detested—   27

. . . . . Richard!

RICHARD III
Act I, sc. 3

Exercise two—Communicate through the Consonants (Consonant Action)

The Role of the Trinity: When consonant action leads, tonal action is confined primarily to the range of the Ybuzz focus, but it can include the intense stage whisper, a rich diluted tonal resonance, and even an

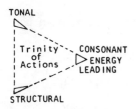

TONAL

Trinity of Actions

CONSONANT
ENERGY LEADING

STRUCTURAL

occasional concentrated tone on a low pitch. The consonants naturally minimize structural action, especially when they provoke an ominous, conspiritorial expression, but minimal good form should nevertheless be maintained on the vowels even though they are not sustained or emphasized.

With consonants in the fore, even Richard II can bite. Consonant action, with its crisp percussion, its whispered sibilance, its resonant legatos, gives perhaps the most natural expression to the anger and bitterness in the falling King's speech, but at the same time, it controls and channels these emotions. Richard can speak incisively with sharp command or he can almost whisper an intensive but controlled anger. You will see that lines 6 and 7 are now neither a request nor particularly reasonable, but a cold challenge to the rebellious nobles and beyond them to Bolingbroke. When this Richard speaks of "my master, God omnipotent," note how much more omnipotent this "omnipotent" is when he lashes it out with the consonant action. God is no longer a friend or a father, but a fellow ruler who fights beside the king and lends him some of His omnipotence. A touch of theatricality in the language throughout the speech may undercut the control and command of Richard's character, otherwise emphasized with consonant energy leading. Look for this and play with it for further exploration.

KING RICHARD:

Refer to p. 178 for guide to markings.—

Concentrate on exploring tempo, rhythm and intensity... note how the whispered sibilance + sustained consonant resonance creates a most natural "low-boil" anger and bitterness in Richard... Use the

We are amazed; and thus long have we stood

To watch the fearful bending of thy knee,   2

Because we thought ourself thy lawful king: 3

And if we be, how dare thy joints forget   4

To pay their awful duty to our presence?   5

If we be not, show us the hand of God   6

That hath dismiss'd us from our stewardship;   7

For well we know, no hand of blood and bone   8

Can gripe the sacred handle of our sceptre,   9

Unless he do profane, steal, or usurp.   10

And though you think that all, as you have done,   11

Consonant action to create and control this anger. Lines 6+7 now ex- press cold challenge ...Line 14 now sees God as a powerful partner...a fellow ruler ———

Feel the syncopated beats resulting from the unorthodox mix- ture of percussive & sustained tones—

Remember, don't be timid!! don't be mechanical!! Play the consonant creatively...For example: in line 29 the s in pastures & the sh in English & the d in blood must be played to project sense as well as feeling——

Feel the play of the violins in the Angel & Angels, the sound effect of the

Have torn their souls by turning them from us,	12
And we are barren and bereft of friends;	13
Yet, know, my master, God omnipotent,	14
Is mustering in his clouds on our behalf,	15
Armies of pestilence, and they shall strike	16
Your children yet unborn, and unbegot,	17
That lift your vassal hands against my head,	18
And threat the glory of my precious crown.	19
Tell Bolingbroke—for yond methinks he stands—	20
That every stride he makes upon my land	21
Is dangerous treason: he is come to open	22
The purple testament of bleeding war;	23
But ere the crown he looks for live in peace,	24
Ten thousand bloody crowns of mothers' sons	25
Shall ill become the flower of England's face,	26
Change the complexion of her maid-pale peace	27
To scarlet indignation, and bedew	28
Her pastures' grass with faithful English blood.	29

* * * * * * * *

Not all the water in the rough rude sea	30
Can wash the balm off from an annointed king;	31
The breath of worldly men cannot depose	32
The deputy elected by the Lord:	33
For every man that Bolingbroke hath press'd	34
To lift shrewd steel against our golden crown,	35

S m must . . . note the special meanings and images which result

God for his Richard hath in heavenly pay　36

A glorious angel: then, if angels fight,　37

Weak men must fall, for heaven still guards the
　right.　38

RICHARD II
Act III, ssc. 2 and 3

Here . . . consonant action lends itself to a legato. Lyrical sense

Note the deliberate sustained tempo— "quite, quite, down" . . . then "sucked the." note the changed tempo in lines 5, 6 + 7

Feel the effect of emphasized bass. fiddle in "O woe is me"

OPHELIA: O, what a noble mind is here o'erthrown!

The courtier's, soldier's, scholar's eye, tongue,
　sword,　2

The expectancy and rose of the fair state,　3

The glass of fashion, and the mould of form,　4

The observ'd of all observers—quite, quite down!　5

And I of ladies most deject and wretched,　6

That suck'd the honey of his music'd vows;　7

Now see that noble and most sovereign reason,　8

Like sweet bells jangled out of tune, and harsh,　9

That unmatch'd form, and feature of blown youth,　10

Blasted with ecstacy: O, woe is me,　11

To have seen what I have seen, see what I see!　12

HAMLET
Act III, sc. 1

Feel the lyric treatment of double underlined con- sonants . . sustained

HAMLET: O, what a rogue and peasant slave am I!

Is it, not monstrous that this player here,　2

But in a fiction, in a dream of passion,　3

Could force his soul so to his own conceit　4

the tendency is for a much slower and deliberate tempo — the legato quality will complement Hamlet's self analytical indulgence ... enjoy the feeling of this quality as you enjoy the indulgence —

note that after the first 9 lines the consonant energy seems to revert to more trigger sharp intensity --

From line 17, consonant energy resolves into a suggestion of help-less self pity — but still vigorous protestation —

Continue with your own mark-ings —

That from her working all his visage wan'd;   5

Tears in his eyes, distraction in's aspect,   6

A broken voice, and his whole function suiting   7

With forms to his conceit? And all for nothing!   8

For Hecuba?   9

What's Hecuba to him or he to Hecuba   10

That he should weep for her? What would he do,   11

Had he the motive and the cue for passion   12

That I have? He would drown the stage with tears,   13

And cleave the general ear with horrid speech;   14

Make mad the guilty and appall the free;   15

Confound the ignorant, and amaze, indeed,   16

The very faculties of eyes and ears.   17

Yet I,   18

A dull and muddy-mettled rascal, peak,   19

Like John-a-dreams, unpregnant of my cause,   20

And can say nothing; no, not for a king   21

Upon whose property and most dear life   22

A damn'd defeat was made. Am I a coward?   23

Who calls me villain? breaks my pate across?   24

Plucks off my beard and blows it in my face?   25

Tweaks me by the nose? gives me the lie i' the   26
        throat,

As deep as to the lungs? Who does me this?   27

Ha!   28 *[handwritten margin notes:]* from line 29... try harsh breathy in- tensity — try stage whisper type self hate ___ Try: cannot be, and cannot be — also lack gall ... with strong emphasis on: pigeon-livered, bitter and fatted-

'Swounds, I should take it, for it cannot be 29

But I am pigeon-liver'd, and lack gall 30

To make oppression bitter; or ere this 31

I should have fatted all the region kites 32

With this slave's offal:—Bloody, bawdy villain! 33

Remorseless, treacherous, lecherous, kindless villain! 34

O, vengeance! 35

HAMLET
Act II, sc. 2

QUEEN MARGARET:

[handwritten margin notes:] Cut with the vivid consonant energy for most venomously in- tense expression --but also use more or less legato treatment for an acerbic sarcasm... a lighter acidity

[handwritten:] Continue with your own markings —

What! Were you snarling all before I came, 1

Ready to catch each other by the throat, 2

And turn you all your hatred, now on me? 3

Did York's dread curse prevail so much with heaven 4

That Henry's death, my lovely Edward's death, 5

Their kingdom's loss, my woeful banishment, 6

Could all but answer for that peevish brat? 7

Can curses pierce the clouds and enter heaven? 8

Why, then, give way, dull clouds, to my quick curses! 9

. . . . stay, dog, for thou shalt hear me. 10

If heaven have any grievous plague in store 11

Exceeding those that I can wish upon thee, 12

O, let them keep it till thy sins be ripe, 13

And then hurl down their indignation 14

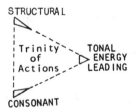

In line 17, try pause after friends, before going on to suspect, using a long incisive sound-effect and sharp double drum beats connecting directly into the word for

Start with line 22- try building into last word with aspirate (stage-whisper) hatefulness — with a harsh, breathy intensity

On thee, the troubler of the poor world's peace!   15

The worm of conscience still begnaw thy soul!   16

Thy friends suspect for traitors while thou livest,   17

And take deep traitors for thy dearest friends!   18

No sleep close up that deadly eye of thine,   19

Unless it be whilst some tormenting dream   20

Affrights thee with a hell of ugly devils!   21

Thou elvish-mark'd, abortive, rooting hog!   22

Thou that wast seal'd in thy nativity   23

The slave of nature and the son of hell!   24

Thou slander of thy mother's heavy womb!   25

Thou loathed issue of thy father's loins!   26

Thou rag of honour! thou detested—   27

      . . . . . Richard!

RICHARD III
Act I, sc. 3

Exercise three—Communicate through the Call Focus (Tonal Action)

The Role of the Trinity: When tonal action leads, structural action is so much a part of the form for the call focus that you cannot be without it. Since the full call tends to modify and even distort the vowels, you will need good consonant action to maintain intelligibility.

STRUCTURAL

Trinity of Actions — TONAL ENERGY LEADING

CONSONANT

The very nature of the call puts distance between the speaker and those to whom he speaks—if not a distance in space, then a distance in station or attitude. When Richard addresses the nobles, with an emphasis on call focus, he speaks down to them however close they may be, from the distance that separates a God-appointed king from his vassals. He neither chides nor challenges—he brandishes the fire of heaven. In lines 6 and 7, he now poses a clearly unanswerable and unthinkable question and answers it with an underlying threat of divine retribution. And "my master, God omnipotent" is no longer beside Richard, protecting him or fighting for him, but on high out of sight, ready to thunder destruction down on Richard's enemies.

The "K" symbol indicates where emphasis through concentrated calls is possible — —

Of course you need not use all of them . . . you have the choice of gentle or angry calls; whether it will be low, med. or high pitch . . . or sustained, staccato; inflected upward, downward or straight ahead . . . Explore the possibilities —

Remember that the call helps establish distance . . . Richard speaks from the distance of a God appointed King — — See how this

KING RICHARD:

We are amazed; and thus long have we stood

To watch the fearful bending of thy knee,   2

Because we thought ourself thy lawful king: 3

And if we be, how dare thy joints forget   4

To pay their awful duty to our presence?   5

If we be not, show us the hand of God   6

That hath dismiss'd us from our stewardship;   7

For well we know, no hand of blood and bone   8

Can gripe the sacred handle of our sceptre,   9

Unless he do profane, steal, or usurp.   10

And though you think that all, as you have done,   11

Have torn their souls by turning them from us,   12

And we are barren and bereft of friends;   13

Yet know, my master, God omnipotent,   14

Is mustering in his clouds on our behalf,   15

Armies of pestilence, and they shall strike   16

Your children yet unborn and unbegot,   17

That lift your vassal hands against my head,   18

And threat the glory of my precious crown.   19

Tell Bolingbroke—for yond methinks he stands—   20

That every stride he makes upon my land   21

approach changes the attack on lines 6 + 7 ... God om- nipotent is not now a peer + partner ... but a mighty spiritual + power- ful ally —

Is dangerous treason: he is come to open   22

The purple testament of bleeding war;   23

But ere the crown he looks for live in peace,   24

Ten thousand bloody crowns of mothers' sons   25

Shall ill become the flower of England's face,   26

Change the complexion of her maid-pale peace   27

To scarlet indignation, and bedew   28

Her pastures' grass with faithful English blood.   29

       *   *   *   *   *   *   *   *

Not all the water in the rough rude sea   30

Can wash the balm off from an annointed king;   31

The breath of worldly men cannot depose   32

The deputy elected by the Lord: 33

For every man that Bolingbroke hath press'd   34

To lift shrewd steel against our golden crown,   35

God for his Richard hath in heavenly pay   36

A glorious angel: then, if angels fight,   37

Weak men must fall, for heaven still guards the   38
    right.

Continue with your own markings — Experiment with them — explore them — and exploit them!

RICHARD II
Act III, ssc. 2 and 3

OPHELIA: O, what a noble mind is here o'erthrown!

Controlled, sus- tained, but not

The courtier's, soldier's, scholar's eye, tongue,   2
    sword,

The expectancy and rose of the fair state,   3 *too explosive calls will illum-inate the eerie, plaintive quality*

The symbol "Y" is used on the Y-buzz vowel when the pitch is quite low—

The glass of fashion, and the mould of form, 4

The observ'd of all observers—quite, quite down! 5

And I of ladies most deject and wretched, 6

That suck'd the honey of his music'd vows; 7

Now see that noble and most sovereign reason, 8

Like sweet bells jangled out of tune, and harsh, 9

That unmatch'd form, and feature of blown youth, 10

Blasted with ecstacy: O, woe is me, 11

To have seen what I have seen, see what I see! 12

HAMLET
Act III, sc. 1

As an experiment, try starting this Hamlet with concentrated call-focus laughter directly into the first word—

The "Y" over words like dream, tears, suggests strong Y-buzz tones on a low pitch rather than calls.

HAMLET: O, what a rogue and peasant slave am I!

Is it not monstrous that this player here, 2

But in a fiction, in a dream of passion, 3

Could force his soul so to his own conceit 4

That from her working all his visage wan'd; 5

Tears in his eyes, distraction in's aspect, 6

A broken voice, and his whole function suiting 7

With forms to his conceit? And all for nothing! 8

For Hecuba? 9

What's Hecuba to him or he to Hecuba 10

That he should weep for her? What would he do, 11

Had he the motive and the cue for passion 12

That I have? He would drown the stage with tears, 13

*Vary your readings!
First, let the pure
tonal energy im-
provise the images
+ your involvement.
Then, keeping Hamlet's
introspective ten-
dency in mind, let
the tonal action
feed that mood.
Then read again
with bitter hatred
of his step-father
as the objective.

note how the inevi-
table injection of
strong structural
action results in
the vowels assuming
most interesting +
varied coloring!

Remember: The only
good call is one that
feels easy, stimulating
+ unencumbered in-
side. The more the
Call is used properly
the more refreshed
+ invigorated, rather
than fatigued, will
you be*

And cleave the general ear with horrid speech;   14

Make mad the guilty and appall the free;   15

Confound the ignorant, and amaze, indeed,   16

The very faculties of eyes and ears.   17

Yet I,   18

A dull and muddy-mettled rascal, peak,   19

Like John-a-dreams, unpregnant of my cause,   20

And can say nothing; no, not for a king   21

Upon whose property and most dear life   22

A damn'd defeat was made. Am I a coward?   23

Who calls me villain? breaks my pate across?   24

Plucks off my beard and blows it in my face?   25

Tweaks me by the nose? gives me the lie i' the   26
    throat,

As deep as to the lungs? Who does me this?   27

Ha!   28

'Swounds, I should take it, for it cannot be   29

But I am pigeon-liver'd, and lack gall   30

To make oppression bitter; or ere this   31

I should have fatted all the region kites   32

With this slave's offal:—Bloody, bawdy villain!   33

Remorseless, treacherous, lecherous, kindless   34
    villain!

O, vengeance!   35

HAMLET
Act II, sc. 2

QUEEN MARGARET: What! Were you snarling all before I came,

Ready to catch each other by the throat, 2

And turn you all your hatred now on me? 3

Did York's dread curse prevail so much with heaven 4

That Henry's death, my lovely Edward's death, 5

Their kingdom's loss, my woeful banishment, 6

Could all but answer for that peevish brat? 7

Can curses pierce the clouds and enter heaven? 8

Why, then, give way, dull clouds, to my quick 9
    curses!

. . . . stay, dog, for thou shalt hear me. 10

If heaven have any grievous plague in store 11

Exceeding those that I can wish upon thee, 12

O, let them keep it till thy sins be ripe, 13

And then hurl down their indignation 14

On thee, the troubler of the poor world's peace! 15

The worm of conscience still begnaw thy soul! 16

Thy friends suspect for traitors while thou livest, 17

And take deep traitors for thy dearest friends! 18

No sleep close up that deadly eye of thine, 19

Unless it be whilst some tormenting dream 20

Affrights thee with a hell of ugly devils! 21

Thou elvish-mark'd, abortive, rooting hog! 22

Thou that wast seal'd in thy nativity 23

Handwritten marginal notes:

Start this Marg. with strong structural action on the 1st + 4th words — However should you be tempted to begin with a 'call' on what + snarling, remember that a very high pitch will be necessary — after which you would be wise to lower the call-pitch progressively, on the succeeding words so as to permit sufficient vocal latitude to come back with a vigorous call on the word *other* in line 2

Warning: No screaming and NO shouting!

The well-focused Ybuzz on "take" deep +Ytors for thy dearest furnishes excellent opportunity for controlled intensity as well as providing a vocal base for the build-up from the low pitched Ybuzz *tones, to your highest, sharpest, most hysterical vocal pitch at the end of the up-slide call on:*

thou destested ...Richard

The slave of nature and the son of hell!   24

Thou slander of thy mother's heavy womb!   25

Thou loathed issue of thy father's loins!   26

Thou rag of honour! thou detested—   27

　　　. . . . . Richard!

RICHARD III
Act I, sc. 3

Exercise four—Communication through the Combined Trinity

By now, your three exploratory interpretations should have shown you the infinite possibilities of vocal life, the individual colors and dimensions given the words by each of the energies, the fullness of expression possible with the trinity. Now put them together and see how the complexity of the character grows. In the speech from *Richard II,* you will see that each of the possibilities you have uncovered with each of the energies is echoed in the complete vocal life of the character. As one energy leads for a time, then abruptly gives way to another, the actor that lies under the surface of the king begins to come through, fully illuminating the inability to *be* anything but only to *play* at being that lies at the heart of Richard's tragedy. Perhaps, as you move from one of his roles to another, you may find, albeit submerged, the fear and panic that every role strives to suppress and that threatens constantly to break through.

KING RICHARD:

Add your own comments and make your own markings — You are on your own — ENJOY it!

We are amazed; and thus long have we stood

To watch the fearful bending of thy knee,

Because we thought ourself thy lawful king:

And if we be, how dare thy joints forget

To pay their awful duty to our presence?

If we be not, show us the hand of God

That hath dismiss'd us from our stewardship;

For well we know, no hand of blood and bone

Possible varia-
tions for the
"K" call symbol:

staccato (abrupt)
K̂ - upward
Ǩ - downward
Ǩ - straight ahead

short (but not
        abrupt)
K↗ - upward
K↘ - downward
K→ - straight

Sustained (lyric)
K↗ - upward
K↘ - downward
K→ - straight

Sustained (emo-
        tional)
K⌇ - up
K⌇ - down
K⌇ - straight

Can gripe the sacred handle of our sceptre,

Unless he do profane, steal, or usurp.

And though you think that all, as you have done,

Have torn their souls by turning them from us,

And we are barren and bereft of friends;

Yet know, my master, God omnipotent,

Is mustering in his clouds on our behalf,

Armies of pestilence, and they shall strike

Your children yet unborn and unbegot,

That lift your vassal hands against my head,

And threat the glory of my precious crown.

Tell Bolingbroke—for yond methinks he stands—

That every stride he makes upon my land

Is dangerous treason: he is come to open

The purple testament of bleeding war;

But ere the crown he looks for live in peace,

Ten thousand bloody crowns of mothers' sons

Shall ill become the flower of England's face,

Change the complexion of her maid-pale peace

To scarlet indignation, and bedew

Her pastures' grass with faithful English blood.

* * * * * * * *

Not all the water in the rough rude sea

Can wash the balm off from an annointed king;

The breath of worldly men cannot depose

The deputy elected by the Lord:

For every man that Bolingbroke hath press'd

To lift shrewd steel against our golden crown,

God for his Richard hath in heavenly pay

A glorious angel: then, if angels fight,

Weak men must fall, for heaven still guards the
  right.

RICHARD II
Act III, ssc. 2 and 3

OPHELIA: O, what a noble mind is here o'erthrown!

The courtier's, soldier's, scholar's eye, tongue,
  sword,

The expectancy and rose of the fair state,

The glass of fashion, and the mould of form,

The observ'd of all observers—quite, quite down!

And I of ladies most deject and wretched,

That suck'd the honey of his music'd vows;

Now see that noble and most sovereign reason,

Like sweet bells jangled out of tune, and harsh,

That unmatch'd form, and feature of blown youth,

Blasted with ecstacy: O, woe is me,

To have seen what I have seen, see what I see!

HAMLET
Act III, sc. 1

HAMLET: O, what a rogue and peasant slave am I!

Is it not monstrous that this player here,

But in a fiction, in a dream of passion,

Could force his soul so to his own conceit

That from her working all his visage wan'd;

Tears in his eyes, distraction in's aspect,

A broken voice, and his whole function suiting

With forms to his conceit? And all for nothing!

For Hecuba?

What's Hecuba to him or he to Hecuba

That he should weep for her? What would he do,

Had he the motive and the cue for passion

That I have? He would drown the stage with tears,

And cleave the general ear with horrid speech;

Make mad the guilty and appall the free;

Confound the ignorant, and amaze, indeed,

The very faculties of eyes and ears.

Yet I,

A dull and muddy-mettled rascal, peak,

Like John-a-dreams, unpregnant of my cause,

And can say nothing; no, not for a king

Upon whose property and most dear life

A damn'd defeat was made. Am I a coward?

Who calls me villain? breaks my pate across?

Plucks off my beard and blows it in my face?

Tweaks me by the nose? gives me the lie i' the
    throat,

As deep as to the lungs? Who does me this?

Ha!

'Swounds, I should take it, for it cannot be

But I am pigeon-liver'd, and lack gall

To make oppression bitter; or ere this

I should have fatted all the region kites

With this slave's offal:—Bloody, bawdy villain!

Remorseless, treacherous, lecherous, kindless
    villain!

O, vengeance!

HAMLET
Act II, sc. 2

QUEEN MARGARET: What! Were you snarling all before I came,

Ready to catch each other by the throat,

And turn you all your hatred now on me?

Did York's dread curse prevail so much with heaven

That Henry's death, my lovely Edward's death,

Their kingdom's loss, my woeful banishment,

Could all but answer for that peevish brat?

Can curses pierce the clouds and enter heaven?

Why, then, give way, dull clouds, to my quick
    curses!

. . . . stay, dog, for thou shalt hear me.

If heaven have any grievous plague in store

Exceeding those that I can wish upon thee,

O, let them keep it till thy sins be ripe,

And then hurl down their indignation

On thee, the troubler of the poor world's peace!

The worm of conscience still begnaw thy soul!

Thy friends suspect for traitors while thou livest,

And take deep traitors for thy dearest friends!

No sleep close up that deadly eye of thine,

Unless it be whilst some tormenting dream

Affrights thee with a hell of ugly devils!

Thou elvish-mark'd, abortive, rooting hog!

Thou that wast seal'd in thy nativity

The slave of nature and the son of hell!

Thou slander of thy mother's heavy womb!

Thou loathed issue of thy father's loins!

Thou rag of honour! thou detested—

. . . . . Richard!

RICHARD III
Act I, sc. 3

VOLPONE: Why droops my Celia?
Thou hast in place of a base husband found
A worthy lover; use thy fortune well,
With secrecy and pleasure. See, behold
What thou art queen of; not in expectation,
As I feed others, but possessed and crowned.
See, here, a rope of pearl, and each more orient

Than that the brave Egyptian queen caroused;
Dissolve and drink 'em. See, a carbuncle
May put out both the eyes of our St. Mark;
A diamond would have bought Lollia Paulina
When she came in like star-light, hid with jewels
That were the spoils of provinces; take these,
And wear, and lose 'em; yet remains an earring
To purchase them again, and this whole state.
A gem but worth a private patrimony
Is nothing; we will eat such at a meal.
The heads of parrots, tongues of nightingales,
The brains of peacocks, and of ostriches
Shall be our food, and, could we get the phoenix,
Though nature lost her kind, she were our dish.

VOLPONE
Act III, sc. 7

VIOLA: Make me a willow cabin at your gate,
And call upon my soul within the house;
Write loyal cantons of contemned love,
And sing them loud, even in the dead of night;
Holla your name to the reverberate hills,
And make the babbling gossip of the air
Cry out Olivia! O, you should not rest
Between the elements of air and earth,
But you should pity me.

TWELFTH NIGHT
Act I, sc. 5

His sneezings flash forth light,
And his eyes glow like the eyelids of the morning.
Out of his mouth go burning lamps,
And sparks of fire leap out.
Out of his nostrils goeth smoke,
As out of a seething pot or caldron.
His breath kindleth coals,
And a flame goeth out of his mouth.
In his neck remaineth strength,
And terror danceth before him.

The flakes of his flesh are joined together:
They are firm in themselves; they cannot be moved.
His heart is as firm as a stone;
Yea, as hard as a piece of the nether millstone.

BOOK OF JOB

There is sweet music here that softer falls
    than petals from blown roses on the grass,
Or night-dews on still waters between walls
    of shadowy granite, in a gleaming pass;
Music that gentler on the spirit lies,
    than tir'd eyelids upon tir'd eyes;
Music that brings sweet sleep down from the bliss-
                                        ful skies.
Here are cool mosses deep,
And thro' the moss the ivies creep,
And in the stream the long-leaved flowers weep,
And from the craggy ledge the poppy hangs in sleep.

ALFRED, LORD TENNYSON
Choric Song 1

I am aware that many object to the severity of my
language; but is there not cause for severity?
I will be as harsh as Truth and as uncompromising
as Justice.
On this subject I do not wish to think or speak or
write with moderation.
No! No!
Tell a man whose house is on fire to give a moder-
ate alarm; tell him to moderately rescue his wife
from the hands of the ravishers; tell the mother
gradually to extricate her babe from the fire into
which it has fallen—but urge not me to use modera-
tion in a cause like the present.
I am in earnest—
I will not equivocate—
I will not excuse—
I will not retreat a single inch—and I will be heard.
The apathy of the people is enough to make every

statue leap from its pedestal and hasten the
resurrection of the dead.

WILLIAM LLOYD GARRISON

MARULLUS: Wherefore rejoice? What conquest brings he home?
What tributaries follow him to Rome,
To grace in captive bonds his chariot-wheels?
You blocks, you stones, you worse than senseless
things!
O you hard hearts, you cruel men of Rome,
Knew you not Pompey?

JULIUS CAESAR
Act I, sc. 1

Beyond a mortal man impassioned far,
At these voluptuous accents, he arose,
Ethereal, flushed, and like a throbbing star
Seen 'mid the sapphire heaven's deep repose;
Into her dream he melted, as the rose
Blendeth its odor with the violet,—
Solution sweet: meantime the frostwind blows
Like Love's alarum, pattering the sharp sleet
Against the window-panes; St. Agnes' moon hath
set.

JOHN KEATS
The Eve of St. Agnes

OTHELLO: It is the cause, it is the cause, my soul;
Let me not name it to you, you chaste stars!
It is the cause—Yet I'll not shed her blood,
Nor scar that whiter skin of hers than snow,
And smooth as monumental alabaster.
Yet she must die, else she'll betray more men.
Put out the light, and then put out the light:
If I quench thee, thou flaming minister,
I can again thy former light restore,
Should I repent me; but once put out thy light,

Thou cunning'st pattern of excelling nature,
I know not where is that Promethean heat
That can thy light relume. When I have pluck'd
                                     thy rose,
I cannot give it vital growth again,
It needs must wither: I'll smell it on the tree—
O balmy breath, that dost almost persuade
Justice to break her sword! One more, one more—
Be thus when thou art dead, and I will kill thee
And love thee after. One more, and this the last:
So sweet was ne'er so fatal. I must weep,
But they are cruel tears: this sorrow's heavenly;
It strikes where it doth love.—She wakes.

                                     OTHELLO
                                     Act V, sc. 2

JULIET: Gallop apace, you fiery-footed steeds,
Toward Phoebus' lodging; such a waggoner
As Phaeton would whip you to the west,
And bring in cloudy night immediately.
Spread thy close curtain, love-performing night!
That runaway's eyes may wink, and Romeo
Leap to these arms, untalk'd of and unseen!
Lovers can see to do their amorous rites
By their own beauties; or, if love be blind,
It best agrees with night—Come civil night,
Thou sober-suited matron, all in black,
And learn me how to lose a winning match,
Play'd for a pair of stainless maidenhoods:
Hood my unmann'd blood, bating in my cheeks, .
With thy black mantle; till strange love, grown
                                     bold,
Think true love acted simple modesty.

                                     ROMEO AND JULIET
                                     Act III, sc. 2

ANTONY: O! pardon me, thou bleeding piece of earth,
That I am meek and gentle with these butchers;
Thou art the ruins of the noblest man

That ever lived in the tide of times.
Woe to the hand that shed this costly blood!
Over thy wounds now do I prophesy—
Which like dumb mouths do ope their ruby lips
To beg the voice and utterance of my tongue—
A curse shall light upon the limbs of men;
Domestic fury and fierce civil strife
Shall cumber all the parts of Italy;
Blood and destruction shall be so in use,
And dreadful objects so familiar,
That mothers shall but smile when they behold
Their infants quarter'd with the hands of war;
All pity chok'd with custom of fell deeds:
And Caesar's spirit, ranging for revenge,
With Ate by his side come hot from hell,
Shall in these confines with a monarch's voice
Cry Havoc, and let slip the dogs of war;
That this foul deed shall smell above the earth
With carrion men, groaning for burial.

JULIUS CAESAR
Act III, sc. 1

LADY MACBETH: The raven himself is hoarse
That croaks the fatal entrance of Duncan
Under my battlements. Come, you spirits
That tend on mortal thoughts, unsex me here,
And fill me from the crown to the toe top-full
of direst cruelty. Make thick my blood;
Stop up th' access and passage to remorse,
That no compunctious visitings of nature
Shake my fell purpose nor keep peace between
Th' effect and it. Come to my woman's breasts
And take my milk for gall, you murd'ring ministers,
Wherever in your sightless substances
You wait on nature's mischief. Come, thick night,
And pall thee in the dunnest smoke of hell,
That my keen knife see not the wound it makes,
Nor heaven peep through the blanket of the dark
To cry 'hold, hold!'

MACBETH
Act I, sc. 5

VOLPONE: 'Tis the beggar's virtue;
If thou hast wisdom, hear me Celia.
Thy baths shall be the juice of July-flowers,
Spirit of roses, and of violets,
The milk of unicorns, and panthers' breath
Gathered in bags and mixed with Cretan wines.
Our drink shall be prepared gold and amber,
Which we will take until my roof whirl round
With the vertigo; and my dwarf shall dance,
My eunuch sing, my fool make up the antic.
Whilst we, in changed shapes, act Ovid's tales,
Thou like Europa now, and I like Jove,
Then I like Mars, and thou like Erycine;
So of the rest, till we have quite run through,
And wearied all the fables of the gods.
Then will I have thee in more modern forms,
Attired like some sprightly dame of France,
Brave Tuscan lady, or proud Spanish beauty;
Sometimes unto the Persian Sophy's wife,
Or the Grand Seignieur's mistress; and, for change,
To one of our most artful courtesans,
Or some quick Negro, or cold Russian;
And I will meet thee in as many shapes;
Where we may so transfuse our wand'ring souls
Out at our lips and score up sums of pleasures,
That the curious shall not know
How to tell them as they flow;
And the envious, when they find
What their number is, be pined.

VOLPONE
Act III, sc. 7

QUEEN MARGARET: Alas, poor York! but that I hate thee deadly,
I should lament thy miserable state.
I prithee, grieve to make me merry, York.
What, hath thy fiery heart so parch'd thine entrails
That not a tear can fall for Rutland's death?
Why art thou patient man? thou shouldst be mad;
And I, to make thee mad, do mock thee thus.
Stamp, rave, and fret, that I may sing and dance.
Thou wouldst be fee'd, I see, to make me sport;

York cannot speak unless he wears a crown—
A crown for York!—and lords, bow low to him—
Hold you his hands whilst I do set it on.

HENRY VI, PART III
Act I, sc. 4

KING HENRY: Once more into the breach, dear friends, once
more;
Or close the wall up with our English dead!
In peace there's nothing so becomes a man
As modest stillness and humility:
But when the blast of war blows in our ears,
Then imitate the action of the tiger;
Stiffen the sinews, summon up the blood,
Disguise fair nature with hard-favor'd rage;
Now set the teeth and stretch the nostril wide;
Hold hard the breath and bend up every spirit
To his full height!—On, on, you noblest English,
Whose blood is fet from fathers of war-proof!—
Be copy now to men of grosser blood,
And teach them how to war! And you, good yoe-
men,
Whose limbs were made in England, show us here
The mettle of your pasture; let us swear
That you are worth your breeding: which I doubt
not;
For there is none of you so mean and base,
That hath not noble lustre in your eyes.
I see you stand like greyhounds in the slips,
Straining upon the start. The game's afoot:
Follow your spirit, and upon this charge
Cry—God for Harry! England! and St. George!

HENRY V
Act III, sc. 1

GONERIL: Come, sir!
This admiration is much o' the savour
Of other your new pranks. I do beseech
You understand my purposes aright;

As you are old and reverent, should be wise.
Here do you keep a hundred knights and squires,
Men so disorder'd, so debosh'd and bold,
That this our court, infected with their manners,
Shows like a riotous inn: epicurism and lust
Make it more like a tavern or brothel
Than a great palace. The shame itself doth speak
For instant remedy; be thou desir'd
By her, that else will take the thing she begs,
A little to disquantity your train,
And the remainder that shall still depend,
To be such men as may besort your age,
That know themselves and you.

KING LEAR
Act I, sc. 4

We hear much of "manifest destiny." That is a charming phrase. It tickles the ears of men; it panders to human vanity; it feeds the lurid flames of our ambitions; it whets the sword of conquest; it is an anodyne for the troubled conscience, but it lureth to destruction. At the last it biteth like a serpent and stingeth like an adder.

Oh yes! "manifest destiny" is a seductive thing. It is the beautiful, the irresistible, the wicked Circe beckoning us on to our undoing. The entire pathway of man since the day when Adam was driven from Eden with flaming swords is black with the wrecks of nations who hearkened to the siren song of "Manifest Destiny," and the epitaph upon whose tombstones is "They were, but they are not."

Hitherto we have been the favorites of Heaven; but let us not tempt fate too far or destiny will grow weary of partnership with us and dissolve it as she did with Napoleon at Waterloo.

CHAMP CLARK
On the Annexation of Hawaii

How long will ye vex my soul,

And break me in pieces with words?
These ten times have ye reproached me:
Ye are not ashamed that ye make yourselves
                                    strange to me.
And be it indeed that I have erred,
Mine error remaineth with myself.
If indeed ye will magnify yourselves against me,
And plead against me my reproach:
Know now that God hath overthrown me,
And hath compassed me with his net.
Behold, I cry out of wrong, but I am not heard:
I cry aloud, but there is no judgement.
He hath fenced up my way that I cannot pass,
And he hath set darkness in my paths.

BOOK OF JOB

OTHELLO: Soft you; a word or two before you go.
I have done the state some service, and they know't;
No more of that. I pray you, in your letters,
When you shall these unlucky deeds relate,
Speak of me as I am; nothing extenuate,
Nor set down aught in malice: then must you speak
Of one that loved not wisely but too well;
Of one not easily jealous, but being wrought,
Perplex'd in the extreme; of one whose hand,
Like the base Indian, threw a pearl away
Richer than all his tribe; of one whose subdu'd eyes,
Albeit unused to the melting mood,
Drop tears as fast as the Arabian trees
Their medicinal gum. Set you down this;
And say besides, that in Aleppo once,
Where a malignant and a turban'd Turk
Beat a Venetian and traduced the state,
I took by the throat the circumcised dog,
And smote him, thus . . .
I kiss'd thee ere I kill'd thee; no way but this,
Killing myself, to die upon a kiss.

OTHELLO
Act V, sc. 2

CHAPTER XII

Vocal Life II—
On Stage

YOU HAVE ACQUIRED a creative vocal life that can explore and communicate personality, whether it be your own personality or the assumed personality of a character in a play. Now you are ready to take that vocal life on stage. You have been working with the energies within yourself, exploring and acquiring the physical sensations of a number of inner actions, and synergizing these parts into an integrated skill that will make the fullest use of the vocal instrument and the communicating self. Now you yourself, with all your skills and insights acting together, are ready to integrate into another larger whole. You will interact with other actors, the spaces of the stage, the lights, the sounds, the stage reality, the audience—with all the assembled environmental stimuli of the temporary stage world. Out of this interaction, something must be created—not just something that happens on the stage, but something that happens from the back of the house to the top of the grid.

You wonder, not unnaturally: Will the use of what you have learned already be affected in any way? Here then are some of the situations that you will encounter onstage and some of the ways—both specific and general—in which they will affect, and be affected by, your vocal life.

The Offstage Voice on Stage

Is there, or should there be, a difference in quality between normal conversational speech and stage speech? Is there really a difference in quality or form between *dynamic* communication on and off stage? The answers are yes and no. What passes for conversational speech and normal behavior can rarely be transferred intact to the stage, and both director and actor should beware of trying to do so, because objective reality pales and becomes dull under the brighter lights or darker moods of even the most representational theatre. It is also true, however, that whatever goes into dynamic communication off stage is part of the actor's craft on stage. When you converse in a new setting with new people, for example, and attempt to communicate your feelings, enthusiasms, beliefs—in short, your own personal character—for the first time, you instinctively increase the creative use of vocal life, not to make a false impression but a more effective communication. The stronger inflections and colors of this speech are very little different from those of the actor at work on stage.

When you speak off stage, whether in quiet conversation or to call across an open space, you instinctively match the amplitude, pitch, and intensity of your voice to the distance between yourself and the listener. If the distance is short, and the speech situation intimate, you tend to reduce to a quantitative minimum the energies involved—tonal action, structural form, and even, to a degree, consonant vitality. With an increase in perceived distance or background interference, you instinctively adjust the intensity and the balance of the three energies to compensate for these changes.

Conditions on stage at first seem quite different from the variability of everyday life. The actor is aware that most of the audience in a theatre is consistently farther away than the audience in an average room and many times larger. When sound is deadened by a full house, the actor, who has been rehearsing in an empty theatre, may feel that his voice suddenly needs a superimposed power and range. To provide this, he may resort to higher pitch and greater volume all the time and so destroy all the creative qualities of vocal life in the attempt to project. To the actor, the communication with the audience is important, but to the audience, no matter how strongly it identifies with the performers, the perceived communication should be between the actors on stage, within the environment they create there. If this communication is conducted continually in a middle to high call focus—as if across wide spaces—the stage illusion is lost.

What the actor sometimes forgets is that the acoustics of an auditorium are planned to supply him with the additional reverberation, space, and resonance that he must supply for himself off stage when he attempts to reach a large audience or span a distance with his voice. Unless these acoustical properties are very poor, he can adapt his use of the trinity of actions to the perceived distances on stage exactly as he does to those off stage. The acoustics will carry this onstage communication across the distances of the auditorium, and the audience will receive a communication that enhances what they perceive as the stage reality rather than one that detracts from it because of what the actor perceives as the demands of the theatre.

For conversation at close range, consonant action leads and the Ybuzz follows closely, the voice staying primarily in the Ybuzz pitch range. The space between the teeth is comparatively small and the structural form actively forward though somewhat reduced. If a particular stage position or special stage business tends to muffle sound for the audience, instead of resorting to volume you must further reduce the size and at the same time improve the form of the inverted-megaphone shape so that you can feel a more vivid, concentrated Ybuzz focus on the small gum ridge area leading into the bone of the nose, while consonant action becomes more deliberate.

For conversation across a room, structural action leads. The tonal focus is strong but spread throughout the low and upper middle range, while an occasional low or middle call comes through for emphasis. This conversational and relatively quiet call quality should always be available to the actor on stage, as indeed it should be available to any trained person off stage.

In a very large room, or when the listener is in another room or some distance away outdoors, tonal action leads and the full gamut of the call focus—higher pitches, sustained tones, sharper accent, and tonal concentration—is brought into use as needed. Full structural form is, of course, a part of the call focus, and since some vowels may be modified, good consonant action must be maintained for intelligibility. On stage, the call is more often a response required by situation or character than by distance: Tonal action leads for energetic or excited communication, for the vigorous build, for addressing large crowds, for calling across or off stage, for creating the illusion of distance in an outdoor setting, for projecting over other voices or noise or music. The heightened emotional quality of classical Greek drama and of many scenes in the Elizabethan drama demands full use of the sustained call focus. Obviously not all plays demand such consistent intensity; but even when the intensified call is used much more sparingly, the actor will find that the well-focused voice will have a natural proclivity for the low to medium call quality. On the other hand, some kinds of intense emotion can be expressed most effectively, retaining dionysian passion as well as realism, by imaginatively working with the sensations of *suppressing* the total energy of the call focus.

The actor must remember that these are not absolute rules, to be followed without deviation, in any of these situations. They only provide a framework, within which the actor must continue to search for the most effective way of making his own communication. If he accepts rules without question, he fails to understand, and improperly applies, the approach. Try suggesting suppressed energy, for example, by addressing a large crowd with consonant, rather than tonal action in the lead, or feel the total energy of the call focus, in a quietly realistic scene, but actively suppress it to create emotional tension; there are thousands of possibilities for creative deviation. The general rules given here are only a base from which the exercises described in Chapter XI can be used for creative character development.

Whatever the situation, never attempt to project your voice to a particular point outside yourself or throw your words out through your lips, for that is tantamount to forcing your voice and creating a torrent of windy breath or abrasive sound. The feeling of the voice used correctly is an inside experience, and when the feeling is there, projection is there; for projection is simply a matter of concentrating the vocal tones in the resonating areas. What you must look for is not a desired result, such as "reaching the top row of the balcony," but the action-sensation that accompanies the result, and the result will take care of itself.

You must also avoid being pushed to what you feel is your vocal limit: Always feel that you have one more comfortable pitch, or just a little more volume, left if you need it—but never use it. When your voice sounds as if there were no more where that came from, you are not only straining toward premature vocal fatigue and general exhaustion, but telegraphing weakness and inadequacy to the listener. In the theatre, an actor who reveals his physical limits to the audience becomes just an actor and loses the chance to become part of the stage illusion.

The Open Stage

A special problem in voice projection for the actor is the changing form of the stage. More and more theatres are moving toward an open stage—either thrust, with the audience on three sides and one back wall, or an arena, entirely surrounded by the audience. With his back to a large part of the audience, the actor is confronted with the complex task of being audible and intelligible to all the audience while at the same time remaining real and natural—and in the relative intimacy of the open theatre, reality and naturalness are often at more of a premium than on the proscenium stage. To cope with this dilemma, the actor often attempts to "open his lips more" or "project his voice out in front of him more"—both poor solutions.

Playing with much of the audience behind you may create problems for certain kinds of acting, but if you have fully assimilated the method taught in this book, you should have little concern about the effective function of your voice and speech on any stage. Even within a proscenium you may find yourself far upstage, facing upstage, crouching or kneeling, or talking to an actor on the ground, but you should still be clearly heard and easily understood, even in a low, quiet voice.

The key is to use as concentrated a tone as possible. Even in intimate, informal, and close-range conversation, use more of the Ybuzz tonal action with a relatively reduced inverted-megaphone shape to produce a darker tonal focus sufficient for any purpose. You will feel the consonant action a little more incisively and the tonal action a little more vividly than usual on the gum ridge and nasal bone, but with these actions in easy, comfortable balance, the combination will not disturb the stage illusion. The Ybuzz is an extremely concentrated form of sound energy, and the energy output is minimal, conveying to the audience an impression of ease and intimacy.

When we tell you not to push for projection and a "stage voice," but to use the trinity of actions on stage as an intelligent extension of dynamic off-stage vocal life, we do not mean to encourage timidity about making energetic use of the vocal instrument. If you hold back when you should not and rationalize by calling it "sensitivity," your voice will not lend confidence, security, or vitality to your role; you will not play with that acquisitive strength, healthy curiosity, and joy that make acting exciting and an actor exciting to watch; you will not be a part of that slightly greater majesty of the stage. If you find yourself in the ambivalent position of being half-trained and uncertain in your voice and speech, your performance will be the confused product of fear and desire glaring at one another.

Vocal Characterization

In Chapter XI, you were given a set of exercises designed to expand your versatility and vocal creativity by application of each of the three vocal energies to the exploration and development of characterization in specific roles. Another approach that may expose even greater resources for characterization in your voice is to communicate and to express emotion through improvisation, not only without a script but without words, using sound alone. In practice, you will do well to use the exercises in Chapter XI and improvisation in close conjunction, alternating from one to the other. The exercises given here might be considered more basic in that they will help you to discover inflections and nuances that you can then apply to work with a script; yet in a way they go beyond the use of words in forcing you to explore even more thoroughly the communicative properties of vocal inflection. However you use them, the two approaches are mutually complementary.

In the work chapters on structural, tonal, and consonant action, you have already had exercises in improvisation with each of the energies alone. In the improvisations that follow, you will combine the energies and go far beyond the earlier exercises. Here you will experiment much further with the expressive properties of pure sound—its melodies, rhythms, and percussive qualities—along with such customarily nonverbal expressions as laughter, crying, and gesture. You will create a synesthesia in which sound *is* content—an orchestration of pure onomatopoeia. The structured exercises with a script and these improvised exercises both utilize the three energies as vehicles and as barriers at the same time: On the one hand, they help you to discover and release new sensations and sound patterns to create new expressions of emotion; on the other, they tend to confine the unbridled expression of emotion by setting boundaries. Used with freedom and awareness, these exercises will further the development of your voice as an instrument for expression as well as a source of new creative ideas.

In the first set of exercises, you will attempt to communicate with pure sound and rhythm:

Sit facing another actor, approximately six to ten feet away. First with the eyes closed, then with eye contact, use only structural action and the stretch vowels to communicate feelings and patterns of thought. Form no words; use only the sounds, but make as much use as you can of variations in pitch, range, laughter, rhythm, melody, and gesture. Use the stretch with abandon, with freedom, with an uninhibiting arrogance, to become aware of the uninhibited use of pure vowel sound communication.

Now do the same exercise with the consonants. Exploit all of the melodic, percussive, and sound effect qualities of the consonant orchestra to communicate thoughts and feelings. Be imaginative and uninhibited. Try to go beyond the expression of specific emotions into the exploration of new patterns of emotive expression and become aware of the communicative possibilities of orchestrated sound.

Do the exercise again with tonal action, using primarily the call focus on all pitches but include the concentrated Ybuzz and +Ybuzz focus. Inject freely all the inflections, intonations, and sustentions of tone that you can find. Use other expressions of emotion—such as laughter and crying—freely. You can begin to turn these into more advanced acting exercises by using the Ybuzz or the call as an object-image with which to try to reach and stay with your partner. Once you have made contact with your partner, twist or drill the Ybuzz object deeper and deeper into his head or heart or back. Try to change him into something else, his feelings into other feelings, his perceptions into different perceptions, his alliances into other alliances.

Now repeat the exercise using all of the actions—structural, consonant, and tonal—not as a finished improvisation but as a continued searching process.

In the next set of exercises, the consonants and call words are used for pure emotive expression:

In real life, emotions such as crying, sobbing, fear, hysteria, and disgust tend to denude, expose, or emasculate the victim. Using the consonants S, F, H, and SH, start out with the objective of not permitting these emotions to show. Suppression is a valuable facet of the actor's expression of emotion; the more he tries to hold back, the more intense and dramatic is the emotion itself. With just the pure sound of the consonants and the feeling it stimulates, you can both control and release the emotion. Clean and properly articulated consonants are not necessary in this exercise. As the consonants progressively permit a greater intensity or projection of emotion, the exercise may impose a breathiness, a jerkiness, a stomach and abdominal pressure, a trembling, and a shaking, quivering, and contorting of the face and body. The intermittent injection of vowel sounds or tones will further heighten the intensity or projection of the emotion expressed with the consonants.

Next, use the consonants M, N, NG, ZH, the Ybuzz, W, V, Z, and R to express wailing, anger, joy, crying, sobbing, laughter, fear, and ridicule. The consonant S can also be used on the last five. As you experiment with these consonants, you will find some of them more expressive and productive than others, but don't ignore the possibilities for new emotive expressions in unlikely sounds. Use your imagination and your improvisational talents and remain keenly aware of what is actually happening. You will find that laughter changes radically, for example, when you go from S to NG, then to M, then to Z, then to R, then to the Ybuzz.

Now use the call words *hello, it's hell, again, away, until, beware, it's good,* and *heaven* to express wailing anger, joy, laughter, ridicule, crying, sobbing, hysteria, fear, and disgust. Use any level or slide or series of tones or placements, but be careful not to strain or harm the vocal mechanism when using maximum pitch or volume. There is little chance of harm if you remember to coordinate the lip opening with the focus sensation on the hard palate and nasal bone, reducing and enlarging both together as the pitch is lowered or raised. Near the top of your voice, the expression of these emotions may require a lip opening close to a smile or the opening for the 6y vowel. Remember to experiment and explore *before* you exploit.

Now combine the expressive consonant exercises with the communication exercises and experiment with expressing and controlling emotion at the same time.

The Correct Use of the Incorrect Use of the Voice

Before you can experiment effectively and safely with extreme distortion of the voice for characterization, you must have complete mastery of the correct and natural use of voice and speech. You will be in a position to explore the creative possibilities of the *incorrect* use of the voice only when the action-sensations that accompany the natural and expressive use of the trinity of actions have become so firmly ingrained in your habit patterns of speech that you are acutely aware of any departure from correct use and of the effort involved in incorrect use. Without this mastery, the possibilities of damaging the vocal mechanism are very real.

As you have learned, when poor conditioning is overcome and the body is functioning as it wants to, the creation of beautiful, resonant tones by natural methods of sound propagation is always an effortless experience. As you learn to recognize the physical sensations of facial form and bony resonance that accompany effortless voice production, you become aware of vocal energy in terms of quality as well as quantity. Breathiness and abrasive throatiness are the sensations of energy moving into effort or input, and their effect, or quality, is unesthetic, while the effortless sensation of vibratory energy in the hard palate and facial bones signals the output of a properly focused sound. For normal speech our goal is maximal output from minimal input.

To achieve this goal, we work toward concentrating the activity of the vocal stream in the bony areas through the specific quality of feeling that this energy produces there. At the same time, we strive to generate and feel *inactivity* in the throat and larynx. We become aware of a *lack* of breathiness in the sound stream and the *absence* of sensation in the throat, because either activity would reflect irrelevant effort and disturbance of natural function and therefore an impedance of the resonant energy that represents useful output.

By learning how *not* to generate sensations of any sort in the throat and larynx—sensations that represent the incorrect use of the voice—you are establishing control over the function of the vocal sound stream in that area. When you learn to achieve and to sense *inactivity* as a *positive* thing, you become more acutely aware of the sensations of *activity*, and able to make finer distinctions among them. This is precisely the skill needed to utilize sound in the throat area for vocal characterization without producing strain, emotional tightness, or physical damage there. The awareness of inactivity gives you the ability to control the amount of activity in the throat with precision, and thus to go just so far and no farther. The balance you strive for in the natural, correct use of the voice is total energy in the resonant areas and total lack of energy, which represents effort, elsewhere; when your skill in that is finely honed, you can then create an equilibrium with effort itself. The correct use of the incorrect use of the voice is not a surrender to total, uncontrolled effort, but a balance between effort (wrong placement) and lack of effort (proper placement), with the wrong placement of the voice always firmly under control.

This concern with the destructive possibilities of the incorrect use of the voice is directed primarily at throat focus or at very high pitch and exaggerated amplitude. The other correct uses of the incorrect use of the voice require only objective listening and creative imagination. Nasal tones, sing-song speech, monotones, excessive lip movement, speaking through clenched teeth, stammers, speaking through one side of the mouth while that side of the face is held in splastic-like rigidity, and other poor speech habits will be used most effectively when your voice and speech skills are fully developed. They will be used with greater awareness and control of the distortion, but the physical distortions involved will not in any way be damaging to the voice.

This controlled use of the incorrect use of the voice is a difficult concept to grasp initially. Complete understanding and effective application will come only when you have fully assimilated the fundamentals and experienced the sensations of focused, resonant sound production—when this experience has become a habit. Only when you have learned the right way to use the vocal instrument as an integral skill will you gain the sure control to do the wrong thing imaginatively and with impunity.

When you feel qualified to experiment in the areas of incorrect use, you will find it helpful to record your initial attempts. Since the sound conduction through your own bones prevents you from judging by ear either the quality of these incorrect vocal sounds or the effects you are trying to achieve with them, you must utilize the tape recorder to hear yourself realistically through air conduction—to hear the different shades and subtle variations in sound that accompany the sensations of incorrect use of the voice as you experiment with them.

There are many possibilities for this kind of experimentation: You can work with nasal, throat, or pharyngeal placement of the voice; you can use a tight or protruded jaw, the side of the mouth, a curled lip, or a stiff upper lip; you can try speaking through a cough, hoarseness, or contracted throat muscles, or speaking inversely on inhalation—you will think of others. Often posture will directly affect the voice: Throw your shoulders back, making them weak and narrow; hollow your chest; affect a distended, lazy stomach—you will find that interesting vocal changes occur. As is true of all of the exercises in voice and speech, these must be performed with both concentration and abandon—they are exercises in exploration.

Building and Topping

To build a scene emotionally, vocally, or physically, and to top the previous moment are really two parts of a whole; the first is a process, the second a single action. Your voice is one of your most effective instruments for either building or topping, and a particularly effective way of training your voice for this use is the wind exercise using the call words *hello, away,* and *until.*

Taking each word in turn, begin on a very low pitch; siren up four or five pitches; then siren down two or three pitches; up again four or five pitches and down again two or three. Continue—all on one breath—until you reach your highest tone with the mouth wide open and then siren all the way down to the bottom of your range again, reaching the smallest lip opening. Think of yourself and the sound as a wind wailing eerily and gently building up intensity.

Remember, however, that important as effective use of the voice is to building and topping, neither of these two instruments of the actor's craft should rely exclusively on increased vocal volume and elevated pitch. For the creative actor, this is only one aspect of the technique and not always the most effective one. Anything that projects a heightening of suspense or a sharp increase of intensity or feeling can be used. A sudden or radical change of pace, whatever the direction, may do the trick. A climax can be topped by undercutting it as well as by riding over it. Anything that maintains a provocative, forward-moving transition, such as variation in tempo, body posture, or facial expression—no matter how quiet and controlled—can constitute effective building. The primary objective must be to continue, to heighten, to intensify, the actor's emotional situation and the movement of the action. You can achieve this by being smaller and quieter as well as bigger and louder. Topping can be many things—a stamp of the foot, a slap, a hiss; a whisper can top an emotional build as effectively as a shout.

But even sound and movement are not essential to topping—a pause can be equally effective, but it must not cause a letdown or break the forward movement of the dramatic moment, unless, of course, the break is the top. When the base level of energy that we sometimes call attention or concentration is maintained, a dynamic pause is not a stopping place but a bridge. This bridge can carry the end of one beat over into the next even as the first is fading away; there is no loss of energy in the space between as long as the actor's concentration is on something coming rather than something ended. The silence creates, not a void, but a thread of tension that draws the actor and his audience onward as effectively as—or more effectively than—a word.

Timing and Rhythm

The dynamic or interpretive pause is essentially a question of timing, and timing is *based* on rhythm—but timing is not rhythm. What timing *is* is difficult to discuss in concrete terms. The extensive definitions usually end in the conclusion that timing is essentially a feeling—a sense of moving or not moving, of speaking or not speaking, at exactly the right moment. Vaudevillians, tragedians, stand-up comedians all assure us that they don't really know the formula for effective timing, that it just happens to them because they feel it, that it happens in a different way in almost every performance.

What the actor feels, what he must feel and move with to keep the energy not taut but constant, is rhythm, his own rhythms, the rhythms of the words, of the production as a whole. Rhythms and tempos, both vocal and physical, can unearth a characteristic or a pattern of behavior for an actor if he lets himself move with them until the rhythm is built into the body. Timing is not a mental process; yet like everything else you do on stage, it must be practiced with awareness and control, but with freedom.

The ability to tap out a rhythm clearly for thirty-two measures is no assurance that you have the capacity to sense that right and elusive moment when action, reaction, or interaction will provide the properly timed beat in a scene. Being able to count is of questionable value in this instance. There may be only a semisecond's difference, or none at all, but on stage it's a lightyear chasm between the pause for a character's own reasons—whether the audience understands them at the moment or not—and the pause while the actor counts "one . . . two . . ."—even if he doesn't move his lips.

Even in music the metronome is a guide to rhythm, not its master, but stage timing can't even be guided by a metronome. A sensitive production of a play is much like a piece of music, but it is music without rigid rhythms, music that beats to the wayward pulse of the world. Spring almost never arrives on March 21, but there's a rhythm to the seasons nevertheless—only you never know precisely where the next beat is going to fall until you're there. The important point, perhaps, is that the production of a play does not have a single rhythm, but an enormous complexity of rhythms of lighting and movement, individual rhythms of actors, and *new* rhythms created as these counterpointing rhythms act on each other.

In musical terms, perhaps the closest approach to the relationship of the actor to rhythm is the jazz singer or instrumental soloist if he is creative and improvisational. Surrounded by instrumental rhythms, he does not conscientiously follow their beat; he finds his own way through them, occasionally with them, more often ahead or behind, playing around them, weaving his own melodic and rhythmic line. Moving freely away from the rhythms around him, he is yet never at odds with them, always aware of them—where they are at the moment, where they will be the next. The actor must find some of this freedom in his search for effective stage timing; it must not be something he follows meticulously, but something he plays with joyfully . . . con brio e con amore.

.The dual concept of relaxed energy and energetic relaxation is useful in timing. The balance and interaction between these two carries a timing and a rhythm of its own. An action, great or small, carries over into a moment of relaxation, which is already a preparation for the action to follow. There is no discrete distinction between rest and action in this concept, but a progressive gradient from one to the other. The continuous apprehension of this shifting continuum of rest and action within yourself, within the situation on stage, will carry you through with timing that acts on, and plays with, but never breaks, the rhythms of the production.

Stage Fright or Stage Excitement

Stage fright and stage nervousness are the unfortunate cognates of stage vitality and stage excitement. They are manifestations of disorganized and random configurations of energy—energy that is not being channeled into the total stage effort but is allowed to disrupt patterns of behavior, memory, coordination, and attention. This energy is crucial to dynamic performance but it can wreak havoc with the actor who is mechanically trained.

The physical sensations of fear that we describe as stage fright are not the private property of the ill-trained or inexperienced actor. They are physiological responses to the body's release of chemical substances into the blood stream in response to many different kinds of environment situation. These metabolic changes increase the *magnitude* of emotional reactions; they do not create the reactions. The result can be either destructive or useful energy. Whether the physiological reactions are channeled constructively or destructively depends on the individual's perception of these sensations in relation to the situation in which they occur—whether he perceives them as feelings of fear, excitement, anger, joy, or diffuse nervousness. Thus, adrenalin, which can stimulate strong and exciting performance when its effects are perceived in conjunction with strong motivation and confidence, can also disrupt performance in the face of fear and uncertainty. Whatever the situation, the chemical processes are always present and the actor can either learn to control their manifestations or be controlled.

Even the seasoned professional will often experience these physiological reactions as nervousness, but nervousness is a form of energy, and energy is essentially characterless; it can perform only the task assigned to it. On stage, nervous energy can be transformed into stage fright—knocking knees, a voice that squirrels into its higher pitches however you fight to control it, indecisive movement, or no voice and no movement at all. This happens because your only connection is with fear and you have lost all contact with yourself. But nervous energy can also be transformed into stage excitement, a quality that vitalizes and lights up your performance, an excitement and a joy that you share with your audience.

To transform nervousness into stage excitement, of course, you must be prepared. All of us have a number of potential responses, and nervousness or energy will reinforce these. But some will be competing responses, incompatible with one another; some weaker, some stronger, and the stronger will be reinforced more strongly and will tend to suppress the weaker. Your vocal life, when fully developed and integrated with emotional and physical life, can become an important key to effective control of stage fright. When you have learned to experience the physical sensations of voice and speech with awareness and relaxed energy and when *these sensations have become an integral part of the physical and psychological sensing devices that monitor other areas of emotional control and expression,* you will have acquired dynamic responses strong enough to overcome irrelevant responses that would undermine your performance. But without proper training, without integration into true vocal life, your voice and speech can work against you: If voice and speech are learned as skills separate from one another and from the acting sense, all three become responses competing with one another, and increased nervous energy on stage will lead to conflict and disorganization of behavior. If techniques of voice and speech have been imposed by rote or mechanical drill, they will become even more mechanical or routine under the pressure of stage performance; *the technique will show,* and when technique shows, stage excitement is gone. If you are poorly trained in voice and speech, whatever the approach, then stress will further weaken this part of your life on stage.

Concentration and Continuity

Energy can also be dissipated by unfocused attention, which is also a kind of competing response. If energy is to be used to create continuous stage excitement rather than disruptive behavior, it must be controlled and used with concentration, not sprayed in every direction like a display of fireworks that fizzles even before the initial "Ahhhhh" of the audience has faded. But you cannot concentrate on nothing, and you cannot concentrate on the act of concentrating. When an actor approaches concentration as an abstract concept and tries to concentrate in vacuo, too often instead of achieving clarification and awareness, he becomes totally inhibited by the effort. It is much like *trying* not to think about a red elephant.

To concentrate, you must begin with something you know about; you must have an object. In doing the exercises in this book, you have begun to learn how to use an image to reinforce the actions you perform and to shut out undesirable images by concentrating on their opposites. In the same way that an image aids in unselfconscious performance of an exercise, the right kind of concentration can lead to unselfconscious performance on the stage—concentration not on *what you are doing* but on *why you are doing it,* not on the response but on the stimulus. Only false emotions can come from concentration on an emotion, and only false concentration can come from attention to the act of concentrating. If an actress playing Juliet concentrates on sorrow in her final parting with Romeo, she can only counterfeit on a single note. But if she concentrates on the memory of the timid-reckless joy of her first encounter with Romeo from the balcony in the garden and lets the loss of that come through, she will begin to find the many subtle qualities of real sorrow. Your vocal life must be constantly stimulated by the moment or by a memory, by a sense memory of a past experience of your own or by an experience within the play—hopefully both.

To concentrate, you must get rid of useless distractions; you must know what *not* to think about. Ideas, impressions, and attitudes unrelated to your stage character or to the stage reality and self-conscious concern about yourself—how you look, how you sound, how the audience is responding to how you look and sound—contribute nothing to your creative life on stage. The actor who knows his part so well that his mind wanders away has just died onstage, although he walks and talks and may even marvelously imitate a man. This is obvious and only the worst kind of actor would expect to get by with so gross an inattention. But neither can he expect to move an audience if the object of his concentration is the effect his stage behavior is having on the audience. Not that the audience is not a part of the experience; the mood created by the response of an audience should indeed become part of the given circumstances on stage, part of the mood on stage; it should influence the rhythms and harmonies of the actors as a counterpoint melody does in music. But you cannot achieve this by keeping an eye on the audience to see if it is being moved. The interaction between an audience and a performance must be something that happens, not something that the actors try consciously to make happen. This may seem a fine distinction, but the end results are as far apart as trying and succeeding.

The objects of attention on stage are the given circumstances of the stage reality and the awareness of your vocal, emotional, and physical life as a functioning part of this stage reality. You must never think that you can get your technique down so well that you are not aware of using it and so can think of other things. The technique that can function in this way is an imitation of true technique, a surface completely independent of acting sense. True technique is an awareness of the action-sensations that help control your vocal life and the inextricable intertwining of these with the action-sensations of emotional recall and control.

And concentration must respond; it must move with the continuity of constant change. On stage—as in life—an object, your relationship to it, your emotions about it, and you yourself are undergoing constant change. Nothing remains what it was a moment ago. In life we usually move smoothly with these changes, not thinking about them; but on stage the wrong kind of concentration, too studied an awareness, can put our responses out of step with the real changes and produce a choppy, segmented performance instead of a smooth continuum. Within a specific speech, you need the same kind of relaxed, responsive attention. A word always comes *from* somewhere and goes *to* somewhere. Your involvement with the heart and soul of the word and the fleeting moment, and how you express it, come from what came before and feed into what follows. You must never utter a word or a speech or perform an action in complete isolation; they are all extracted from something and inserted into something else.

One thing is certain: Whether your concern is with a characterization or with a problem in concentration, there are many possibilities available to the actor who understands and uses his voice and speech according to the concepts articulated here regarding vocal and verbal life; but there are no gimmicks or easy formulas; a brilliant performance cannot be handed to the actor on a silver platter—he must work for it.

Warm-up Drill

Before you go on stage or into rehearsal, or when you get up in the morning, run through the following series of vocal exercises to prepare yourself for the performance or the day ahead. These exercises will help tone up, not only your voice, but your body and your concentration.

1. Ybuzz

step 1. Sustain an easy, calm, and vibrant Ybuzz on five or six of your lowest pitches.

step 2. Slide the Ybuzz up and down over a very small range.

step 3. Sing a melody on the Ybuzz, using only the lower third of your vocal range.

II. Ybuzz into +Ybuzz

step 1. From the Ybuzz, slide into the +Ybuzz on a pitch slightly higher than that of the Ybuzz itself. Don't dilute the tone; feel the beginning of the +Y fully focused in the bone of the nose.

step 2. Recite the alphabet, maintaining the Ybuzz tonal stream on all EE and A sounds—don't forget the H. If the structural form is good, the letters O, Q, U, and W should bring a low, quiet call sensation.

III. The Call

step 1. Do a series of easy but dark calls on medium pitches, using h'LLO, aWAY, unTIL, aGAIN, plACES.

step 2. Do the wind exercise on h'LLO, aWAY, unTIL.

step 3. Do the vendor's calls realistically and musically on a medium pitch level. Call "Strawberries . . . watermelon . . . cockles and mussels . . ." etc. Don't sing them—be a vendor, not an entertainer.

IV. The Stretch

step 1. From a Ybuzz, slide into the stretch vowels for diluted focus. Feel the dilute focus resonating throughout the mask as the rich Ybuzz diffuses into—#5, #6, 6y, ⅀, #4, #3, #21, #1, and #51. If the structural form is good, the last four will come closest to a calm, dark, low-pitched call.

step 2. Smoothly and with spontaneous tempo, count energetically from one to twenty; then recite the months of the year and the days of the week.

V . . . End up with:

A few comfortable but short sustentions of the medium call on h'LLO, aWAY, unTIL, plACES.

A vibrant, clean Ybuzz until you are ready to go on!

Some Final Reminders

Don't listen to your voice or your speech, on stage or off stage—listen only to others. Listening to yourself can only make you nervous and self-conscious; it is energy dissipated. Listening to yourself on stage tends to shut out what and who is around you, to disconnect you from the stage action; it becomes part of a vicious cycle of fear and withdrawal into greater fears, which totally disrupts stage excitement and stage illusion.

Don't spit and spray when you speak—at least don't make a practice of it; it is unesthetic, self-indulgent, and almost totally unnecessary, and it impairs good, clean diction—wet speech makes artistic consonant action very nearly impossible. Your fellow actors will certainly find the experience artistically disconcerting and an impedance to spontaneous emotional life on stage. A dry mouth and throat is one of the manifestations of nervousness, but a mouth full of saliva does *not* indicate that you are relaxed. Both underactivity and overactivity of the salivary glands are reflections of physical and mental discomfiture. Those with underactive glands must learn to collect saliva skillfully—to maintain a reasonable oral moistness—*and to swallow* the saliva in order to lubricate and relax the throat; those with overactive glands must form the habit of swallowing frequently to prevent flooding of the mouth. The key in both cases is to coordinate vocal action with swallowing, which is in itself a natural relaxing technique. But actors, speakers, or singers who have been taught to "throw" their voices *out* to an audience will often find it difficult to swallow in the process and will necessarily throw a fine spray as well. The vocal and verbal controls and relaxation devices inherent in the Lessac system, however, are the exact opposite of the force and pressures displayed by the voice throwers. If you rely on maximum forcefulness with minimum force—if you project a tonal stream rather than a breath stream—you are unlikely to spray your listeners or your fellow actors.

Don't rely on muscular tension to support your voice—don't contract your buttocks, tighten your abdominal muscles, or grip with your toes. The practice of tightening the muscles in one part of the body to offset tension in another is unrealistic, unscientific, and harmful. It should be obvious that if you consider the person as a whole, not a collection of unrelated parts, tightness in *any* part of the body only induces impingements and fixations in other parts.

Keep your body in good physical condition with some form of fairly strenuous, regularly scheduled exercise and a good sensible diet. Your voice reflects that condition. Don't eat a heavy meal —and *never* eat chocolates or nutty, syrupy, or sweet foods—just before a performance. Smoke or drink lightly—or better still, not at all. If you must have a hard drink, have only one—a short one—and make that do until the entire performance is over. Eat half an apple before going on—it soothes and cleans the throat.

As temporary relief when your throat hurts and you can't get to a doctor, try gargling every two or three hours with hot water—not scalding hot—mixed with a quarter teaspoon of salt, a quarter teaspoon of bicarbonate of soda, and an aspirin; when the pain is assuaged, leave out the aspirin. If gargling is inconvenient, I have found that chewing aspirin gum is helpful.

Don't force your voice—don't mistake volume for projection or strength of tone.

Use the Ybuzz to enrich and protect the lower third of your voice; with it, your voice should easily go at least four or five half pitches *below* your customary low conversational tones.

Real learning begins with feeling the experience in most human functioning and particularly in the development of skills. Learning continues only through successful doing—*not* through intellectual grasp.

Don't let your technique show. Any drill brought to mechanical perfection is most difficult to apply creatively. No actor—and for that matter no one else—ever feels any experience precisely the same way twice; therefore never do a speech or an action exactly the same way twice; instead, be a part of what is happening on stage, contributing and responding to it.

Be a teacher as well as a student. You learn best and get the most ideas from teaching. Be your own teacher to begin with, and become a practice teacher by working with other students.

CHAPTER XIII

The Whole Person

Communicates

*T*HERE ARE MANY WHO BELIEVE that in communication through speech, as well as in writing, the content is what really counts. But Heywoud Broun once said: "People respond *less* to ideas than to particular vocal tones"; and Heaver[1] notes that "psychiatry is still far more preoccupied with *what* the patient says than with *how* it sounds as it is said" and disagrees with that preoccupation. The "what" illuminated and informed by the "how" is the dynamic communication, and that communication comes through in the inflection as much as in the literal meaning of the word; sometimes even more. A simple "hello" can express warmth, welcome, surprise, lechery, insincerity, reluctance, distaste; it can be formal or informal, pleasant or unpleasant. The word remains the same in every instance; the inflection changes the communication.

Any form of communication is meant to produce a response, and by its very nature, speaking is meant to produce an immediate response. The speaker looks to the response of his audience as a measure of success or failure, and he in turn responds to that response, so that true communication, even when only one person is speaking, is still an interaction; both the speakers and the audience are simply a part of a still more significant whole or Gestalt. This is as true in conversation at home, in the office, or behind a counter as it is in the more formal setting of classroom, stage, pulpit, platform, or conference room.

The Many Sides of Speaking

To obtain the greatest response, you must remem-

---

[1]Heaver, Lynwood: Spastic dysphonia: psychiatric considerations. Logos Bulletin of the National Hospital for Speech Disorders, vol. 2, no. 1, April 1959.

ber that speaking is not a single but a multiple activity. There are the implicit, unseen influences, the source of stimulation—the things outside yourself such as the situation, the place, the mood of your audience whether large or small—and the quality of listening within yourself—to your own purposes and convictions. These are intangible parts of the speaking experience, as important as the words you use; while the three overt physical deliveries—vocal and facial expression and body gesture—are the outward manifestations of these intangibles. Each of these overt deliveries speaks its own language, but each must supplement and support the others.

In an inadequate performance, however, these overt activities may oppose or contradict one another. Often a speaker's facial expressions will unwittingly betray private thoughts and emotions at variance with his words and even the tone of his voice; or his voice will bellow or snap without relevance to his words or his manner; or gestures and movements, either ill-advisedly deliberate or nervously unconscious, will distract his listeners with stilted or aimless signals.

But something invaluable is lost if one of these activities is neglected, if the face is inexpressive or the arms hang limply at the sides or the voice drones. Everything must be working for dynamic oral communication—the inner energies, the interaction with outside stimuli, and the physical deliveries, *plus* command of language and ideas.

The Vocal Delivery

However important the multiple activities of speaking and their integration with one another, the voice—the tonal instrument responsible for quality, projection, and auditory communication—is the essential means of gaining and holding attention and getting a satisfactory response. If this instrument is not played effectively and skillfully, none of the other deliveries can have their full effect.

The skilled violinist brings to his playing a wealth of qualities—virtuosity, imagination, emotion, interpretation, training, practice, and personal response to the source of stimulation—but the vehicle is the violin itself. The caliber of this instrument determines the quality of the expression that it can give to the qualities of the violinist. In oral communication, whether utilitarian or artistic, the quality of the voice, the instrument, is even more important because the instrument *is* the instrumentalist and the instrumentalist is the instrument. Every voice, unlike every violin, is potentially a Stradivarius. *Proper use trains, and proper training sharpens, both the instrument and the instrumentalist at the same time.* The quality of one cannot be separated from the quality of the other; voice cannot be separated from speech.

I do not mean to detract from the importance of ideas, organization, grammar, and choice of language. Certainly without well-organized content the voice will have little to communicate, and certainly poor grammar and word usage will hobble even the best ideas. But the aim of this study is to help develop the vehicle as an inner process which is an essential part of the entire internal event. I lay stress upon the transmitting medium because while we live, voice and speech make the communication that leads to strong relationships, a sense of personal fulfillment, and an awareness of individual worth.

In the five activities common to the art and science of voice and speech—source of stimulation, listening within oneself, vocal delivery, facial delivery, and body gesture—I place vocal delivery, supported by structural, tonal, and consonant energies, at the hub: It searches out and takes from the first two, while it contributes to and follows through into the the last two (Fig. 59).

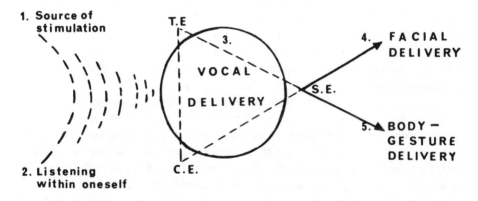

Figure 59. Schematic representation of the elements in communication.

The Facial Delivery

Next to voice and speech, the most revealing communication is that of the eyes. Even at a considerable distance, you can sense whether someone's gaze is directed at you or at something an inch to the side of your head; you can tell when he looks at you and when he shifts his gaze; yet the movement of the eye is the smallest fraction of an inch. To the listener, then, failure to communicate with the eyes or a communication opposed to that of the words is far more apparent than the speaker realizes. The eyes and the facial expressions carry the most profound and subtle meanings; yet the fact is that many speakers and performers never realize what expressions and nuances, what overtones and undertones, what their eyes and faces are saying or refusing to say.

I recall the reaction of a minister, a student of mine, when I drew back the curtains that concealed a wall mirror in my studio while he was working on the delivery of an important sermon on the subject of peace on earth. He was shocked to find that his face was consistently contorted with frightening grimaces that could only be interpreted as expressions of hate.

. . . and the perplexity of the New York City councilman who couldn't understand why he was never taken seriously when all the while he wore a wide grin that seemed permanently fixed, inanely mocking his words.

. . . and the indignation of the society woman when I told her that her habit of speaking from one side of her mouth made her look and sound hard, tough, and insincere.

The initial shocks were painful but in each case a serious knuckling down to a short but intensive training program worked miracles.

In the chapter on structural action, you have learned the advantages of the facial posture that accompanies the inverted-megaphone stretch, the cosmetic value, the hygienic value, and the vocal value. Now you must become aware of the value of facial expressiveness in reflecting mood, motivation, friendliness, sincerity, seriousness of purpose— or lack of these.

In the early days of television, some announcers and salesmen were suddenly caught up short when they could no longer hide as voices behind an eyeless radio. There was a glazed and transfixed insincerity to their facial expressions while they waxed emotional over the news or a performer or a product. Conscious that radio was a purely verbal communication, they had made no attempt to develop the communication of facial expression, had perhaps tended to lose the art of facial expression in concentration on the voice. When television came along and revealed their faces, they were unable then—and some still are—to integrate facial expressiveness with vocal expression; where they were conscious of the new need for both, the two were often separate and contradicting entities.

Nor is a *lack* of facial expression much better than the wrong expression. A poker face may win at cards but it seldom wins a debate. Too many people go through half a lifetime or more before they realize that their smile has genuine charm that can win or disarm their listeners; they put people off with a look interpreted as cold or severe when that look might be warmed in an instant with a simple smile. Nothing can take the place of the facial expression that reflects honest conviction, a sense of humor, seriousness of purpose, or a liking for people.

Just as I have said that you must not practice your voice and speech exercises too carefully, you must not try too carefully for facial delivery. Facial expression is a subtle thing and if you work too consciously to arrange the face, you will probably achieve a false or exaggerated arrangement. Let the facial delivery flow from, and become a part of, the vocal delivery, illuminated by the same emotions and purposes that stimulate, and are stimulated by, the vocal delivery.

Body Gestures

A gesture, like a word, must have something to say and should say it well. If a gesture, as well as a word, adds nothing, it may well subtract something. What it has to say should underline and add to what the words have to say. If a gesture is justified in the context in which it is used, repetition never becomes mechanical; if it is not justified, even a single use is too much.

For effective communication, gestures must be used easily and with conviction. A vehement use of the body—the bull-like stance with the upper torso pushed out over the speakers' stand as if the speaker were about to charge through, the finger that points or jabs unceasingly, the fist that mechanically crashes down like a gavel—is aggressive or bullying, and the audience may be cowed or it may respond with its own aggression. The too sudden or half-hearted gesture betrays ambivalence—the desire aborted by uncertainty. But avoidance of the gesture because it is often misused is a poor solution.

No one can teach you the gestures to use. All a teacher, coach, or director can do is teach you the concept of using the whole person for full expression. He can try to break you of being self-conscious; he can train the controllable factors, loosen you up, expand your understanding, sharpen your sensitivities, widen your outlook, and dignify your moral and ethical values by reinforcing your personal sense of right and wrong; in short, he can help develop a stronger and better motivation for a more mature and more effective mode of expression. But you must create for yourself gestures that say what you want to say in a natural, believable way. Otherwise they will form nothing more than an artificial and contrived pattern.

The Natural Communication

Gestures, vocal intonations and inflections, and facial expression are universal, as universal as humor, creative expression, or dynamic discussion; they spring from these qualities and usually occur in direct proportion. They reflect mood and sensitivities and they tend to diminish or disappear altogether in an atmosphere of regimentation or fear.

Much like words, they do not always mean the same thing when used by different people or in different places or even by the same people in different circumstances.

But like anything else, all of these activities, when used repetitively, can develop into patterns of behavior that lose spontaneity and become habit. I am not speaking of the free use of gesture and expression with awareness but rather of mechanical or automatic repetition. This kind of repetition can type an individual or characterize an entire group.

No gesture or intonation or expression of any kind is the exclusive behavior pattern of any one group or individual: a poker face is not necessarily Indian; a severe countenance not necessarily Texan; a drawl not necessarily Southern; an upward inflection not necessarily French; vigorous shaking of an upturned, cupped hand not necessarily Italian; a flat, uninflected utterance not necessarily American. All of us can and do use similar gestures, tones, accents, melodic lines, and expressions with effective and desirable results at one time or another; yet all of them are associated unfavorably with various groups—partly because we develop stereotyped habits of thinking of others; but also because we develop stereotyped habits of use.

The actor reaches the highest degree of his artistry when he succeeds in enlarging and projecting without distortion the simplest, most natural behavior. The public speaker, the teacher, anyone who would have an effect on someone else, has a similar task but an easier one. The actor who attempts to project a natural behavior pattern is usually working with the behavior of someone not exactly, or not at all, like himself; he must *be* someone else. The rest of us have only to be ourselves, to control and exploit the various physical energies and the various deliveries while being simply and naturally ourselves.

The task should be easier but the teacher of voice and speech must often spend much time demolishing the concept of the dual standard. The novice in the art of speaking retreats from his own natural behavior when he faces an audience because of fear, nervousness, insecurity, and lack of proper training and control. He may know what he wants to say; he is often very articulate and has an excellent command of language, but he feels that he must be someone else, that he himself is not good enough when facing an audience. You cannot become an accomplished speaker overnight, but when you have developed and integrated all your skills and abolished stereotyped habit patterns, the whole person that you communicate most effectively will be yourself—yourself at a peak but still yourself.

CHAPTER XIV

How to Give a Talk

*T*HERE ARE FEW gifted extemporaneous speakers. Legendary figures like Mark Twain and Will Rogers come to mind, but even among professional lecturers, excellent speakers are scarce. What seems to be talent is more often much training or experience—or the happy possession of a photographic memory. Even those with the latter, however—and even the extemporaneous speaker—must prepare, if not on paper, then in their heads.

In writing a speech, and in delivering it as well, you should continually ask yourself four simple questions?

Why am I delivering this talk? Why are *you,* rather than someone else, particularly qualified to speak on this subject or on this occasion or to this audience? The answer to this question must be clear in your mind and must be reflected both in word and spirit, especially during the introduction. You want to relate yourself, your subject, and your audience at the very beginning and then keep that relationship throughout. It can be done directly or indirectly, by fact or anecdote or whatever attention-getting device you choose.

What am I going to say? Have you done a reasonable amount of research? Do you feel that you know your subject? Is there logical continuity to your arguments? Have you considered all the opposing arguments? Have you thought of balance and variety?

How am I going to say it? Do you want the effect to be persuasive? . . . thought provoking? . . . informative? . . . arousing? Will you best achieve your end by being witty or very serious? Do you know where the climaxes are and how to build them?

What result do I want? Do you want some specific action? If you want to start a petition, raise money, build support for an unpopular issue, get votes, you should keep this end in mind from the beginning. Does the conclusion of the speech effectively involve the audience?

And remember always that what may be a brilliant article for reading may not be an effective instrument for vocal delivery.

Whether an audience is one person or a thousand (and often, during preparation or training, a critical audience of one may be a more crucial test than a larger group), successful communication depends upon a chain reaction. The speaker is first motivated by his own sense of purpose, values, and attitudes, and then fed by the mood, behavior, and response of the audience; while each listener first receives the communication in the light of *his* experience, understanding, and inclination, and then responds under the influence of his impression of, and personal attitude toward, the speaker. You must learn to look upon the audience as an asset not a liability. Not every audience—and perhaps not everyone in any audience—will agree with every speaker, but a genuine, persuasive communication carries the possibility of swaying an audience toward the speaker's views, while a stiff, awkward presentation is more likely to turn them away.

Those who can speak extemporaneously and do it well are fortunate because this is the natural speaking situation and the freshest, most direct communication with an audience. But most of us, when called upon to speak in public, must depend upon memory, a manuscript, or organized notes. Nevertheless, a speaker must never merely recite or read to an audience. For his communication to be dynamic and to elicit a positive response, he must keep three qualities that come naturally to the extemporaneous speaker: (1) maximum contact with the audience, and here eye contact is all important; (2) words that are not merely spoken but arise from an active thought process; and (3) all the characteristics, quality, and variety of natural discourse.

How to Memorize a Speech

Much has been written about, and there are many institutes and courses devoted to, the improvement of the memory. Most of us need help. You can probably benefit from learning how to use association of ideas, graphic reminders, and all the other mnemonic devices, and by all means use them whenever they function as helpful aids. But this approach to memory is of secondary importance in memorizing a speech.

The most important task is to retain the spontaneity, the freshness, and the naturalness of individual, face-to-face communication, while committing words and ideas to memory. This admonition would be mere cliche if I were addressing myself only to actors—they know, or should know, that mere recitation of memorized lines is not good enough; but for the public speaker, the minister, the rabbi, the priest, the business man, the salesman, and the teacher, the need to learn this is real.

What you must try to preserve in memorizing is not the word alone, but the thought process—the process of stimulation and response. You should be concerned, not with the word itself, but with the meaning attached to the word; the expression of this meaning through the use of pause, inflection, hesitation, intonation, emphasis, accent, or pitch level; and the linking of these meanings into a continuity of ideas. You must be concerned with the support given the words by facial expression and body gesture.

These important supplementary supports fade and ultimately vanish during the process of mechanical word-for-word memorization. With every mechanical repetition stuffed into the portion of the brain concerned with memorizing, the impulses delivered to that portion concerned with creativity become weaker and fewer. The stimulus of meaning and the response of natural, effective interpretation are lost and replaced by stereotyped, meaningless vocal and physical mannerisms. Sooner or later you become nothing more than a repeating machine, a plagiarist of yourself. Words that were an expression of an active thought process when the speech was written—words intelligently created, honestly motivated, necessary to say—become smudged carbon copies of thoughts. The excuse that you can inject nothing new into the delivery of a speech because you're bored with it or tired of repeating it is a confession that mechanical memorization has robbed the speech of its vitality.

Since memorizing is almost always a mechanical, noncreative process, I have tried to develop techniques with which memorization is a byproduct of working with the simulated elements of immediacy, spontaneity, and realistic source of stimulation. These are elements the actor must always work with, and the task of memorizing and delivering a speech is similar to that of the actor.

The talented and experienced actor tries never to memorize words as such. After reading through a script once or twice, he first commits to memory not words, but information, all the information that he can glean from his lines about the character he is to portray. He evaluates him, seeks justification for his existence on stage and his interaction with the rest of the cast; if possible, he visualizes and memorizes the stage setting and his stage business in that setting. During this process he of course explores and works with the text, but he never memorizes word for word; instead he thoroughly familiarizes himself with, and commits to memory, the important ideas, actions, interactions, continuity, and desired results; he creates a thought process for the character, constantly asking himself: "Why am I saying or doing this? . . . What do I want to accomplish? . . . How shall I say it or do it?" In time, by exploring the script and by rehearsal on a realistic level of doing instead of repeating, he *does* come to speak the playwright's exact words, but he speaks them creatively, as if they were his own, out of thought and motivation.

The task of the speaker is similar, with one important difference: Where an actor memorizes a role in order to discover and project the personality, motivations, and ideas of someone else, the speaker memorizes his speech in order to project his own ideas and his own personality. With this advantage, the speaker need not engage in the extensive research into character so vitally important to the actor, but in all other respects his task is the same.

The step-by-step procedure for creative memorization that follows is intended to be a flexible formula. You may alter and modify it to fit your own needs and purposes, but however you change it, use it to avoid the trap of mechanical repetition and routine drill.

Step one. After writing the speech, read it; then jot down, for memorizing, the larger ideas or concepts, the continuity of these ideas, and the justification for the continuity: Why do these ideas follow one another in this particular order? What key thought in each paragraph makes it follow logically after the last and lead into the next?

Step two. Now read the speech aloud in sections as if you were facing a class of bright college students and explaining the subject to them in anticipation of a question and answer period after each logical thought sequence. With this in mind, you will try to impress upon them, not just the words, but the meaning of the words; your reading will include only the spontaneous emphasis, pauses, accents, inflections, intonations, and gestures that grow naturally out of that meaning. This approach on every reading is the major factor in avoiding stereotyped mannerisms; in emphasizing a point *to* someone, or expressing a feeling to someone, or teaching someone, you never use the same accent or inflection quite the same way twice. There is a freshness behind the delivery of each word, a spontaneous meaning. You do not commit to memory, along with each word, a single way of repeating that word.

Step three. After reading each section, put the text down. Using only the notes you began in step one, explain again to your imaginary class or special audience the section or paragraph you have just read. Don't hesitate to use whatever parts of the written text you remember, but at the same time, don't hesitate to ad lib and augment the text during this explanation. The point of this step is free expression. Note in your outline any breaks in continuity, any point you have forgotten, any new phrase or sentence or explanation you particularly like. Such spontaneous material is often better than what you wrote and can be used to strengthen the written speech. Without permitting yourself to memorize in the traditional manner, you have, without realizing it, committed quite a lot to memory and during the process you have tested the validity and worth of your speech. You have asked yourself the "why," "what," and "how" of the actor, and this listening within yourself, this indirect questioning, sets up the guideposts to creative memorization.

Step four. Return to the text and again deliver the section you are working on to your class. This time, however, refer to the text *only* when necessary, and each time put a reminder of what you have forgotten into your notes. Keep the manner of the informal classroom lecture that may be followed by questions. If you find that despite your precautions, a repetitive pattern is developing, change—in your mind—the character or intellectual level of your audience.

Step five. Put the text aside again; take the outline with all the reminders in it and deliver the section of the speech from these notes. If absolutely necessary, you may glance occasionally at the text and jot down the necessary reminder in your notes.

Step six. After going through steps two through five for each section, deliver the entire speech to your imaginary class in the same way, but this time don't look at the text at all. Whenever you get stuck, put another reminder on the outline sheet. From now on you should have everything on this sheet necessary for confident, secure delivery of your speech.

Step seven. Continue to work from your notes, and whenever you feel confident that any reminder is unnecessary, delete it.

Step eight. The last step is the preparation of the outline cards to be used during the actual delivery of the speech. These cards will contain only the notes you really need, but because of the way you have developed and arranged them, they will be *all* you need for confidence and security. Use whatever devices you need—two colors, capitalization of important words, indentations, separation lines, white space—to make the notes leap to your eyes the instant you need them.

This process may at first seem involved, but experience has proved to me that it takes less time than the usual method of mechanical memorization, and it accomplishes much more. You do not repeat the same pauses, the same accents, the same inflections, the same gestures, as you repeat the words; instead, in every step you explore new possibilities, and you find that they are all good. This knowledge arms you with alternative choices that will let you go, interpretively and expressively, where the stimulation of the the moment takes you. Confident that your speech not only is, but will sound like, a natural, spontaneous expression of your thoughts and ideas, you will never tire of hearing and delivering it. Even if you give the same speech a dozen times before different audiences, you will be trained, like an actor, to deliver it as if you were giving it for the first time, with the ideas, the motivations, the varieties of expression still fresh. You will feel the pleasure and excitement that a skilled extemporaneous speaker takes in communicating with an audience, and they will highlight the projection of your personality and the overtones of your voice. Working creatively, with relaxed energy, you will not be afraid to think on your feet.

If time is short, an alternate procedure can be used that falls somewhere between memorizing and reading:

Step one. Write the text out in full three times. This will give you an opportunity to improve the contents as well as to memorize them. Deliver the speech aloud before rewriting it the last time.

Step two. Type the final draft in triple space, leaving a wide right-hand margin—as much as three inches.

Step three. Underline important words and phrases for special emphasis.

Step four. Put cue words and key phrases in the right-hand margin. They will be a direct help in recalling the text and the continuity of ideas and will also help you to find quickly a particular point in the script.

Because, with this procedure, you will spend less time in preparation, you must be even more acutely aware, in delivery, of your words as immediate expressions of thought rather than a rehash of an idea you once had. Always remember that the meaning comes not from the word but from your inner self; a word is but an empty symbol.

How to Read a Speech

The speaker whose eyes are glued to a manuscript or whose head bobs rhythmically up and down like that of a happy parakeet cannot possibly provide the three basic requirements: contact with the audience, an active thought process behind the words, and a natural style of discourse. He relates to the text, not to the audience; his preoccupation with the reading process makes an independent thought process impossible; and his rhythms, tempo, intonations, and accents, left to themselves while his eye seeks out the words, are usually less than natural. There are a few rules, however, that can help put the desired qualities into a reading:

Rule one. Never really read to an audience—speak to them. You may decide to read from a manuscript because you have no time to memorize and cannot trust your spontaneous choice of expression, but the effect must never be that of reading. Your purpose is to deliver a message of some sort, to talk to your audience, explain to them, report, lecture, convince, inform, or entertain—but never to read. The pauses, inflections, accents, emphases, gestures, facial expressions that are part of the face-to-face conversation are just as essential to the reading of a speech. Ask yourself throughout: "Do I sound logical and reasonable to *myself?* . . . Am I making the meaning of the words real to me?" If you are, there is an excellent chance that the meaning will be real to your audience.

Rule two. Never break eye contact with your audience unnecessarily. For effective communication, the most important time to look at the audience is at the beginning of a new sentence or thought. When an orchestra conductor signals an instrumentalist to resume playing, they look at one another; they coordinate and communicate through eye-contact. The conductor looks down at his complicated and perhaps not too familiar score to find the place for the signal *before* it is time to give it. In the same way, when reading a speech, you should look down to read ahead as you finish the end of a phrase or sentence, so that you can look up as you begin the next. Thus, in reading Lincoln's Gettysburg Address, you would look at the audience as you begin: "Four score and seven . . ." then look down at the next phrase on ". . . years ago . . ." so that you can maintain eye contact as you go on, ". . . our fathers brought forth upon this continent . . ."

Rule three. Learn to read whole phrases at a glance and to read ahead. This is a musician's trick: The pianist or violinist never looks at the measure he plays, but four or five measures ahead. In reading a speech, you too must train yourself to take in four or five words at a time; or better still, you must learn to take in thoughts and key words rather than every word, so that you can *speak* thoughts rather than mere words. With this skill, you will look down less and communicate more with the audience.

Rule four. Keep your manuscript as near the top of the lectern as possible so that eye movement alone is necessary for a glance at the text. If it is near the bottom, you must bend your head each time, and you will emphasize the break in contact with the audience.

Rule five. Keep continuous track of your place in the text so that your eye doesn't have to search for it. This is done best by keeping one hand—preferably the left—on the manuscript with the index finger following the line or lines being spoken, while the thumb points to the next section or paragraph. These should be at most fifteen double-spaced lines apart.

Rule six. Always simulate natural behaviorisms or even seeming weaknesses in speaking. Let yourself pause that split second to think of the better word; look down occasionally to create the effect of thinking on your feet; when the inspiration strikes, ad lib a word or two or repeat a phrase for emphasis. The extemporaneous speaker does these things naturally; when reading, you can take advantage of these naturally effective techniques to glance at the script for reinforcement. These techniques are of cardinal importance, but they must be used from strength, from a thorough knowledge of your subject. If that knowledge is faulty, these techniques will be painfully artificial, but without them, your reading will be *too* smooth, too unvaried. It may be paradox, but it is nevertheless true that the most artistic speaking performance is the most human and the most revealing of these seeming human frailties. The more you labor for perfection, the more mechanical you will seem—the less human and the less artistic. The delivery of a speech, whether from manuscript or memory, must never proceed with a constantly recurring pattern nor a steady, uniform vocal line. Like the ticking of a clock, this kind of delivery will dull the senses, hypnotize an audience, or put it to sleep. The speech must be punctuated, its even flow interrupted. This is natural behavior, and the projection of a natural behavior pattern is the ultimate goal of any artistic performer.

Rule seven. Never shift or flip your pages audibly or noticeably while reading. It distracts the attention of the audience and breaks your contact with them.

So, read your speech if you must, but give the impression that you choose your own words, that you say them for the first time, that they rise out of a thought process. A speaker must address an audience as if he expects an answer, a reaction—he must communicate *with* them.

CHAPTER XV

Some Observations

on Voice and Speech Therapy

*A*CCORDING TO OFFICIAL SURVEYS, nearly ten per cent of all Americans, or almost seventeen million, suffer from serious speech defects or voice abnormalities. There are the stutterers and lispers, those with cleft palates and lips, functional voice disorders, severe articulatory defects, paraphonia, many of the dysphonias or aphonias, cerebral palsy, certain aphasic conditions, and many others. These are the prisoners behind great walls of silence; these are the ostracized and rejected.

When denied the opportunity to develop the tools for normal communication, even the less severe cases often become emotionally unstable and retreat still further behind neurotic defence mechanisms. Whether the cause or the symptom is considered of primary importance, emotion is a major ingredient in most voice and speech problems. The victims feed on fear, hostility, denial, repression, ridicule, and these charged emotions become punitive and self-sustaining, a destructive kind of protective barrier that prevents any normal or satisfactory social behavior. According to Dr. J. S. Greene,[1] voice and speech disorders "constitute one of our major medical and re-educational problems," and the problem appears to be a multiple one.

In the first place, speech and voice defects are not a single kind of condition. They may have a functional, organic, physiological, or psychoneurotic basis.

In the second place, the necessary teamwork is sadly lacking in voice and speech therapy. When doctors, analysts, psychologists, and therapists do try to work as a team, the attempt is often ineffective because the team members know too little of one another's specialties, and they are either unable or unwilling to develop a program that will effectively accommodate and integrate all of them. If, in addition, one member or another pulls rank to become head, rather than a member of the team, a truly concerted approach becomes all but impossible.

In the third place, despite the many excellent studies on the disorders themselves, there is still too little agreement about, and too little flexibility toward, treatment procedures. The current literature is full of controversy about etiology and a good deal of confusion as to whether one treats the symptom or the underlying cause. There is considerable agreement that effective therapy must take into account the whole person but much less agreement as to who shall do the job.

The multiple bases of voice and speech disorders are an inherent part of the problem and cannot be eliminated, but the lack of sophisticated teamwork and the controversy over cause and symptom are distractions that should be eliminated. If the whole person is to be treated, the symptom must be considered an integral part, not only of the problem, but of the causes as well. It is not enough to treat the cause and assume that the explicit behavior patterns of the symptom will go away, that consideration of the symptom is not germane to the task of reeducation and rehabilitation. At the very beginning, the symptom may be simply an outward expression of an inner cause, but by the time these disorders come to treatment, the symptomatic behavior patterns have pervaded and begun to interact with the causes. Symptom and cause affect one another qualitatively and quantitatively, and the symptom tends to become self-propagating, to become part of the cause, increasing the complexity of the entire syndrome and its resistance to treatment.

The matter of jurisdiction depends, it seems to me, upon circumstance, provided that the talent and training of the team are approximately equal. If, in hysterical aphonia for example, the psychoanalyst, through his scientific probing of the mind, can relieve the emotional disorder to the point where the voice is restored, the patient's security and pleasure in this improvement will aid in the succeeding stages of adjustment. This is an important breakthrough, but no more important than if the voice and speech therapist effects the same vocal improvement through *his* scientific methods of voice and speech training. A properly trained voice and speech therapist might restore the voice more quickly, bringing the patient more quickly to the point where he can experience the psychoanalytical process more deeply and cooperate more fully.

But more important than *who* makes the breakthrough is *how* progress is reinforced at the time of the breakthrough. Does the team work together as a team, making full use of all the skills of all its members, during that crucial period when treatment can finally be directed at both the cause *and* the symptom—when the entire organism can really be treated as a whole?

Here precisely, it seems to me, is where a breakthrough often breaks down. Even where there is a coordinated work schedule, the approach is too often segmented, the members of the team insulated against one another, and genuine interaction and integration almost nil. In a program strongly oriented toward psychoanalysis, a weekly half hour of voice and speech therapy may be worse than none at all: It tends to destroy integrity in teaching and leaves no time for the "rooting" of a skill; it is often no more than a burden, a tease, or a bore to the patient. The development and growth of new vocal and verbal habit patterns cannot be achieved in less than two or three hourly sessions a week. On the other hand, a total lack of psychotherapy may prevent progress however intensive the work of the voice and speech therapist. With some patients, the analyst and therapist may achieve the best results by working closely together in joint sessions; with others, this might be precisely the wrong procedure; some patients will benefit most from a multiple therapy program; others may require a consecutive arrangement. There is no single best approach, no single best way of coordinating the skills of the team. Every patient must be approached as an individual with an individual problem that requires individual treatment, but I feel that a team dedicated to considering the patient as a whole, a team whose members are not concerned with rank or status, will not find it difficult to agree upon diagnosis, program, and procedures.

Unfortunately, the weakest link in the team is often the representative in voice and speech. It is not at all unusual to find a specialist in speech who knows little or nothing about voice training or a voice expert who knows little or nothing about speech. Either one is only half trained. You might as well try to work with two schools of physical therapy, one devoted to developing muscle tissue with no knowledge of muscle function, the other to training muscle function with no knowledge of muscle physiology. With this kind of fragmentation within a single area, the hope of integrating all areas of voice and speech therapy in a true team approach goes glimmering. Every expert on the team must certainly be thoroughly trained in every aspect of his own discipline, and in addition he should have a working knowledge of every other discipline represented on the team.

When Dr. Paul Moses[2] says that "the ideal speech and voice specialist should be a combination oto-laryngologist, psychiatrist,

---

[2]Moses, Paul J.: Speech and voice therapy in otolaryngology. Eye, Ear, Nose and Throat Monthly 32:367-375, 1953.

psychologist, speech teacher, singing master and experimental phonetician," I assume that he speaks with tongue in cheek. There are few such supermen around in this age of departmentalization and particularization. Nevertheless, I must agree with Dr. Moses in spirit if not in letter. He is certainly correct when he says that "the physician who specializes in this field must acquire some knowledge of these other subjects." But it is just as necessary —and it should be just as easy—for the voice expert with a Ph.D. to acquire this additional knowledge as it is for the man with the M.D.

To rephrase Dr. Moses' ideal into a more practical goal, I believe that the ideally trained voice and speech therapist should be a combination of speech teacher, singing master, voice specialist, speech therapist and experimental phonetician—and from my point of view, this does not mean a man with five different specializations but rather a man with a strong and integrated proficiency in *all* aspects of one area of specialization; only when all are mastered can one become an expert or specialist or master teacher.

In addition, he should have a working knowledge of otolaryngology, neurology, anatomy, and psychology. It will take time and ambition, but it is not an impossible goal. I would guess that many speech teachers are more lacking in proper singing and voice techniques than in the collateral knowledge. This is where they fail to meet any reasonable definition of the "ideally trained." Where voice and speech are considered separate, there still exist confusing and conflicting ideas in both areas, with the result that their proper relationship and interaction is not understood and is therefore neglected. Certainly if we say that the physician is in no position to rehabilitate vocal disorders alone because of his lack of voice training and superficial knowledge of exercises, we cannot consider the speech therapist capable of handling the task without proper and exhaustive vocal training. If, on the other hand, the speech therapist with two semesters of college exposure to voice is considered qualified, then *any* physician, with his scientific background, should certainly do a better job—but not an adequate job. A smattering of articulatory techniques and vocal exercises is as dangerous in the hands of the physician as a smattering of anatomy and psychology is in the hands of the voice and speech teacher; each is professional in his own field but at best an amateur outside.

But however well-rounded any expert becomes, no one person will do it all. The otolaryngologist will still call in the singing master; the singing master will depend upon the analyst; the analyst will seek the help of the therapist; the therapist will get information from the testing clinic. If there is to be no superman to do it all, there can be no effective alternative to the organized and integrated efforts of the team of creative specialists.

The therapeutic suggestions and observations given for specific conditions indicate my own experience and general emphasis in treatment procedures. They suggest an approach but the details are flexible. The therapeutic application of the Lessac system must be flexible, and this flexibility must come from a thorough grounding in its principles and methods. In therapy, more than in any other application of voice and speech training, superficial knowledge can be dangerous. Even to *understand* the application of the principles, let alone to apply them, you must refer frequently to the work chapters to be sure that you understand the principles.

Cleft Palate Speech

From my discussion of the distinct difference between the breath stream and the sound stream, it should come as no surprise that I consider blowing exercises, to improve articulation or eliminate nasality, a waste of time. I have found through experience that when the patient, whether he has had the obturator or palatal operation, is taught to feel the vibratory sensation of the Ybuzz or the call, he will not only develop habit patterns that eliminate all or most of the nasality, but will find it much easier to learn systematically to puff out the cheeks, yawn, and blow at objects. In other words, I teach a major part of the necessary breath control and directional use of the breath stream by deliberately avoiding concentration on breathing exercises at the beginning, and thus avoiding the pressures and muscle tension that result from them. The first concern is tonal and structural control.

The next step is consonant action. Because the emphasis is on the sustained, easy legato of the voiced continuants, the almost breathless sustention of the voiceless continuants, and the light, springing, drumbeat technique of the percussive consonants, breath again plays a secondary role. Only after the trinity of actions has done its work is it desirable to work on breathing exercises as such.

For developing articulatory skills with the cleft palate, I consider the experiments listed by McWilliams[3] to be of decided interest. I would agree with him that consonant action provides "improvement in over-all speech efficiency," but only when the patient speaks just above a whisper. As soon as he attempts normal tone, pitch, and projection, the vowels in the words pull his voice right back to objectionable nasality or nasal unintelligibility. Because of this correlation of nasality with attempts at articulation, I do not agree with McWilliams that articulatory skills can

---

[3]McWilliams, B. J.: Speech pathology and therapy. Journal of the College of Speech Therapists 2:6, 1959.

be stressed "as the major goal" in cleft-palate therapy. Proper vocal therapy must come first: The patient must achieve the physical controls for structural and tonal action before correction of consonant articulation can assume major importance.

Stuttering

My comments on the treatment and reeducation of the stutterer are based on the belief that symptoms and causes are cognate forces, each interacting with and upon the other to create a single dynamic gestalt. Goldstein[4] puts it another way when he says that the stutter symptom "is to be considered as an expression of the emotional distress into which the patient comes when he is aware of his defect."

The stutterer has been analyzed and a number of his specific problems identified: 1. He expends energy excessively. 2. He has breathing difficulties. 3. He suffers from multiple muscle spasms and body tensions. 4. He is given to facial contortions and fixations and compensates with unreliable temporary distraction devices. 5. His speech is too fast. 6. His pitch is too high. 7. He has a limited vocal range and speaks apathetically. 8. His physiological function — heartbeat, respiration, circulation, metabolism—is irregular or deviant. 9. He displays neurotic behavior. 10. He suffers an intense conflict between his feelings of apprehension and fear and the social factors in his environment. These factors and others, including the primary cause, become a habit-forming syndrome of behavior, both defensive and offensive.

On the other hand, it is generally accepted that the stutter disappears when a stutterer sings, when he takes part in ensemble or choral speech, when he cannot hear his own voice, when he speaks or reads to himself or to small children or animal pets, when he speaks in a foreign language, or whenever he finds himself in any totally relaxed, totally unthreatening and noncompetitive situation.

The contradiction facing us here—and the source of hope as well—is that seemingly fixed habit patterns of behavior, growing out of a disturbing and complex disorder, can disappear at once and normal, positive behavior take over in somewhat unrealistic circumstances; the stutterer is not being judged—he need not fear ridicule, pity, or curiosity—in these situations. The therapeutic problem, then, is to create those favorable conditions that will permit the stutterer to seek adjustment on higher levels of reality. I have found that many of the techniques used in my system of

[4]Goldstein, Kurt: Language and Language Disorders. New York, Grune & Stratton, 1948, p. 81.

voice and speech training will work to this end, and I have developed the following approach, based on the needs of the stutterer:

1. *The stutterer must learn to breath correctly and easily.*

Done correctly or naturally, the process of inhaling and exhaling is both relaxing and energizing. Whether accompanied by speech or not, whether full and complete or partial, it promotes at the same time a sense of physical security and a feeling of physical vitality. It provides the basis for excellent posture, more space for the internal thoracic organs, a fresher and larger volume of tidal as well as residual air, and a more efficient oxygenation of the blood. Correct breathing activates more of the organism and contributes to more efficient systemic functioning.

Even if some muscular tension is reduced, correct breathing will rarely if ever substantially affect the stutter, but it will contribute, in a general way, to a more favorable therapeutic environment. Correct breathing is only natural breathing and training for it need only reflect the natural functioning of the body when it is not subjected to faulty conditioning; it is the same in speech or in singing as it is in any other activity or at rest. Since it is not a special and difficult skill, the stutterer will have little or no difficulty in establishing proper breathing habits by the methods outlined in Chapter IV; it will take him no longer than anyone else to accomplish this—usually from two to four weeks—despite spasms and other muscular difficulties in the abdominal, diaphragmatic, and thoracic areas.

2. *The stutterer must acquire a tonal and vocal continuity that defends against—and at the same time aggressively and physically attacks—spasticity, blocks, and fixations.*

The stutterer will find the tonal action of the Ybuzz a lubricant that induces a smooth, sailing or gliding action into his speech; it will be his most certain ally in the attempt to liberate himself from the locked and fixed condition that strangles his speech. Consonant action will provide a secondary method of relaxation through the specific treatment of the continuants and the anticompression technique of the percussive consonants. Both of these actions are assisted by the vital structural form of the inverted-megaphone stretch.

3. *The stutterer must find a way to liberate himself from facial contortions and grimaces and body tension.*

Structural action is also of cardinal importance here. In the physical sensation of the inverted-megaphone stretch, with its easy, symmetrical facial musculature, the stutterer will find a positive guard against facial contortions and grimaces. From the achievement of this simple facial posture and its carry-over to vowel formation, he will feel, perhaps for the first time, a qualitative and quantitative easing of body tension and increase in muscle comfort and muscle tonicity. These actions will serve the stutterer as a functional crutch—more efficient than unreliable distraction devices—which in time will melt intrinsically into the general pattern of habit-formed behavior and cease to be a crutch.

4. *The stutterer must learn how to reduce tension.*

The mandatory equilibrium of the Ybuzz and the moderate calls and the relaxing, yet dynamic and creative, treatment of consonants in consonant action provides the stutterer with weapons to counteract muscular tension, pressure, and undesirable contractions. Furthermore, structural action removes the primary muscular action from the mandibular area and reassigns it to the maxillary area. This improves the spatial and directional form of the vocal sound box—by which, remember, I mean the oral cavity, not the larynx—and changes mandibular function from a tight action that helps strangle speech to a pliant action that helps to free speech. These techniques, along with the exercises in relaxation given in Chapter V, will teach the stutterer how to relax consciously as a dynamic, doing process: and these first experiences with success will permit the pleasure principle to become established and to contribute to the learning cycle that leads to desirable new habit patterns.

5. *The stutterer must overcome a tendency to speak too rapidly.*

When the trinity of actions is mastered, it constitutes a physical gauge that prevents objectionable or impractical tempos in speech. To feel each of the actions properly requires a specific length of time; thus, if every action-sensation is fully perceived, voice and speech will be produced with maximum efficiency and clarity, and no possible speed will be excessive.

6. *The stutterer must extend his vocal range and overcome a tendency to speak apathetically.*

Serious and consistent application of the principles of tonal and structural action will develop full vocal range and quality in anyone—in the stutterer as easily as in any normal speaker or singer. Not only is this no problem, but it is a part of the educative process that corrects the stutter. The monotony that may be induced in speech by passive methods of relaxation is prohibited by the principle of energetic relaxation and relaxed energy described in Chapter V. If this principle is followed, vitality, projection, and variety are inherent in the speech act.

7. *The stutterer must find a way to reduce his fears, depressions, and defence mechanisms.*

In my experience, the procedures presented here go a very long way in themselves to reduce physical tension to minimal proportions. When the stutterer is taught methods that give him a sense of pleasure and accomplishment to replace the painful devices he used before, the pleasure-pain balance swings dynamically in favor of the former, inducing comfort, confidence, and control. By contributing to the relief of physical tension, the voice and speech therapist helps create a climate conducive to the relief of mental anxieties and emotional fears, and thus helps eliminate the need for destructive defences against these fears.

In the final analysis, the stuttering patient must be provided with vocal techniques that he can practice precisely *during* the onset of stuttering. As he feels the spasticity and tensions coming on and then receding in response to his conscious and deliberate use of one or more of the trinity of actions that he has learned, he no longer feels himself a victim of the old habit patterns, but rather their conqueror and the architect of new and more efficient habit patterns to replace them. Only then, as he strives physically to overcome the conditioned imperfections, can he judge his progress objectively. His fears cannot be conquered merely by telling him repeatedly that he is not really a stutterer—that he only does more of what every normal person does sometimes.

The subject of stuttering is beset with theories, most of them of doubtful value: I cannot accept the validity of the theory that there is a predisposition to stuttering; nor do I believe that the stutter disorder is synonymous with—or no more than a severe manifestation of—the occasional blocking that everyone experiences in the face of confusion, fatigue, or unfriendly stimuli. I also suspect that the occasionally observed coexistence of twinning or sinistrality with stuttering is coincidental rather than evidence of a significant relationship between these phenomena. Nor does my experience bear out the contention that lack of coordination is a constitutional characteristic of the stutterer.

But whatever one believes, most of these theories are irrelevant to the *treatment* of stuttering. As I have said, I believe that the relationship between cause and sympton is a fluid one—that secondary symptoms can become causes in themselves and that primary causes can be exacerbated by symptoms and so become a part of the symptomatology. Whether stuttering is diagnosed as a functional, organic, or neurotic disorder, one thing is rather clear: The overwhelming majority of stutterers will require vocal and physical reeducation, and this must be carried out with skill and understanding of the process involved.

Dysphonic Voice Disorders

Voicelessness can have many causes: hoarseness and fatigue, nodes and contact ulcers, dysfunction of the abductor muscles, and hysterical, habitual, or functional aphonia. I will not discuss each type specifically, but in general, the task of reeducation in voice and speech, whether as postoperative therapy, a substitute for surgery, or an aid to psychotherapeutic treatment, is two-fold: (1) to relieve pressure and strain on the vocal cords specifically and the laryngeal musculature and nervous system generally; (2) to separate the vocal wheat from the chaff—the sound stream from the breath stream.

To accomplish the first half of the task, silence for a period of two or three weeks may be beneficial, but only as preparation for a positive program of training. The silence should not be total: During this period, an active program of breathing exercises should be punctuated by practice in sustaining the sound effect consonants—the S, SH, TH, F, and H. We also begin on the second half of the task at this point by teaching the patient how to reduce the breath to imperceptibility whether he makes voiced or unvoiced sounds. Toward the end of the period of silence, practice in sustaining other consonants can be added, first the N violin, then the V cello, the M viola, the NG oboe, the ZH bassoon, and the Y French horn.

The next step is to work for gradual and flexible effectuation of vocal cord approximation during the voicing of vowels. This attempt to get free-edge vibration of the vocal membranes must be accompanied by an appreciable reduction in the breath pressure and vocal force that the patient has been accustomed to using in vocal production. It is a delicate operation for anyone who takes on vocal therapy, since the objective at this point is two-fold: (1) to institute a therapeutic procedure that will effect a cure, and (2) to establish a disciplined and positive method of voice training—it is a medicine and a food at the same time. The clinician must be a voice specialist who understands the qualitative and quantitative process of voice production as it applies to singing as well as to therapy; he must be able to hear expertly and demonstrate accurately and effectively; he must be both doctor and maestro of the vocal skills and arts, one who can handle *voices*, and not necessarily a doctor of medicine, whose competence is pathological or psychological diagnosis and the handling of the stethoscope and administration of drugs. Consequently, the clinician—fully aware that in dysphonia or aphonia the vocal membranes resist occlusion or approximation because of nodes, inflammation, fixation, or hysterical compulsion—must teach the patient the initially subtle experience of divorcing the breath stream from the sound stream, which means educating him in the perception of bone-conducted vibratory sensation as a desirable, free-flowing energy; at the same time, he must help the patient to recognize the undesirable vocal effects of muscle contractions, abrasive noises, and sibilant and breathy sounds.

After the work on the consonants, voice therapy centers first around the lower half of the Ybuzz range, utilizing the EE, as in *leave,* the French U, as in *sûr,* and a very low-pitched OO, as in *food.* Then the rest of the Ybuzz range is taken up, the EE fusing into a low-pitched O, as in *goad,* which is shaded toward the OO; and the +Ybuzz A, as in *came,* which is shaded toward the EE. The sustentions are short at first, then increased in duration as voice is restored. During these exercises, the vibratory tonal action in the bony areas must be the only sensation of the sound stream at work; it must not be diverted into activity in the mouth or throat, and there must not be the slightest sensation of the presence of breath—this is the point where the bone-conducted perception helps develop that tonal equilibrium that brings with it such a salutary feeling as to improve vocal cord flexibility and increase the spontaneity of membrane occlusion. As the voice improves, higher pitches, other vowels, and mild calls are added; then the tonal action is carried over to specially constructed phrases and sentences.

In many cases, proper voice and speech therapy can eliminate the need for surgical removal of nodes on the vocal cords; nodes that regress in this fashion do not recur because the patient has established new and improved vocal habit patterns. When a node is removed by operation, however, it will usually reappear if the vocal conditions that caused it are not removed. A thorough reformation of faulty habit patterns is necessary, and the traditional, inspirational or permissive postoperative vocal therapy is not enough.

Other Voice Disorders

The principles and concepts of voice and speech discussed in this book are fundamentally valid under any circumstances and therapeutically applicable to a wide variety of voice and speech disorders. They bring order and security to the use of the vocal mechanism and a keen awareness of the participation of the resonating areas and the structural relationships and physical sensations involved in natural voice production. These traits are salutary in themselves and have a salutary effect on many vocal ills, whether physical or psychological in origin.

The only area in which the approach is of uncertain value is mental retardation and certain kinds of brain damage. In the total picture of voice and speech disorders this is a small corner.

My experience with small children has also been

limited. I have found that the rate of progress in voice training is in direct proportion to the student's, or patient's, conscious and intelligent understanding of the method. It would be necessary, then, to invent and develop games, exercises, and additional techniques especially for use with very young victims of voice and speech disorders. To do this, of course, the teacher or therapist must have a thorough understanding of the principles of biodynamics given here and must personally have mastered the physical techniques.

Appendices

I. A Guide to Pronunciation

The chart below gives a Lessac phono-sensory symbol for each of the diacritical markings used to distinguish sounds in *Webster's Collegiate Dictionary*. Most of the consonant sounds are designated by the same alphabet letters in both Webster's and the Lessac system; only the exceptions are shown here. The key words are those used by Webster's. A detailed explanation of acceptable variations for each sound is given in the dictionary's guide to pronunciation. Each Lessac symbol represents an economical choice from the acceptable variants used by Americans.

Vowels

Webster	Lessac	Key Word	Webster	Lessac	Key Word
ā	+Ybuzz	haze	ō	#21	old
á̱	+Ybuzz	chaotic	ŏ̱	#21 (unstressed)	obey
â	N³n	care	ô	#3	orb
ă	#6	add	ŏ	#4	odd
a̱	N⁴	account	ŏ̃	#4 or #3	soft
ä	#5	arm	ȯ	N⁴	connect
a̲	#6	ask			
ȧ	N⁴	sofa	oi	3y	oil
			ōō	#1	food
ē	Ybuzz	eve	o̬o	N¹	foot
ḙ	N²n	here			
é̱	N²	event	ou	#51	out
ĕ	N³	end			
ĕ̱	N⁴	silent			
ẽ	N¹ or N⁴—final R optional—or weak R; if ever stressed, it becomes strong R	maker	ū	consonant Y plus #1	cube
			ú̱	consonant Y plus #1	unite
			ủ	consonant Y plus #1 (unstressed)	menu
ī	6y	ice	û	R-derivative	urn
ĭ	N²	ill	ŭ	N⁴	up

Consonants

Webster	*Lessac Consonant Instrument*	*Key Word*
ch	CH crash cymbal (T SH), no sustention of SH	chair, march
j	DG Chinese cymbal (D ZH), no sustention of ZH	judgment, pigeon
ts	TS after-beat cymbal, no sustention of S	tracts, adopts, scientists
dū̆	dy, aspirated D plus Y	verdure
ty̆	ty, aspirated T plus Y	stature
t̶h̶	TH clarinet	smooth
'	prepare consonant before mark; execute consonant after mark. Indicates syllabic N and L	pardon (pard'n) eaten (eat'n) rural (rur'l)

II. Accent Elimination

By now, the use of physical action-sensations, rather than hearing, as the guide to good speech should have eliminated a good many of the sounds and patterns that we think of as "foreign" when they appear in English speech. With this technique, the student to whom English is a second or third language can, if he wishes, eliminate all traces of these accent patterns; this can be particularly useful to the actor or to some speakers, who find any accent a handicap. He can, on the other hand, retain as much as he likes of the native flavor of his speech and yet speak clear, understandable American English if he concentrates on perfecting certain specific American sounds.

The use of structural action on the #21, #51, and #6 vowels and the use of tonal action on the Ybuzz and +Ybuzz will already have given a native American quality to the pronunciation of most of the vowels by promoting the physical control of their formation. In the same way, most of the techniques taught in this book will be useful, but here I would like to give special consideration to some specific techniques that I feel will be of value to the foreign student: (1) the #1 vowel, (2) the neutral vowels, (3) the R and the R-derivative in relation to the R, (4) the V and the W, (5) the S and the Z and the two TH's.

1. *The #1 vowel.* Treat this vowel as a diphthong. Begin with the smallest lip opening; then as you complete the vowel sound, close your lips to a still smaller opening as if you would attempt to go from a #1 to a #½ position. In a sense, you begin with the #1 vowel and end with the lip position for the W: you→(w) . . . dew→(w) . . . show→(w) . . . do→(w) . . . spoo→(w)n . . . refu→(w)se . . . beau→(w)ty.

Think of this vowel as being as much a diphthong as the #21 or #51 except that the lip action begins from a much smaller opening.

2. *The neutral vowels.* Remember that these are short, gruntlike sounds that are not to be associated with the stronger #1, Ybuzz, #6, or #5 vowels. To avoid this tendency to expand the sound, color one neutral vowel with another (see the sentences in Chapter VIII):

Color the N¹, as in *stood*, with the N⁴, as in *stud*, to avoid pronouncing *stood* as *stewed*.

> *Example:* The GUHD-LUHKING CUHK TUHK a GUHD LUHK at the BUHTCHER with the CRUHKED FUHT who STUHD . . .

Color the N⁴, as in *stud* or *tuck*, with the N¹, as in *stood* or *took*, to avoid the pronunciation *stahd* or *tahk*.

> *Example:* WOONCE (once) NOOTHING BOOT HOONGRY DE-STROOCTION SOOCCEEDED, THOO BLOOD OOV (of) DOOZ-ENS . . .

Color the N², as in *fill*, with the N³ as in *fell*, to avoid the pronunciation *feel*.

> *Example:* MESTER SMETH and HES SEX ASSESTANTS DEDN'T FENESH their VESET EN THES CETY TELL . . .

Color the N³, as in *fellow*, with the N², as in *fill*, to avoid the pronunciation *fallow*.

> *Example:* The VIRY BIST and IFFICIENT MIN OF THE RIGI-MINT BILLIED THIMSILVES toward the IDGE of the PRICIPICE . .

In using the neutral diphthongs, you will note that an R consonant always follows the vowel sound; disregard the R completely and end the word with the neutral vowel in the early stages of training. Later, when you have developed complete facility with the American R, you will be able to pronounce this consonant very clearly whenever it links directly with a vowel at the beginning of the next word; at the same time, you will continue to deemphasize the R whenever it precedes a consonant.

3. *The R and the R-derivative.* As a preparatory exercise toward developing complete facility with the R trombone, practice emphasizing and sustaining the R after every R-derivative vowel as if the vowel sound before the R did not exist: The c-rly w-rking g-rl b-rst into an unreh-rsed fl-rtation . . .

Practice this on the R-derivative sentences:

The curly working girl burst into an unrehearsed flirtation in order to divert the determined attentions of a certain third person.

The dirty worm squirmed nervously and furtively when the early bird returned.

The pert nurse had the nerve to flirt with the perturbed surgeon.

The sum of thirty dollars spurred the surly clerk on to finish the irksome work for the foreign firm by the third day.

The disguised chauffeur peered through the door but did not stir; suddenly there was a whirr as the alert girl hurled the unsheathed dirk at the trapped murderer and emerged triumphant.

Continue to practice emphasizing the R in the exercises below. When you have thoroughly assimilated the American R, *then* return to the instructions in Chapter VIII to deemphasize the R and play the normal R-derivative vowel instead.

step 1. As you emphasize the R trombone in the R-derivative, sustain the consonant sound for as long as you can, and check to make certain that *both* undersides of the tongue are gently but firmly pressed against the inside of the upper teeth, or better still, against the inside upper gum; only with the tongue in this position will you produce a clear, buzzing, trombone-like vibration.

step 2. Again emphasize the R in the R-derivative, and check, while you sustain it, to make certain that the front half of the tongue forms a hollow with the front blade, or tip, curling slightly upward; make certain that the vibrations of the R trombone gather in this hollow and resonate out through the roof of the mouth and on through the nasal bone and forehead. Remember to keep *both* undersides of the tongue against the upper teeth or gums.

step 3. Establish the R and sustain it as long as possible, constantly working to increase the trombone buzz and improve the tongue position.

step 4. Establish the R and sustain it with the lips protruded into a pout; then sustain the R again, alternating the lips between the pouting and the normal position.

step 5. Establish the R and sustain it; then slowly separate the jaws as much as you comfortably can while still holding on to the genuine R trombone vibration. With practice, you will achieve maximum separation of the jaw while maintaining tongue contact for the R.

step 6. Establish the R and sing a melody on the strong trombone-like vibration.

step 7. Establish the R and then with a quick jaw action turn it into a series of repetitions that sound like the continuous growling and barking of a dog.

step 8. Establish the R and then connect it, without any separation, into the different vowels:

#5 as in *rah*	Ybuzz as in *read*	N^1 as in *rook*
#4 as in *rod*	+Ybuzz as in *raid*	N^2 as in *wrist*
#3 as in *wrong*	R-derivative as in *earn*	N^3 as in *rest*
#21 as in *Rome*	3n as in *roar*	N^4 as in *rust*
#1 as in *rude*	N^1n as in *Ruhr*	
	N^2n as in *rear*	
	N^3n as in *rare*	

step 9. Establish the R and while sustaining the trombone-like vibration, interject the tympani drumbeat B eight or nine times; do the same with the F, M, P, V, H, NG, and W; now do the same with the T, G, CH, SH, S, D, K, L, SK, ST, SP, and SF, even though it seems a little more difficult to hold the sustained R vibration. In this drill, you will find yourself saying words like *were, cur, purr, and stir.*

step 10. Now read the R sentences holding every sustainable trombone-like vibration for two or three seconds whether it begins a word or follows a consonant. The sustainable R's will be underlined; an underlined final R is to be linked directly into the vowel at the beginning of the next word. The object is to hold the consonant until you are conscious of the trombone-like vibration rather than the consonant R—only then should you continue on to the vowel. Now repeat the sentences holding the R for one second, then a half second, and finally read them normally, still feeling the trombone-like vibration.

The red-headed roving rogue with brown breeches and green shirt, ran round the ragged rock in the road, broke through the rambling brush, and scrambled out of sight.

The French literary critic regarded as the slanderer of the American writer rewrote the frightfully reactionary article.

The reluctance of all mankind to confront disagreeable truths is one of its notorious and unfailing characteristics.

The growing crowd in the street was struck as if in a trance at the trapped crack pilot, striving to break through the gruesome, monstrous, well-trained attack.

Apparently outmaneuvered by the numerically superior cavalry regiment, the men of the heroic band were forced to retreat to their original line of attack.

        4. *The V and the W.* These two sounds are often substituted for one another in English by foreign students. Just remember that the V is the vibration of the cello and that the W flute begins with the #1 vowel. As you read the practice sentences, concentrate on *feeling* the cello vibration and the vowel-like sensation of the flute—don't listen. A few F sound effects are also combined with the W flute.

I have wooed the cave woman over.

They strive woefully.

We've warned you.

I've wanted it.

We've weeded the garden.

Eve wished she could go along.

Love wept tears.

Save wear on tires.

Steve waxed angry.

They were tough wounds to heal.

The calf wouldn't move.

These are enough woes.

Half-worn and half-wasted the staff wanted a rest.

I was very well aware, Victor, that your fervent avarice varied willfully with your well-timed vexatious moods.

Between us we've wiped out the entire history of the world, said War to Famine.

Unsolved poverty can venerate values and convictions that will give the invisible devil unconceivably feverish convulsions.

Of everyone present, Valerie was the most vivacious.

Since we've brought with us a variety of velvet velours, we've been avalanched by vociferous visitors.

        5. The S and the Z and the two TH's. The S sound effect, the Z bass fiddle, the TH sound effect, and the TH clarinet are all discussed extensively in Chapter X, but the foreign student will benefit from further practice in distinguishing these sounds. In the practice sentences, the unvoiced S and TH sound effects are underlined once, the voiced Z bass fiddle and TH clarinet twice. As with the V and the W, concentrate on the correct feeling of the consonant-instrument and not on the sound.

Sally's sister Sadie sips sodas sitting sideways.

The restrictions on the restricted strike were strictly observed.

Is there someone here who will say something to stifle this silly, stupid sentence?

Neither the penicillin nor the chlorpromazine administered during the past six weeks caused any noticeable or recognizable recession in the series of sepsis cases.

The reluctance of both masters and masses to confront disagreeable truths is one of the notorious and unfailing characteristics of mankind.

Captain Caesaro paid a stiff price for the prize he seized on the high seas.

With three fifths of their wealth thus thoroughly withering away, the worthy venture breathed its last breath.

The thoughtless, toothless, faithless old thing thought she was certainly not thoughtless and felt that she had kept the faith, but agreed that she might be better toothed.

These trying thoughts will reinforce you with a thousand thrilling resolves.

The wrestler writhed in pain as the doctor bathed the sixth cut on his thigh and vowed that henceforth his everlasting theme would be: "Health is worth more than wealth."

The beliefs and thoughts of youth can serve until death if guided by both faith and truth.

III. A Note on Syllabification

        Both the student to whom English is native and student to whom it is a foreign language would benefit from some re-evaluation and reform of the manner in which English words are divided into syllables. The conventional practice is formal and academic, arbitrary and inconsistent, and it contributes little to realistically good diction; we teach one way and speak another. I would like to suggest that in English, as in Spanish, every syllable of a word begin with a consonant, wherever possible. Even in words that are, of necessity, divided between vowels, a consonant sound is implicit: *Reinvest* is really *re-yin-vest,* and *coincide* is *co-win-side.*

Practice the words below that have been divided in this manner and see how much more conducive to the natural pronunciation these divisions are than the conventional divisions. Where the consonant at the end of a syllable has a retarding effect, the consonant at the beginning encourages an easier forward flow of verbal sound and facilitates connected speech. When you have run through the divided words, divide the rest into syllables yourself, using this proposed method. Two identical sounding consonants are pronounced and divided as one, and certain consonants are combined with the R and the L to produce a smoother and more connected speech. In a cluster of consonants, use your own educated preference, as long as at least *one* consonant begins the next syllable.

con-si-dered	i-llus-tra-tions	experiment
un-sy-mme-tri-cal	un-com-pro-mi-sing	resurrection
po-si-tion	re-cog-nize	reactionaries
a-ny-time	clarification	corollary
i-nno-va-tions	specific	ruination
di-ffe-rent	specificity	treacherous
pre-li-mi-na-ry	foreigners	intelligibility
i-mmea-su-ra-bly	megaphone	resonances
i-rre-gu-la-ri-ties	illustrate	establishes

IV. Student Comments

The following excerpts are from self-evaluative comments submitted during the past years by a number of students already acting professionally, some of them for quite a number of years. They are included in the hope that these personal experiences will indicate to others some of the additional applications and byproducts of these techniques. The problems of these young actors may be yours; their solutions may be your encouragement.

As a personal note, I should add that teachers who have experimented and lived with a technique for a long while may still have much to learn from the new and exciting beginning insights that students bring. For example, twenty years ago when I was perfecting this approach, getting ". . . high on pot," to which one student compares his experience with the Ybuzz, was not really relevant to my experience; yet I can understand and resonate with the comments that reiate these aware-nesses to new experience. The new generation is turned on to a new set of sensations and a new kind of involvement that may be even more relevant than the sensory experiences I have described in this book.

Read these excerpts, not as comments to be taken solely for their own content, but with the same sense of searching and explor-ation that I have urged consistently throughout the book. Find new impulses in them for new experience of your own—find that special perceptiveness to everything that makes wandering through ignorance with awareness a fascinating and productive experience.

1. *B. P.*

". . . In preparing the John Proctor role in Arthur Miller's "The Crucible," I found it necessary in the last scene for Proctor to cry out his agony and weep for his name. Any actor or acting student who has ever expended the high degree and kind of emotional and physical energy necessary to make this particular scene moving, will recognize immediately that exact articu-lation cannot be achieved by concentration alone. From somewhere—from habit or some unrecognized neural response—a relaxation of the face must come in compensation for the paroxysm of muscles that normally occurs to the actor when his involvement is strong enough to make an audience believe what it is seeing and hearing. Without any knowledge of the use of structural action per se, I experienced that action without sacrificing any degree of conviction in Proctor's intolerable situation or his pain. It came as a genuine compensation in muscular position. The character-in-pain created facial tensions and muscular fixations resulting in an actor-in-trouble. The forward stretch of the face replaced the drawn, tight muscles, making it possible to articulate intelligibly and sustain my characterization. The relaxation achieved through the use of the forward stretch, albeit accidental, freed my tongue and lips to speak, and increased my ability to focus concentration more deeply on the stimulus which was allowing me to play the words, emotions, and movements selectively, specifically, and honestly. It is apparent in this case that emotion created a need for structural action, and that action in turn fed the emotion.

"As a result of having now acquired an understanding and feeling of the 'trinity of actions' it is clear that what was achieved by accident is actually necessary to an actor's technique and can be used, indeed, *must* be used, if the vocal instrument is to be protected against misuse, and the art itself is to grow in an atmosphere and foundation of freedom. The application of these actions is geometric in its possibilities and consequently limitless—the vocal action problem calls for the proper 'actions' and 'action' contributes to feeling the emotion, and so on in a self-feeding cycle . . ."

2. C. K.

". . . I think that I have already discussed with you my feelings about the freedom that your voice technique has given me in my work—a reliance and a confidence in my own voice as a usable instrument, which is new to me. Before, I always felt that I had to be good despite my obviously poor vocal tool. I feel this way less and less, as I begin more and more to incorporate the voice as a tool. But there are other practical effects that the technique has had on my work as an actor—things which I will now endeavor to explain. In acting, I may have a line or speech such as one in 'The Chinese Wall.' The intention of that speech may be 'to figure out these monsters.' Now, I as an actor who must play the scene (as Romeo in this case) must fully play that intention—must know what I am doing ('to figure out, etc.'), and why I am doing that (in this case we are trapped, Juliet and I, in time, surrounded by strange people from other times, places, epochs, etc.)— and I must also know how I am doing it. This is where the three sides of the technique, the three actions come into play. It is now clear to me that a conscious or unconscious choice of one of these actions for a word or emphasis adds a tone which supplies part of the how, which an actor must take into consideration before he can fulfill the acting of the what-why-how trinity of that intention. The trinity of what, why and how is backed up by the trinity of vocal actions of your technique, as an almost indivisible support. So that 'to figure out these monsters' if done in consonant action, steers the actor toward the realization of the apparent danger of the situation with the quiet intensity which this action supplies to words and moments. If done with full structural action the same intention is realized in another way— say with the quality of a deeper realization of the problem, but of a more possible hopeful and positive solution 'to be figured out.' And, finally, if done in call focus there would be a much greater emphasis obviously, as well as an implied 'calling out' against the fates which have placed them in this precarious and dangerous situation. These are only possibilities, mind you, and there are many of them. Moreover, there should be no thought that this involves a technical or 'purely outside' cliche and approach. It's just that one feels the other, takes from and nurtures each other in a perfectly natural and life-nature process.

"There is one other way that this technique can influence the acting (if indeed the two can be separated into individual categories at all) and that is: If during the early searches of what (and why) you are doing at a given moment, you happen to deliver the line with say, an unconscious use of call focus, you may through an intuitive use of the how in an intention, go on to discover the values of the moment which in turn may then lead one to the conscious knowledge of what (and why) you are doing at that moment . . ."

3. *S. B.*

". . . When doing the Ybuzz with the attention on the 'opening' just above the bridge of the nose, I began to feel—after making it work almost consistently for a few minutes—almost as if I were high on pot. I get dizzy, feel almost suspended in air—not in another world, but more as if my feet are a few inches off the ground.

"In learning how to feel rather than listen I am beginning to hear something special in other people. I listen to them but I am *listening differently* and it relates to the technique of 'feeling' when *I* speak. In a way, this is somehow related to the thought processes that should and sometimes do occur when the method is functioning properly. The reality of the line is there, relating to something or someone outside myself (excellent for relaxation for me) yet at the same time the mechanics of the technique are so obviously a part of me my point of concentration is outside me but the sensation of the technique working properly is within me, and the freedom coming from this awareness or 'feeling' enhances the focusing of my concentration. Which comes first—the chicken or the egg—it really doesn't matter. What matters is that it happens simultaneously and one enhances the other . . . yesterday I had a very important audition, everything worked great through a feeling of real control. They asked me to sing a ballad which I never did before in my life. I must have done it very well—this was quite a remarkable experience . . ."

4. *F. D.*

". . . In acting we talk about connecting with an object or partner as an aid in releasing nervousness and tension. Dealing with props, furniture and partner allows nervousness to drain off into them and thereby relaxes you and frees you to work in your pre-planned manner (i.e., to let the good work show).

"So too with vocal exercises this morning, 3/11/63—the 'We are not weak, sir' selection.

"In dealing with who I was—a young officer stating his opinion to his commanding officer—and in dealing with the vocal and verbal sounds and the understanding and interpretation of what I was saying—I was unable to be nervous in public.

"Simply by dealing with voice technique, acting and interpreting the selection and trying to make it clear to you (my partner) I didn't have time to *feel* nervous—or better still, the nervousness or excitement aided the expression of the piece. Not until I finished did my ears burn and did I feel embarrassed—then there was nothing to do but be nervous.

"I feel though that the technique of sound is secure enough in me now to use it to convey an idea, a state of mind or heart. I am optimistic about this marriage occurring within me. I mean we're making healthy progress . . ."

5. *P. R.*

". . . Probably my main goal in life is a fuller, more expressive, more alive me. In order to achieve this, I must use myself fully. I mention this as I realize that one is able to use oneself only insofar as one *allows* use of oneself. This is a problem of considerable size with me right now and one which must be solved in order to achieve the fullest, most exciting use of myself in life and theatre.

"The study of acting and voice have brought to my attention many personal questions (and a few answers) that I did not consciously know existed but which I had subconsciously resisted. I feel strongly that the positive approach which comes from your particular training in voice and speech (and from the method of acting I am studying) will be instrumental in the solving of these particular problem areas.

"Both voice and acting have brought to my awareness a particular treasure I think I once had but which I have (for reasons unknown at this moment) pushed away to the deeper recesses of my inside and labeled 'not for use in everyday life'—*and that is the marvelous joy of expressing my deeper feelings.*

"The discovery that I have a big vocal instrument (when I allow it to function) is very exciting. Also discovering I can express deep emotions (when I allow myself to) is exciting.

"As you point out there is no mystery about where the sounds come from when the physical understanding of vocal use is there. It is this knowing that when correctly approached with physical understanding one can have no doubts as to the availability, power and strength of one's voice, which takes the first pressure off and starts the germ of confidence in one's vocal effect upon others. The very act of opening my mouth and speaking words with a feeling of the focus through the roof of my mouth (I should say hard palate) gives a thrill of excitement and pleasure—and makes me want to keep talking just because of the wonderful sensation.

"Just a final thought—knowing the power of what it is to really use one's voice is comparable to the power of knowing one's 'action' or objective in a scene. There is a sense of confidence, a through-line, a directness, an actual forwardness in approach which does cause a forwardness in appearance . . ."

6. *M. C.*

". . . I feel the three principle we've been studying both in the exercises and in the show, and I am beginning to become aware of them in my conversation—especially consonant action.

"The two main advantages of using these actions in connection with interpretation are, 1) the freeing power and 2) the experimenting power.

"1) Since I've begun to feel consonant action in the Hostage, I've not had to worry about projecting to the back of the house ('pushing')— but now I'm free to play it casually and in an off-hand, quiet way and I'm heard. The same free principle is true of the Call Focus. The confidence in knowing my control over a shout or call gives me the freedom to allow my emotions to inform it. When I started to apply the Stretch during my arguments with Leslie, I found that my anger and conviction in the argument increased.

"2) In scene work, the experimenting with these actions and combinations of them has induced experimenting with interpretation. When I force myself to call a speech I find the place where I might want to call. The same is true of consonant action and the stretch. Playing with these forces one to play with interpretation and not settle for one's first impression (usually conventional and cliche).

"Also, the energy that this work demands greatly helps to intensify the intentions, the sensory feeling of the stream of speech feeds the emotions and the experience—(the action being acted) . . ."

7. *A. B.*

". . . While working on the Shakespeare sonnets, approaching them through each of the three actions (structural, tonal, and consonant), I have noticed different words and phrases coming to my attention from the drill of each separate action. By the time I have read through the sonnet, using each action separately, I am able to understand more clearly the whole sonnet because of the various words and phrases brought to my attention during the drill work . . ."

8. *N. F.*

". . . Last Tuesday, during the filming of the picture, I experienced something very new and exciting. This has nothing to do with the use of the voice and speech but rather with the use of the body. In my scene I had to slowly, very slowly, descend a long, curving staircase. I thought about the work we did involving breathing, body posture, walking, etc., and I tell you Arthur, for the first time in my life I felt that my back was projecting and maintaining a characterization. You see, the camera was shooting me from the back throughout the entire scene—not a single shot of my face. The excitement of knowing that there was dynamic projection and involvement, even though the audience could see only my back, was a revelation. I felt as though I had become a better actress overnight . . ."

9. *F. L.*

". . . I believe I feel the interrelation of all the parts to the central whole . . . I feel how each of them comes into play in my daily life and in my work: 1) tonal focus for emphasis or for distance, or for effects (or emotions) of monumental pitch and intensity; 2) the form following close behind tonal focus, and interrelated to it. The form (which uses a 'spread' tone throughout the upper facial mask, rather than the concentrated placement of it through the hard palate to the nose and bridge of the nose, as in tonal focus) has its usage in developing that rich, dark tone we hear so much about but seldom can find embodied as a part of an individual's vocal equipment. Form, when used as comfortably as I now see it was intended to be used, produces this dark tone, already well-placed by call focus, and helps in keeping the tone forward thru the principle embodied in forward direction. Thus the form (or structural action) has its use in normal conversation and in rhetoric, and in stage work as the median between the other two actions; 3) finally consonant action, which, again, is never far behind the other two actions, and which has given me such improvement in clarity as three years of 'diction' lessons would (and could not). Consonant action has its greatest usefulness in passages of great intensity (and possible rapidity) but also great quiet. Based, as it is on its concept of musical instruments and orchestral effects, one finds not only the aforementioned clarity coming into one's voice, but also great precision and lightness as the musician has when he plays . . ."

10. A. P.

". . . I'm beginning to feel the taste of words and how the sensory approach to words themselves (not just the ideas they express) affects my gut and imagination. This approach gives me clues to interpretation which are different from the clues I get from my intellectual understanding of the ideas.

"I've never experienced this before. I've been thrilled by the speaking of some English actors who seem to know the sensory powers of words, in the way that we're learning. I don't remember that in any American actor. I'd like to know if there are some you can think of.

"When I did Juliet's "Gallop Apace," feeling the words, intensified the voluptuous quality of the speech when I was doing it for stretch; doing it for consonants gave me her impatience; working on tone and call focus, her longing. Playing it, I would incorporate these three—as well as the discoveries made through feeling the words themselves. That's wild! . . .

11. *B. L.*

". . . After working on a scene yesterday, I was told by a few people how remarkably beautiful and 'open' my face had become. I said that much of this was due to my voice and speech training. Naturally, I got the feeling from these people that I had not understood what they said. I had—How much of this change is voice and speech and how much is growth in acting I could not say for sure. It had been a hand-in-hand progression. I do know several of the elements that brought on this remark and which are attributed to Lessac:

"a) The physical appearance of my face due to the structural action.

"b) My forwardness and relative security stemming from the confidence I feel that I will be listened to because of the new positive quality in my voice, due to the tonal action.

"c) Plus the over-all confidence gained from knowing that inside of me, subject to my command (through physical awareness) is a lovely voice. I know I have a marvelous and reliable tool at my command to express anything I want to from my inner self.

"I say this, of course, with the knowledge that there is much to be done before I have perfected the instrument and my use of it—but I am on that road . . ."

12. *D. P.*

". . . If we recall the maxim, great art conceals art . . . and add to it that the concealment is not only from the audience but from the actor himself, we stand in a better position to observe organic application rather than mechanical application.

"I have observed in my own work and in the work of others, for example the evolution and extension of an emotional expression in the simple use of structural action. The need to communicate being so strongly motivated qualitatively and quantitatively that the simple stretch involved not only the area of the facial muscles, but brought the whole body into action. This feeling of the total involvement of the instrument (in *this* case the actor) is what is meant when the actor is no longer conscious solely of the employment of technique to gain his objective. He knows his objective has been gained, however, by the satisfaction of a completed emotional release— achieved not only psychologically but physiologically as well.

"When the desire to communicate brings with it the additional element of artistic necessity we may find the concentration on one process of the trinity to be of almost magical help. For example, in a series of Proust readings prepared by myself for radio, I wanted to characterize the narrative with the physical and mental conditions of Proust the narrator. I felt that a relaxed, lethargic, affluent, drowsy sound was what I wanted. In order to achieve this without sacrificing clarity, I concentrated on the use of consonant action. Not only did this guarantee intelligibility, but the playing the different consonants added yet another dimension to the vocal characterization and to variety. Upon reflection the actor is then able to analyse the use and blending of actions and techniques which at first seemed to serve only one purpose . . . perhaps to be heard, to be free of a throaty tone, etc. But with proper emotional motivation being served by structural action which allows a natural functioning of the instrument, he finds a freedom not only from mechanical obstacles, but an opportunity for freedom of artistic expression never before realized . . ."

13. *J. R.*

"I was having a reunion with a World War II buddy whom I hadn't seen in over twenty years. As we were sitting in the convivial environment of a well known restaurant, reminiscing and trying to catch up on our respective personal lives, I began to note a sense of dissatisfaction with my voice . . . a sense of uneasiness as I became more and more aware of vocal strain. I suddenly realized that I had reverted to my old speaking patterns, and along with this realization came a prick of conscience about not using structural action. I then made a rather forced effort to speak with more of the forward look. However my body didn't seem to want to cooperate at all—it was perfectly content to speak along in the old patterns without the slightest interest in any other vocal effort. I then began to feel an odd sense of inner tension: it seemed as if one part of me wanted to speak differently, while another part reacted as though it couldn't care less. The result of this ambivalent condition was a further depletion of my vocal energies with an increasing awareness of additional strain in my voice. Then an interesting thing happened: Rather than permit my functioning to be taken over by negative energy, I began to think of a motor purring gently and smoothly, and I found myself applying this image to my vocal apparatus, and began shifting into a vocal 'purr' which was of course a Ybuzz-like sensation and without any sense of strain or obvious effort I smoothly shifted into my newer speech patterns. The experiment proved quite successful for when the vocal change occurred, it happened with a fuller tonal action. But what struck me as really interesting was this: when I tried at first to shift into a stronger structural action, the moving from one extreme to another was uncomfortable and the body vetoed it; but when I started with a gentle 'purr' of the tone in the palate and nose, and then added a very small megaphone shape my body, and of course all of me, began to take a real interest and feel much better, and the discussion took on new life. I noted that the change was pleasant and then invigorating like getting a 'second wind' which the body seemed to enjoy. Furthermore, it was interesting to observe that the more the body enjoyed the newer vocal sensations, the easier was it to swing into the other energies of structural and consonant action."

Index

Abdomen strengthening, 41
Accent elimination, 266-271
    neutral vowels in, 96, 97-98, 267
    R in, 267-270
    R-derivative in, 104, 267-268
    S and Z in, 271
    structural vowel #1 in, 266-267
    TH in, 271
    V and W in, 270-271
    weak form in, 106
Accents, regional, xvii
Acoustics, as aid to projection, 222-223
Acting
    call in, 110-111, 184, 200-206, 274, 277, 279
    connecting with object in, 275-276
    consonant action in, 183-184, 194-200, 274, 277, 279, 280
    forward direction in, 230, 277
    intention in, 274-275
    interactions in, 221, 231, 234
    rhythms of, 231-232
    structural action in, 182-183, 188-194, 274, 277, 279
    vocal life in, xi, 181-189
    voice and speech as, vii, 188
    with body, 278
Acting technique(s)
    awareness of, 235, 279-280
    mechanical, 233, 238
    use of, off stage, 179
Action(s)
    nonvoluntary, xiv, 13, 17, 80
    related to rest, 43, 44, 232
    semivoluntary, 13
    voluntary, xiv, 13, 17
    See also Consonant action; Energy; Structural action; Tonal action; Trinity of actions
Action-sensation(s)
    control of, xii-xiv

    of breathing, 30
    of consonant action, 130-131
    of effort, 228
    of results, 224
    of structural stretch, 17, 65-69
    of tonal action, 19
    of use of voice, 228
    See also Feeling
Actor(s), 280
    careful, 186
    interactions of
        with audience, 234
        with stage circumstances, 221
        with stage rhythms, 231-232
    limitations of, 224
    mechanically trained, 232
    method of memorization, 247-248
    problems of, 221-225, 228-235, 272-281
    rhythms of, 231-232
    task of, 244
    use of rules by, 223, 224
    voice and speech for, 180-181
Actor's choice, 185
Ad libs, 248, 251-252
Aging, and facial posture, 63
Air conduction, 13-14, 15
Alphabet, 92, 125-126
Ambivalence
    betrayed by gesture, 243
    in use of voice, 225
    overcoming, 280-281
American R, 168, 267, 268
American speech, xviii, 23
Announcers, television, 242
Antony, 215-216
Aphonia, 254, 262
Arena stage: *See* Open stage
Articulation, with cleft palate, 257-258
Audience
    communication with, 222-223
    interaction with, 234, 239, 246

in CH, 161
Shakespeare, William, 186, 187, 189-
    211, 212, 214-220, 277, 279
Silence, in dysphonia, 262
Singers, 21, 128
    as speakers, xviii
    jazz, 231-232
    opera, 111
Singing, xiv-xv, 22
    call focus in, 110-111, 128
    choral, N in, 133
    consonants in, 130, 184
    for children, 5-6
    tonal action in, 111
    vowels in, xiv, 130
    See also Voice
Sinistrality, related to stuttering, 261
Sinuses, 10, 11, 14, 19, 80
Siren drill, 118-120, 122
Soft-palate yawn, 45-46, 111
Sore throat, 237-238
Sound, expressive properties of, 226
Sound box
    human, 11, 260
    instrumental, 11
Sound stream
    actions of, 10
    compared to water hose, 113
    control of, 113
    in tonal action, 83-84, 112
    in Ybuzz, 83-84
    physical sensation of, in dysphonia,
        263
    vs. breath stream, 29-30, 257, 262
Sound waves
    as physical forces, 79
    control of, 12, 79
    misdirected, 113
Southerners, use of neutrals by, 97-98
Source of stimualtion, 240, 241, 247
Spanish speech, 125
Speaker
    as singer, xviii
    interactions with audience, 246
    task of, 244
Speaking
    extemporaneous, 245, 246, 252
    facets of, 239-243
    monotony in, 252
    preparation for, 245-246
    qualities in, 246, 250
    thought process in, 246, 247, 250
    vocal delivery in, 240-241
Speech, xiv-xv
    American, xviii, 23

apathetic, in stuttering, 258, 260
as inner experience, xvii
bad habits of, 4, 6
British, 23, 124
connected, 172-176
consonants in, xiv-xv, 184
formal
    call focus in, 112
    neutral vowels in, 96
French, 23
intelligibility in, 20, 22, 176
Irish, 124
Italian, 23
Russian, 23, 124, 125
Scotch, 124
sloppy, 131
Spanish, 125
speed of, 62, 173
    in stuttering, 258, 260
standard of, xvi-xviii
sustained, as singing, 128
See also Conversational speech;
    Stage speech; Vocal life; Voice
    and speech
Speech therapist, 254
    qualifications of, 255-256, 262
    weakness of, 255, 256
Speech therapy: *See* Therapy, speech
Speeches
    memorizing, 246-250
    reading, 250-252
    writing, 245-246
Speed
    of breath vs. sound, 10
    of speech, 62, 173
    in stuttering, 258, 260
Spelling, neutral, 99
Spine, 19
    curve of, 40, 52
Spitting, 237
Stage, vocal conditions on, 222-223
    See also Open stage; Proscenium
        stage
Stage excitement, 232-233
Stage fright, 232-233
Stage reality, 222-223, 235
Stage speech, 184
    tonal action in, 125, 223
    vs. offstage speech, 221-224
Standard of speech, xvi-xviii
Stanislavsky, Constantin
    on consonants, 183
    on relaxation, 43
Stanley, Douglas, 29-30
Stereotypes, 244